WITHDRAWN

HARVARD LIBRARY

WITHDRAWN

KIERKEGAARD & POSTMODERNISM

Aparté:
CONCEPTIONS AND DEATHS OF SØREN KIERKEGAARD

TRANSLATED WITH
AN INTRODUCTION
BY KEVIN NEWMARK

SYLVIANE AGACINSKI

Kierkegaard and Postmodernism

GENERAL EDITOR
Mark C. Taylor, WILLIAMS COLLEGE

ASSOCIATE EDITORS
E. F. Kaelin, THE FLORIDA STATE UNIVERSITY
Louis Mackey, THE UNIVERSITY OF TEXAS AT AUSTIN

OTHER WORKS IN THE SERIES—

Points of View: Readings of Kierkegaard
by Louis Mackey (1986)

A Question of Eros: Irony in Sterne, Kierkegaard, and Barthes
by John Vignaux Smyth (1986)

Kierkegaard and the Problem of Writing
by Pat Bigelow (1988)

APARTÉ

CONCEPTIONS AND DEATHS OF SØREN KIERKEGAARD

Sylviane Agacinski

Translated with an introduction by
Kevin Newmark

University Presses of Florida
FLORIDA STATE UNIVERSITY PRESS
TALLAHASSEE

The Florida State University Press is grateful for support for this publication from the Frederick W. Hilles Publication Fund of Yale University and from the Cultural Ministry of France.

University Presses of Florida is the central agency for scholarly publishing of the State of Florida's university system, producing books selected for publication by the faculty editorial committees of Florida's nine public universities. Orders for books published by all member presses of University Presses of Florida should be addressed to University Presses of Florida, 15 NW 15th Street, Gainesville, FL 32603.

Library of Congress Cataloging-in-Publication Data
Agacinski, Sylviane.
  [Aparté. English]
  Aparté: conceptions and deaths of Søren Kierkegaard / Sylviane Agacinski; translated and with an introduction by Kevin Newmark.
    p.   cm.—(Kierkegaard and postmodernism)
  Translation of: Aparté.
  Bibliography: p.
  Includes index.
  ISBN 0-8130-0887-5 (alk. paper): $24.95
  1. Kierkegaard, Søren, 1813-1855—Criticism and interpretation.
2. Postmodernism. I. Title. II. Series.
PT8142.Z5A5613   1988
198'.9—dc19   87-24072
                                                            CIP

Originally published as *Aparté: conceptions et morts de Sören Kierkegaard*, La philosophie en effet (Paris: Aubier Flammarion, 1977).

Copyright © 1988 by the Board of Regents of the State of Florida

Printed in the U.S.A. on acid-free paper. ∞

CONTENTS

Foreword, by Mark C. Taylor ix
Taking Kierkegaard Apart, by Kevin Newmark 3

On a Thesis 33
Irony as a Subject?——Socratic Irony–Pure Negativity——The Double Valorization of Negative Dialectics——Apology for a Seducer——Politically Blameworthy Irony——The Nontragic Death of Socrates——Irony: Nondialectizable Negativity——The Serious Side of the Thesis: The Defense

Economies of Sacrifice 79
Passion, Panic——The Logic of the Hero——Phantasmatics——The Cut——Sacrifice to the Letter

Apartés 127
To Write *Aparté*——Regine——Isaac-Job——Recollection——Detachment——Old Age——Husband and Father——The King Who Got Slapped——Repetition——The Fruitful Idea——The Breaking of the Inveiglements——Mime——The Singer Elvira and Repetition——Farce——The Sublime and the Ridiculous——Woman——Sexual Indifference——The Family——The Animal——Cannibalism: The Devourers and the Devoured——The Martyr's Desire/The Desire for Martyrdom——Hegel——The Secret——The Police——Money——Profit——Number——Imperialism——In the Margins

v

of Marx——Notabene: Prefaces——Ventriloquism——Language——Names——The Legacy of the Father——The Suspicion——Periander——A Scene of Rape——The Phantom——The Family Vault——The Mother——In Memoriam: Accounting for the Father

Selected References 259
Index 263

Man was made for eternity: woman leads him into an *aparté* (*Journal*, 4:581).

As Jewish women regarded being without children as a disgrace, so the Christian ought to regard being without tears (which, like children, are the gift of God) as a disgrace and pray and pray, as did Rachel, that God will open the womb and viscera of the spiritual man and in the inward movements of the heart give proof of its conception (*Journal*, 1:176).

Foreword

It is impossible to translate *"aparté"* or to translate this word clearly, precisely—properly. Derived from the Latin *a* + *pars, aparté* means, *inter alia,* an aside, words spoken by an actor, a private remark. Following a usage first suggested by La Ménardière in *Poétique* (1640), *"aparté"* designates a theatrical convention in which an actor addresses the audience in order to clarify his designs, while the other actors who are present pretend not to hear the words spoken. So understood, an *aparté* is, in the words of F. Soulier, *"un entretien à l'écart."*

This "definition" only compounds the difficulties of translation. How is one to render *"entretien"*? While *entretien* can designate, among other things, maintenance, upkeep, preservation, living, livelihood, conversation, talk, interview, conference, sermon, or homily, *entretenir* (*entre,* between + *tenir,* to hold, keep, etc.) can mean to hold between, hold together, keep in repair, provide for, feed, converse, talk with, or entertain. And how are we to understand *écart:* stepping aside, swerving, mistake, fault, deviation, digression, variation, difference; *à l'écart:* aside, apart, in solitude, in a lonely place? For those who, unlike the actors on stage, have ears to hear, other sounds echo in *aparté: part,* share, part; *partir,* to set out, depart, crack, crash, die; *parti,* gone away, gone off; *partie,* part of a whole, party, diversion, amusement, game, match, contest, client, opponent, adversary, parcel, lot; *partage,* portion, division; even *apartheid.* If we recognize these nuances (and others not [yet] spoken), *aparté* might be translated "aside" or "apart." But something would still be missing. What does (the) translation lack? What slips between the lines and is not said? What remains untranslated because it is untranslatable? What is left unsaid because it is unsayable? Is there always something cryptic about translation?

If it is impossible, or almost impossible, to translate *aparté*, then is it possible to translate *Aparté*? Perhaps it is better to leave the *conceptions et morts de Søren Kierkegaard* untranslated. Perhaps . . . but one cannot be certain. It is, after all, possible that Kierkegaard's *conceptions* (is this word a translation—if so, is it a translation from French to English or English to French, and can these terms or this term [we cannot be sure if the word is one or two, even when it is singular] translate *Be-greb* [*greb*, grasp, snatch, clutch], which might or might not translate *Be-griff* [*Griff*, grip, grasp, hold, catch] and vice versa?) are already translations—translations of *something else*. As Rodolphe Gasché points out: "Not only does all translation into a foreign language rest on the very possibility of the double translation already at work in any language, but all translation of whatever sort is 'rooted' in the asemic by the very dissymmetry of this double translation and therefore in that which cannot legitimately function as a 'root': in the nonlanguage conditions of language."[1] If nonlanguage always conditions language, then language is, in some sense, already translation, and thus translation is always a translation of a translation. If, however, translation of whatever sort is "rooted" in the asemic, then translation is inevitably mistranslation. Language, in other words, is forever foreign language—language that is foreign to that which is foreign to it. The translator, who is always a writer, and the writer, who is always a translator, face the impossible task of transcribing something else—a certain difference, which repeatedly resists assimilation and thus is never present though it (how should this "it" be translated [*il, elle, ça, es, den,* or *det*] and what does "it" translate?) is not precisely absent.

---

1. Rodolphe Gasché, "Roundtable on Translation," *The Ear of the Other: Otobiography, Transference, Translation; Texts and Discussions with Jacques Derrida*, ed. C. V. McDonald, trans. P. Kamuf and A. Ronell (New York: Schocken Books, 1985), 112.

Foreword

From one point of view (and there are many others), the writing-translating of *Aparté—conceptions et morts de Søren Kierkegaard—Aparté—Conceptions and Deaths of Søren Kierkegaard* is a rereading of Kierkegaard as a writer-translator. According to Sylviane Agacinski (SA), Kierkegaard is preoccupied with the impossibility of translating the nonlanguage conditions of language. Through relentless indirection and countless *apartés*, Kierkegaard struggles to evoke that which language implies but cannot contain. Even when speaking in "his own" voice or writing in "his own" name, Kierkegaard's language remains the discourse of an Other. Sometimes Kierkegaard names this Other "God," sometimes "Father," sometimes "the Unknown." There are always other "names" for this uncertain Other. For SA, the discourse of the Other haunting Kierkegaard's writings transforms not only his works but his very life into an irreducibly cryptic text. The unreadability of the Kierkegaardian corpus calls into question Hegelian *savoir absolu*, which, in the wake of *Glas*, we can abbreviate *Sa*. The text of SA, or more precisely SA's translation of SK's translation of the asemic Other, subverts the book of *Sa*.

Aparté—Conceptions and Deaths of Søren Kierkegaard is one of those rare works that forces one to reread books that have become all too familiar in new and different ways. Agacinski weaves together philosophy, theology, psychoanalysis, and literary criticism to create a brilliant text that defies not only translation but also classification. Both more and less than a commentary, Agacinski has written a work that simultaneously deepens critical discourse and extends the implications of many of Kierkegaard's most important insights. After reading *Aparté*, it is impossible to read either Kierkegaard or the languages of criticism in the same way. The publication of Kevin Newmark's outstanding translation of *Aparté* (which, of course, he does not translate) opens a new chapter in Kierkegaard research and provides an occasion for the reassessment of the significance of Kierkegaard's writings for contemporary philosophy, theology, psychology, and literary criticism.

Mark C. Taylor

INTRODUCTION

Taking Kierkegaard Apart

By Kevin Newmark

How does something like Sylviane Agacinski's book on Kierkegaard happen? Considering how very unlike it is to anything on Kierkegaard written in English, it seems to take us by surprise, to burst upon the American scene like a storm, and we could easily describe the present publication of *Aparté* in the same disruptive terms Agacinski herself uses to refer to the well-known but little understood Kierkegaardian concept of repetition: "It's like a tear or rip that blows or blows up, pops, pierces, opens and shows up. There it was, and now here it is. It happens." Like repetition, moreover, the translation of *Aparté* into English seems to relate itself to something that was already there, in this case a certain Søren Kierkegaard, but in such a way as to shake things up, to tear them apart so that we become aware of the repetition and an unknown or unnoticed original at one and the same time. And since we did not know it was there originally, such a process of translation cannot be thought of in the dialectical terms of "recollection," which goes backward in order to coincide with an origin that is actually there, but must be called instead a "repetition," which, as Kierkegaard reminds us, goes forward from nothing to produce itself at the same time that it repeats (itself). Discovering Agacinski on Kierkegaard, then, is like discovering in Kierkegaard an opening or mobility that is different from what we have become used to finding there and always again expect to find there; it repeats or translates a Kierkegaard that many of us can't recollect was there in the first place. It disrupts our habits as well as our linear concept of temporality. How does something like this happen?

It happens, of course, through an act of reading, and the kind of reading practiced by Sylviane Agacinski is so remote from us, so foreign to the Anglo-American tradition of Kierkegaard studies that it stands in need of some sort of introduction. No matter how original a book like *Aparté* might appear in the French context of Kierkegaard studies, it could never have seemed to come as completely out of the blue there as it would here in the United States. For reasons that are as demographic as they are ideological, the study of Kierkegaard in this country has been conducted first and foremost along theological lines, either by professional theologians or by individuals who have looked to Kierkegaard as a source for identifying and clarifying spiritual questions and crises. There have been exceptions, of course, and especially of late widely divergent approaches to Kierkegaard have begun to make their appearance on the scene, but it remains true that by and large the point of entry into the texts of Kierkegaard here in the United States takes place by way of a theologically grounded discourse, and whether we like it or not, it is against the background of an interpretation that takes for granted the ultimately transcendental value of Kierkegaard's work that all other readings have had to define themselves. A representative if not formative case in this respect is David Swenson, one of the pioneering thinkers who helped introduce Kierkegaard to an American readership. It would be difficult to overestimate the emblematic value of his own discovery of Kierkegaard and the conversion scene that followed. It is as though the narration of how, in a moment of spiritual crisis, he once happened upon a Danish edition of *The Concluding Unscientific Postscript* tucked away in a dusty corner of a Minnesota public library, and how as a result he stayed up all that night and the following day to read it through without stopping, was meant not only to retrace the occurrence and resolution of his own spiritual crisis but also to anticipate the overall reception of Kierkegaard in this country as the province of the believer rather than that of the philosopher or critic.[1]

---

1. The fact that the story is told twice in the introductory material to the current edition of the *Postscript*, once by Swenson's widow and then again by his editor, serves to emphasize its almost hagiographic character. The editor's description is worth quoting: "Having nothing

Swenson was later to team up with another of the earliest American readers of Kierkegaard, Walter Lowrie, a retired rector of St. Paul's American Church in Rome, and together they were responsible for the majority of texts translated into English for the first time. While their joint efforts were to result in the impressive publication of the standard Princeton editions, it was left to still more influential professional theologians like Reinhold Niebuhr and Paul Tillich to extend the reach of Kierkegaard scholarship in a subtle but firm way in the United States. It may be true that both these names are conspicuously absent from the standard references in Kierkegaard studies, but through lectures, articles, and reviews, and merely through the kind of cachet they lent the name Kierkegaard by associating it with their own transplanted versions of a negative theology particularly well-suited to a postwar culture, they helped to awaken curiosity about the Danish thinker and encourage broader examination of his texts. Tillich, who eventually held a teaching post at the University of Chicago, had fled Nazi Germany near the beginning of the war, leaving a chair at the University of Frankfurt, where one of his students had been Theodor Adorno. One cannot help wondering just what the American reception of Kierkegaard would have been like had it occurred more along the interpretive lines of someone like Adorno, whose interest in both literature and the European philosophical tradition of dialectical thought certainly made his approach to Kierkegaard less theologically straightforward than Tillich's, and who had, in fact, actually written his doctoral thesis with Tillich in the early thirties on the place of Kierkegaard's aesthetics within his philosophy as a whole.[2]

> to support him except the faith his mother had taught him as a child, he happened to be attracted by the quaint title, 'Concluding Unscientific Postscript to the Philosophical Fragments.' He took it home, read it all night and all the next day, with the profoundest emotion; and in this book he found support for his stalwart Christian life" (xi).
>
> 2. Adorno's thesis, "Kierkegaard: Konstruktion des Ästhetischen," was first published in 1933. It has not been translated into English and seems to have had little effect on later readings of Kierkegaard. As one of the few serious discussions of the aesthetic as a philosophical category rather than as a value, it deserves analysis not only with respect to Kierkegaard but also in its own right.

The mere mention of the name Adorno in connection with Kierkegaard, of course, begins to reveal how different were the configuration and development of Kierkegaard criticism in Europe than in the United States. Almost without exception, the American reception of Kierkegaard, already associated with such thinkers as Tillich, Niebuhr, Barth, Bultmann, and Buber, remained for quite some time firmly tied to the immediately pragmatic questions of an individual's spiritual life within or without a specific community of believers and for this reason was far less speculative and contextually rooted than some of the contemporary interest in Kierkegaard in Europe. It was not until the early seventies, in fact, when some of the urgency and even fashionableness of the first inquiries had begun to fade and when pressures from the increasingly sophisticated interpretative tools provided by literary and linguistic analysis made it seem appropriate to place both the philosophical and religious dimensions of Kierkegaard's writing within a general examination of the *mode* of their communication prior to their meaning or value, that the study of Kierkegaard in this country was prepared to encounter in a productive way the kind of readings that had been taking place in Europe at least since the early forties. Not until the appearance of Louis Mackey's *Kierkegaard: A Kind of Poet* in 1971, some forty years after Adorno's thesis on the status of the aesthetic in Kierkegaard, is the question of Kierkegaard's "indirect communication" thematized in a way that could draw wide attention to the possibility of reading Kierkegaard from a rhetorical point of view prior to a theological or hermeneutical perspective.

In this respect, one of Mackey's most promising insights concerned his perception of the necessity of proceeding to a reading of Kierkegaard by way of "the tools of literary criticism," which meant in turn that Mackey would try to distinguish his interpretation from earlier work in English through his self-conscious decision to read the texts of Kierkegaard "closely and sensitively, with a view not only to *what* they say but even more to *how* they say it." Despite a certain lack of rigor in following through with his program and a resulting overemphasis on the "sensitivity" of his reading at the expense of its "closeness," which served to contain or offset some of the more radical effects of Kierkegaard's "indirect communication," Mackey's effort to identify in this manner a distinction between *what* a text means and the *way* that it means, or between the text's theology (or philosophy) and its poetics (or rhetoric), marked an important moment in the study of Kierkegaard in the United States and announced the direction that would increasingly be taken in the best of the work that was to follow. Nonetheless, it would be impossible to imagine the most interesting of Kierkegaard's newest American critics—Mark Taylor, Henry Sussman, John Smyth, Ronald Schleifer, and Paul Bové, to name a few—being able to produce their own work without the crucial contact they have all had, in one way or another and with varying results, with recent developments in the way that philosophy and literature are read in Europe, and especially in France.

This is not to say that there is nothing in the French reception of Kierkegaard that parallels the religious preoccupations operative for so long in the American context. The ready example of Pascal within the French philosophico-religious tradition of thought could hardly have escaped attention in certain circles, and even the use made of Kierkegaard within popularized versions of French existentialism was as often geared toward holding out to philosophy a transcendental buoy as it was toward creating a genuine opportunity for reading Kierkegaard's texts with any real philosophical rigor. But the ironic fact that for many French intellectuals Kierkegaard was assimilated to the weighty German philosophical tradition beginning more or less with Kant and culminating in Hegel was bound to offset these tendencies to a certain degree and pave the way for a highly original reading of Kierkegaard.

Such, indeed, is the case of Maurice Blanchot. Combining an interest in German literary figures such as Rilke and Kafka, whose work was most profoundly, if obliquely, marked by an acquaintance with Kierkegaard, with a power of philosophical reflection that is rooted in Kierkegaard's most important philosophical predecessor and successor, namely Hegel and Heidegger, Blanchot is singularly well prepared to attend to the complexities of reading Kierkegaard. In fact, Blanchot has written rather sparingly on Kierkegaard, a few pages here and there, hardly a sustained interpretation of him as a whole or even of individual works. But when he does refer to Kierkegaard, it is always with a kind of uncanny authority and always in regard to two essential issues. First, according to Blanchot, it is important to recognize that Kierkegaard *does* think "dialectically." The Kierkegaardian concepts of "faith," "sin," and "anxiety," for instance, are not to be regarded as returns to some sort of ineffable immediacy but rather as fully reflected concepts that present themselves to Kierkegaard on the far side of dialectical thought. Second, Kierkegaard's "dialectic" is quite obviously not the same as Hegel's, and the way in which Hegelian dialectical thought is challenged by Kierkegaard's peculiar form of dialectic has something to do with his theory of *language*.

Thus, in a short essay on Kierkegaard's *Journals*, Blanchot insists that, for Kierkegaard, the fundamental problem is that of "communication," the possibility of revealing truth adequately in the medium of language. It is because of the structural impossibility of communicating truth directly that Kierkegaard, again according to Blanchot, is led to thematize in such a sustained manner the "secret" that would eventually cause him to suffer doubly from his own need and inability "to speak," and also to theorize in a more general way on the necessity and effects of the Christian writer's remaining "incognito" and "pseudonymous." Seen from this perspective, it is actually the theory of language as indirect communication that *produces* those familiar elements in Kierkegaard that we most readily attribute to his subjective particularity and its existential crises and not the other way around. In Blanchot's reading, it becomes possible to glimpse the profound irony that would turn Kierkegaard's "existentialism" into a subjective mask whose sole reason for being is to help make explicit the impersonal consistency of his theory of language. For Blanchot, then, it follows that a prerequisite for any legitimate approach to the question of the "self," the "secret," and even of the "truth" in Kierkegaard's writing, be it speculative or religious, would be a careful examination of the complexities of his linguistic theory of indirect communication.

As a consequence, Blanchot's reading goes a long way toward unsettling in an unexpected and radical way the more or less traditional understanding of the ascending movement linking Kierkegaard's three "spheres" of existence. Rather than retracing a hierarchy in which the single individual would be subjectively free to choose between the relatively independent spheres that move upward in linear fashion from an aesthetic (or prephilosophical) to an ethical (or philosophical) stage, and finally on to the religious (or postphilosophical) stage, Blanchot's focus on the question of "communication" serves to place the three categories in a *differential* relationship of communication or signification in which each stage is structurally possible only by reason of its entering into a play of relative distance and proximity with respect to the others. Following Blanchot, then, we begin to suspect that the ordinary conception of the three stages as an existential *movement* or history, the progression of a self-conscious subject along the road of experience, is already a kind of rhetorical device or figure in the narrative form of an allegory. Namely, such an allegory would tell the story of how Kierkegaard's subjective spheres of existence were the putting into a sequential narrative of a differential structure of signification that is not necessarily either temporal or subjective. Within such a nonnarrative structure, the *form* of communication (which is partly, though not entirely, a question of *aesthetics* since it is concerned with the outward form or sensuous appearance of the communication) and the *meaning* of the communication (which would at some point become *religious* truth as inwardness) are maintained indissolubly in a relationship of nonadequation as the result of a *philosophical* theory of indirect communication or, better, as the result of a purely *linguistic* predicament (that the communication of truth is by necessity indirect).

This would mean, of course, that the question of the relationship between the aesthetic and the religious in Kierkegaard could become accessible *only* through a prior consideration of the linguistic constituents of a philosophy of (indirect) communication. Blanchot himself makes this abundantly clear by stating unequivocally that the quandary of the "Christian witness of truth" in Kierkegaard—to be stuck between the necessity of speaking *religious* truth and the impossibility of speaking it in any but the *aesthetic* language of the poet—is the logical outcome of the purely *linguistic* impossibility of direct communication. If Kierkegaard's ultimate persona for the witness to truth was "a kind of poet," that is *not* because particular individuals—and especially Kierkegaard himself—lack either adequate courage for a commitment to faith or a full understanding of dialectical thinking, but rather because a theory of language as indirect communication *requires* for its representative an aporetic image such as that of the "religious poet." To some extent, then, the actual figures of the "poet" and the "man of faith" are contingent; they are there only by reason of their asymmetrical relation to one another, which can as a consequence become illustrative of the more far-reaching philosophical problem of truth. They are merely different sides of the same (linguistic) coin of indirect communication, which can say what it means (religious truth) only by not saying it, that is, by saying it in a form that is not immediately recognizable as what it is (poetic language). "There is communication," in Blanchot's own enigmatic formulation of Kierkegaard's writing situation, "only when what is said becomes the sign of what must be hidden. Revelation consists entirely in the impossibility of a revelation."

But where, we must ask at some point, does Kierkegaard's (philosophical) theory of indirect communication come from? Why should there be a structural impossibility of revealing truth adequately in the medium of language? And in the wake of such questions as these we must also wonder whether it would suffice to answer them by merely resituating Kierkegaard's theory of language in a more fundamental region, that is, by making it depend on some kind of extralinguistic model like a *theological* concept of sin or a *psychoanalytical* or *political* theory of the unconscious. These are some of the questions that have remained until now in the shadows behind the suggestive but limited remarks of a handful of readers of Kierkegaard like Blanchot. Sylviane Agacinski, who in *Aparté* brings these and other questions into focus by passing them through the crucible of Jacques Derrida's philosophico-linguistic project of deconstruction, develops along the way one of the most brilliantly original and important full-length studies of Kierkegaard yet to be written in any language.

*
* *

Agacinski is fully aware of the fact that by far and away the most crucial text for a determination of Kierkegaard's theory of language and the place in it of indirect communication is his Magister thesis, *The Concept of Irony.* Not only is it the text from which the others "originate" in simply genetic terms (since it is the first major published work); more important, it is the one text whose subject matter could be said without exaggeration to be overtly linguistic. "Irony" may not be as easily reducible to a clearly defined set of characteristics as are, say, the universally recognized and discussed Mutt-and-Jeff pair of tropes, metaphor and metonymy; but as the term that names the possible discrepancy between an expression's *saying* and its *meaning*, it is beyond question that irony belongs as much as they do to a general theory of language and, more specifically, to the special province of rhetoric. As such, and in a way that remains to be determined, it could be said that *The Concept of Irony* implies, explains, and produces Kierkegaard's entire authorship.

It is no mere accident, then, that *Aparté* begins with a long and programmatic chapter on that text, since all that Kierkegaard (and Agacinski herself) will go on to write has its source in the previous interrogation of irony. But "beginnings" and "sources" are precisely what are problematic here, for the question of irony is no sooner raised by the philosophical inquiry than it is beset by the no means negligible problem of irony's definition: What is irony, where does it come from, and how far does it go? Agacinski thematizes the question right from the start in a way that is as subtle and duplicitous as irony itself.

First of all, and in the form of a kind of leitmotiv that will run through the entire chapter, Agacinski sketches out the place that is assigned to irony within the discourse of philosophy. Inside the historical framework of Western philosophy, irony always appears as a moment of negativity that can be endowed with a subjective consciousness in order subsequently to be able to enter into a process of self-development. Irony is the freedom of subjective thought, the negativity of the particular that opposes itself to the universal but that also, in coming to know itself as free and potentially arbitrary, imposes objective limits on its own freedom and thus prepares the way for a positive content to succeed it. In this way, irony becomes a major category in the evolution of philosophical thought traceable from Socrates forward to the German romantics (Schlegel, Tieck, Solger). For Hegel, the passage from Socrates to the romantics takes place by way of a negative dialectic in which increasing levels of self-conscious subjectivity would finally end up in the "absolute freedom" (but concomitant lack of earnestness and solidity) characteristic of the German thinkers on irony.

However, the disparity that appears in Hegel between Socrates' "too little" subjectivity and the romantics' "too much" subjectivity remains a problem only as long as our perspective fails to include the mediating moments of a diachronic movement. Once the ironic point of view has been isolated and limited to being part of a larger historical process, it ceases to be threatening for a dialectic of mediated negativity. Socrates did not *yet* know that the negativity of his subjectivity would become part of a larger development and history, while the romantics have somehow *already* forgotten that the negativity of their subjectivity is only part of a history. From the standpoint of history, there is very little difference between the two, since ultimately the historical process itself will provide its own antidote to whatever excess or deficiency is part of irony's negativity, and this despite the threat of irony's potentially repetitive nature to become monotonous and boring. Hegel's treatment of the late-romantic Solger is in this regard emblematic of the entire procedure. Like the contemporary example of this theoretician of ironic negativity whose "life was broken off too soon for him to have been able to reach the concrete development of the philosophical Idea," irony's negativity is always "onesided," either excessive or deficient, and in a historical sense always *premature*. Its very onesidedness also implies a positive complement that, no matter what the historical period in question, will follow on its heels and cancel its negativity.

To some extent, this perspective will also hold true for Kierkegaard, whose thesis on irony closely parallels Hegel's treatment by making very ostensible use of "the world historical validity of irony" in order to organize the crucial passage from an analysis of Socrates' nascent or negative subjectivity to an analysis of irony's overly self-indulgent subjectivity after Fichte. But whereas Hegel seems willing to vacillate in his evaluations by referring somewhat haphazardly to the possibility of a positive (nonironic) Socrates and a negative (ironic) Socrates, positive romantic irony (Solger) and negative romantic irony (Schlegel), one of the main objectives of Kierkegaard's thesis is to separate these value judgments once and for all in order to avoid any unnecessary confusion by determining them with all possible precision and consistency. In this respect he will have to appear as more Hegelian than Hegel himself. At any rate, it is precisely the possibility of defining the difference between Socratic and romantic irony in terms of an axis of positive and negative values that are *also* historical moments within a development of subjectivity (even if, in this particular case, the development takes the inverted form of a degradation) that allows Kierkegaard to distinguish definitively between "good" and "bad" irony. Such a scheme of historical values will finally account for his being able to recognize and assimilate a timely irony of the past (Socrates) while still being able to reject outright an untimely irony of the present (the romantics).

It follows that in order for irony to be "good," its negativity—like Socrates' questions—has to be "timely," that is, it has to correspond to the needs of the historical moment in which it originates. In the case of Socrates, this meant that the empty substantiality of the Greeks was *ready* to be negated and replaced by the dawning subjectivity of Socrates. Otherwise, the negativity of subjective play is merely gratuitous and of no "use" whatsoever, like the arbitrary playfulness of the romantics that empties objectivity of its content but is not geared toward replacing the void it creates with any ideal positivity of its own. One of Kierkegaard's clearest formulations of this necessarily dialectical conception of subjective irony is as follows: "To the extent that this irony is world historically justified, the emancipation of subjectivity takes place in the service of the Idea, even though the ironic subject is not clearly conscious of this. This is the genial quality of an irony that is warranted. As for an unwarranted irony, on the other hand, it may be said that whosoever shall save his life shall lose it. But whether irony is warranted or not can only be adjudicated by history" (*The Concept of Irony,* 280). In this way, all of irony's negativity can be put in its rightful place, assigned its necessarily *past* moment in history (Socrates), or else deprived of any place whatsoever (the romantics).

This would be one way of understanding the concluding chapter of the thesis, "Irony as a Mastered Moment—The Truth of Irony." History functions here as the gradual accumulation of individual layers of consciousness, a means of ordering from a higher perspective the negativity of subjectivity's irony in order to reduce the "more or less" of various stages to homogeneity and eventually to the "truth" or "mastery" of a philosophical thesis. To return for a moment to our point of departure, we could say, philosophically speaking, that Kierkegaard's theory of indirect communication results from his theory of subjectivity, which, in turn, is a dialectical theory of mediated negativity. The sequential narration or "history" of this negativity—whether it be in philosophical, theological, psychoanalytical, or even political terms—also includes the promise of its sublation. To some extent, then, it would be perfectly conceivable to read Kierkegaard's own textual evolution from *The Concept of Irony* to *The Point of View* as the gradual development of a given subjectivity from its beginning in indirection or irony toward its culmination in the potential to speak in its own name or voice.

All of this is more or less straightforward and more or less easily read in the texts of both Hegel and Kierkegaard. So by entitling the first section of her book "Irony as a Subject?", Agacinski seems to place herself in a wholly predictable way within the context of a traditional philosophical inquiry of irony, which always links the question of ironic negativity with the question of the self-conscious subject and his (potentially infinite) freedom. "Irony as a Subject?", then, could be taken to ask about the kind of "subjectivity" that assumes the form of irony, and the title could almost be translated as *"Who* is the subject that is made out of irony?" We must not, however, overlook the fact that Agacinski adds to this heading a note that extends the question in a somewhat different direction by asking about the context of a *thesis,* in other words, an institutionalized act of *language* in the form of a proposition or meaningful statement. Rather than asking about irony's "subjectivity" or about the relationship between irony and the subjectivity of the subject, the title redirects itself by way of an unobtrusive footnote and actually goes on to ask the dryly scholastic question "Is irony a fit *subject* for a *thesis?"* To ask about the conditions in which subjectivity can be ironic is one thing, but who cares about a list of possible thesis subjects? Nonetheless, what is truly interesting and potentially disruptive in Agacinski's question, which seems to begin in one place only to end up in another, is precisely the way she displaces slightly the question of ironic "subjectivity" from the field of *historical* and dialectical development by putting it side by side with the necessarily *linguistic* element that will eventually reveal itself in any examination of irony.

For, by the time the marginalized form of the footnote has been reconnected to the question of the heading, the category of the "subject" has expanded considerably and now includes not only the existential category whose dwelling place is within a historico-philosophical theory of self-consciousness but also the rather bloodless "subjects" and "predicates" scattered throughout the impersonal field of *grammar*, without which no meaningful discourse whatsoever could come into being. Rereading the title, we cannot avoid noticing an effect that could only be ascribed to Agacinski's own irony: a question that seems to ask about the all-important relationship between irony and subjectivity ends up asking only about grammatical subjects and their predicates. What Agacinski does here implicitly, and later in the same chapter with more insistence, is to ask whether irony, considered as a grammatical "subject," can ever be made compatible with the meaningful production of a "thesis"; that is, she is asking about the place of irony within a particular form of language, or language considered from a particular point of view. For example, in the proposition "Irony is a fit subject for a thesis," the grammatical subject is "irony," and it merely fills a particular syntactic slot that, from a purely grammatical point of view, could just as easily be occupied by "Danish philosophers who limp" or "Greek philosophers who drink hemlock."

The question here no longer has anything to do with self-consciousness or history; or rather, if it has to do with self-consciousness and history, it is solely on the basis of a possible relationship between *grammar* (subject, predicate, attribute) and *meaning* (thesis, proposition, statement). What would it *mean*, the first heading of *Aparté* seems to ask, for the subject of a proposition (say, "Kierkegaard is a fit subject for a thesis") to be *irony*, to *be* ironic, that is to say, not to be as earnest and directly understandable as the earnestness and directness of the meaning of the proposition must require of it? The question seems to ask whether "irony" is a fit subject for a thesis, but if its own "subject" is ironic, how can it hope to know *what* it means by asking such a question? Would not the "meaning" of any proposition or question necessarily be threatened by the possibility of its being predicated upon a subject that was "ironic"? And how can we determine which subjects are ironic ("irony," "Kierkegaard," "Socrates," etc.) and which are not ("earnestness," "Hegel," "Plato," etc.)? In its most general terms, the same question could be asked in this way: If the relationship between a grammatical subject and its proposition can always be one of "irony," then how can we be sure that grammar (for instance, the "subject") and meaning (or the "thesis") can ever be made compatible, can ever be made to coincide in a direct way? We know, for instance, that for philosophy irony *is* a meaningful subject, and considered as a form of self-consciousness, it is *the* subject of philosophy. But in addition to the story of irony's (subjective) place within philosophical discourse that is hinted at by the first (philosophical) paragraphs of *Aparté*, there is also the rhetorical question of the heading "Irony as the subject of a thesis?" And this heading also points to the possibility that *any* proposition, insofar as it is necessarily predicated on a purely grammatical subject that can always be "irony," may also remain forever beyond its own power to signify in earnest, may also be condemned to not knowing whether it is or is not ironic, that is, whether its own "subject" is connected or disconnected from its intended meaning and, finally, whether the question of the subject of irony must occur in the mode of a heading or a beheading.

The distinction Agacinski brings into focus here, of course, is one between *consciousness* and *discourse,* or between philosophy and its language, or, to return to the terms used above, between *what* a text says and the *way* it must say it. It may in fact be true that subjectivity, considered solely in terms of self-consciousness, requires a moment of negativity that will itself be negated in the process of its own self-development, and that this moment can conveniently be referred to as "irony." As long as we restrict ourselves to asking about this irony in terms of consciousness, we may rely on a dialectical process like that of history to reduce the negativity involved in the individual ironic moments by eventually organizing them into a totality in which they become bounded and therefore understandable. But once we begin to ask about the status of a purely grammatical subject within a discourse of meaningful theses or propositions, we have left such assurances behind and can no longer be certain that we are dealing with questions having anything to do with either self-consciousness or history as understood in their traditional philosophical senses. No doubt the question of Socrates' history and self-consciousness could be an interesting and possibly fruitful subject for debate, but it would be a far different matter to argue that the grammatical subject that allows such propositions to be stated—"Socrates," "Kierkegaard," or "Irony"—has either consciousness or a history. That irony could name *both* a negatively subjective moment in the history of self-consciousness (Socrates or Kierkegaard, for instance) *and* the grammatical category that puts into question the articulation of a subject ("irony") and its predicates (meaning conceived of as the possibility of a *serious* "thesis") is truly ironic. For the two mutually exclusive meanings of irony thus conceived enter into a self-obliterating relationship between the self *as* consciousness and the self *as* grammar, and so the (necessarily rhetorical) question that asks about irony as a "subject" makes it forever impossible to decide whether irony is what allows consciousness to come into being or what prevents it from ever taking place.

At any rate, one of the places where these questions surface in a more developed and contextualized way in Agacinski's own reading of *The Concept of Irony* is in her use of Kierkegaard's reference to the engraving of Napoleon: "There is an engraving that portrays the grave of Napoleon. Two large trees overshadow the grave. There is nothing else to be seen in the picture, and the immediate spectator will see no more. Between these two trees, however, is an empty space, and as the eye traces out its contours Napoleon himself suddenly appears out of the nothingness" (*C.I.* 56). Appearing rather coincidentally within the dismissive presentation of Xenophon's Socrates, this brief sketch, or skit, is itself like the engraving of Napoleon it describes, and it will eventually allow us to read all the principal elements of a radical and comprehensive theory of irony, of which Kierkegaard's entire authorship is but an elaborate extension. We should recall that, in its context, what is at issue is not merely "seeing" the head of Napoleon or rather not seeing it as "mere" head. Kierkegaard introduces the reference to the engraving by saying, "Allow me to illustrate my meaning with an image" and thus tells us the story of the head not for its own sake but rather as a means of understanding his meaning more easily. Napoleon's head becomes a *figure* for what, in this case, just happens to be the difficulty involved in understanding the meaning hidden in the ironic words of Socrates. In order to tell us that there is no direct access to what is in Socrates' head, Kierkegaard avoids telling us what is in *his* head; instead he tells the story of another, mute, head, that of Napoleon.

This one moment in *The Concept of Irony,* which itself uses indirect communication in order to raise the question of the possibility of communicating truth or understanding, also includes a figure for subjectivity and its negativity, and so it can legitimately be taken as emblematic of virtually the entire Kierkegaardian project. Kierkegaard wants us to "see," that is, to *understand,* that seeing the head of Napoleon come out of the empty space of nothingness in the engraving can be taken as a figure for "hearing" or understanding the meaning of Socratic irony, or indirection. The appearance of subjectivity, clearly marked in the making visible of Napoleon's head, thus comes to be linked metaphorically not only with the initial subjective negativity that is traditionally associated with Socratic irony but also with the possibility of mastering this irony retrospectively through an act of understanding: "Napoleon himself suddenly appears out of the nothingness. . . . It is the same with Socrates' replies. As one sees the trees, so one hears his discourse; as the trees are trees, so his words mean exactly what they sound like. There is not a single syllable to give any hint of another interpretation, just as there is not a single brush stroke to suggest Napoleon. Yet it is this empty space, this nothingness, that conceals what is most important. As in nature we find examples of places so curiously situated that those who stand nearest the speaker cannot hear him, but only those who stand at a fixed point often at a great distance; so also with Socrates' replies when one recalls that in this case *to hear* is identical with *understanding,* not to hear with misunderstanding" (*C.I.* 56–57, emphasis added).

Irony would be like such an engraving, or rather irony would occupy the place that is empty in the engraving, the empty space from which the head of Napoleon pops up without anyone's having noticed. Inside a picture, irony occupies the empty space, the space in which the picture could no longer be said to be a picture but also an empty space which, ironically enough, produces *more* picture and more *subjective* picture (Napoleon). Drawing on Jacques Derrida's trenchant critique of representation in *La Dissémination,* Agacinski points out that the metaphor of painting, the image, or the engraving in this case, has always been used to characterize the *mimetic* relationship between thought and idea that is crucial to Western metaphysics. Some form of imitation or analogy is what guarantees a relationship of adequation between presence and representation and allows to take place the particular kind of recognition necessary to the philosophical discourse of truth. But, Kierkegaard tells us by way of the indirect figure of the Napoleonic head, the relationship between the words of Socrates and the "idea" he is trying to communicate is not one of resemblance or mimesis. This is Socrates' irony, and insofar as it is an empty space, insofar as there is literally *nothing* there, it tears or interrupts the process of painting, representation, perception, mimesis, or metaphorical exchanges based on resemblance. Irony does not imitate anything, it is not part of the metaphysical system of mimesis, and yet out of this empty space *within* the metaphysical system of mimesis, the image of the subject (Napoleon) bursts forth. Irony is not mimetic, but it seems capable of producing mimesis as an aftereffect. Irony is also not primarily subjective; if anything, it is more like the death of the subject, since it first hovers over the *grave* in this engraving. The story of the engraving tells us: that irony is not mimesis but that mimesis follows irony; that irony is not subjective but that subjectivity appears in the wake of irony; and finally, that the only access we have to irony is through both mimesis and subjectivity, that is, through the mimetic "like" of analogy and the "Napoleonic" figure of subjectivity—since here irony is "like" an empty picture of "Napoleon." How are we to understand such an ironic process?

Perhaps we should look again at this curious picture, or since irony is not mimetic, not painterly or representational, perhaps we should not "look" at it as one looks at an image but rather try to "read" it as one reads a text, for instance, the text of Socratic irony. We should recall, in fact, that *as* figure, the painting of Napoleon is a substitute for text; the painting is a figure for Socrates' words. Is there any place in this picture where its own status as a figure for language as textuality rather than painting is inscribed? In fact, language as textuality, as what has to be *read* rather than experienced, is precisely what has been occulted in the narrative of this textual image. For there *is* something to be read in the empty space, and it is something like the proper name, "Napoleon," the minimal inscription, which usually takes the form of a name on a tombstone, that must spell out the death of Napoleon's empirical subjectivity in order to mark this spot as his final resting place.[3] It is this space, then, above the inscription of subjectivity's death that is necessarily implied in the fact that this is an engraving of a grave, that irony works to produce an afterimage of subjectivity. Is the image of Napoleon that appears after his empirical death a form of philosophical idealization, a giving up of empirical immediacy in order to accede to the ideal realm of philosophical thought? Or, in Kierkegaard's own words, is the irony that prepares or produces such an image still functioning "in the service of the Idea"? In order to begin to sketch out an answer to these questions, we must ask where precisely Agacinski turns to the issue of language as inscription rather than representation or, in more specific terms, to the relationship between the proper name and subjectivity.

The last section of the chapter "The Serious Side of the Thesis: The Defense" opens with a citation of the first heading, "Irony as a Subject?" Is it merely a coincidence that the section that will discuss the general "citationality" of inscription is itself introduced by a citation of the earlier question of the subject as grammar? Is there a link between a reduction of subjectivity to the linguistic status of grammatical subject and the law of iterability that applies to all writing, to all language as a system of signs rather than images? Could this "link" possibly have something to do with irony? "The possibility of writing is also the possibility of irony: it is the possibility of detachment." The inscription or writing on the grave *is* irony, then, insofar as it performs the same interruption of mimetic, i.e., self-evident, connections between man and nature as does irony. And to the extent that all writing is ironic, i.e., nonmimetic, and dependent on the mechanical codes of merely grammatical subjects and predicates to signify the possibility of self-conscious subjectivity, it is also, and by necessity, indirect. Kierkegaard's special theory of indirect communication, then, is also a general theory of language as irony.

What makes such a theory of language a theory of *indirect*

---

3. For a reading of the grave as an inscription to be read rather than experienced, see Andrzej Warminski's "Missed Crossing: Wordsworth's Apocalypses," *MLN* 99, no. 5, 994.

communication is that, unlike the faithful image of Napoleon that will eventually appear between the trees, the inscription of the name cannot be *seen* here any more than it is literally possible to "see" or "hear" irony.[4] To the extent that it does not represent or imitate, all writing is an "empty space" in the picture. As such, a name must be *read* rather than perceived directly by the eye or ear, that is, must first be placed within an arbitrary but infinitely repeatable, i.e., recognizable, code, a grammar. But at the moment the self, as name, becomes dependent on the systematic but merely formal laws of a grammar, it gives up any illusion of speaking for itself, speaking directly in its own voice, and hands itself over to a process of recognition that is *mechanical* rather than self-conscious. This is why, within language conceived as a system of notation, it is never possible to determine with certainty whether the "subject" is a mind or a machine, that is, whether it is the "citation" of a merely grammatical or ironical rather than a thinking subject. Writing as nonmimetic inscription, insofar as it requires the mechanical underpinnings of a grammar, is itself the question of "irony as meaningful subject," the question of the possible disarticulation of grammar and consciousness. The turn toward language as a system of inscription, as an engraving of names rather than, say, a representation of trees, is an *aparté*, a

---

4. A reference to this same passage on 56–57 of *The Concept of Irony* also occurs early in John Smyth's discussion of Kierkegaardian irony in *A Question of Eros: Irony in Sterne, Kierkegaard, and Barthes* (Tallahassee: Florida State University Press, 1986), 108. By taking the analogical reference to "hearing" Socrates for granted as the possibility of an "ideal communication" of irony, Smyth can gesture toward a "contextualized performative" aspect of irony that would not be at all the same as irony's positing power, a language power that will be discussed later in this essay. The fact that the "ground" of this particular figure of "hearing" is composed of the distinction, by no means simple, between words as "meaning" and words as "syllables" should alert us to the complexity of the question and the necessity of examining the figure as a problematic figure of "reading" rather than Smyth's ideal "perception" in which "all the indeterminacy of interpretation . . . is resolved in the objective dialogical features of 'the situation and the reply.' "

turn away from a metaphorical chain of resemblances between mind and matter in which it is always possible to determine what one is seeing or hearing. Writing, then, is always the writing of a tombstone, because within language conceived as inscription, it is always possible that the "subject" is the death of the subject, that is, a hollow citation to be read rather than a living voice to be perceived. To quote Agacinski herself, it is always possible "that the subject would not be thinking whatever it is it is arguing."

What is the status of a "subject" that argues (a thesis) without thinking? Such a "subject" would seem to be a purely grammatical epitaph for self-consciousness, because it continues to exist as subject independently of any thought or consciousness. It is the grammatical subject that remains cut off or disconnected from the meaningful propositions it is in the process of pronouncing. And yet this is not the end of the story, and the purely grammatical subject cannot adequately account for the fact that the picture, the image, the entire metaphorical chain of subjective attributes suggested by the appearance of "Napoleon himself," actually does occur here: "Napoleon himself suddenly appears out of the nothingness, and now it is impossible to make him disappear. The eye that has once seen him now always sees him with anxious necessity." What the eye sees when it looks at Napoleon, of course, is *itself* in the image of the other, that is, and above all, it sees itself *as* the image of metaphorical resemblance between inside and outside. This is the scene of self-recognition in which the figure of Napoleon reflects the gaze of Narcissus, and so it is no wonder that the eye that has once seen itself in the commanding image of Napoleon will continue to look for its mirror image with increasing anxiousness. For only at this moment when the self can recognize itself as an image of subjective consciousness rather than a mere inscription of a grammatical category (the ironic subject) can it begin to enjoy the self-conscious freedom that is traditionally, if somewhat hastily, associated with irony. Kierkegaard himself speaks in this regard of the ironist's "enjoyment" at being able to direct all of his activity back into himself at every moment: "the ironist moves proudly as one terminated in himself—enjoying" (*C.I.* 176). For the pleasurable intoxication most often attributed to the ironist is certainly not to be looked for in the mute name inscribed on a tomb, but rather in the heady *freedom* to find himself again and again in a Napoleonic image of his own making and at his own pleasure.⁵

However, there remains something curious about this passage, and it is not the fact that the self would look repeatedly for itself with anxiousness or even anxiety, because such a reaction is easily accounted for from within a subjective consciousness, even if it were a pathologically obsessive one. But that the look would occur by *necessity* is somewhat surprising here, since, very much like the arbitrary but systematic element in the grammatical "I," the concept of necessity takes the act of self-reflection away from the willfulness of a self and once again turns it into a wholly mechanical form of repetition that remains outside of any subjectivity, whether conscious or unconscious. For this reason it would not be legitimate to equate the image of Napoleon that occurs over the grave of the empirical subject with the philosophical "subject" of idealism, Hegelian or other. To say that the subject looks for himself "by necessity," or that it is "impossible" for him to make the image of his self disappear (or appear), is also to say that he is not really a subject in any philosophical sense of the term, since such a "subject" would have no power over what he is doing and would much rather be the mere *product* of forces beyond his control and understanding. There is no doubt that the image of Napoleon does occur on the far side of the grammatical reduction of the subject, but it cannot be said for this reason alone that this new image of subjectivity is any less mechanical than the nonmimetic and citational "subject" of grammar that preceded it. What *is* different here is that this mechanical subject does not read itself as a mere name but instead *mistakes* itself for Napoleon. To be reduced to the status of a grammatical subject is bad enough, but to be turned into a grammatical subject that entertains Napoleonic delusions of grandeur is the height of irony.

---

5. Kierkegaard's understanding of the Narcissistic pleasure involved in ironic consciousness is inherited from Hegel's critique of the romantics' interpretation and use of the Fichtean absolute *ego*. The eye that recognizes itself by looking into the face of the Napoleonic image is a kind of figural corollary of Fichte's "I = I," whose ultimate aim would be to recuperate the negativity implied in Napoleon's death by bringing it into a balanced equation with the positive self-recognition of the living I.

And we must not overlook the fact that it is precisely out of the space of irony in this text—"out of the nothingness"—that the "necessity" of Napoleon's image originates: "Napoleon himself suddenly appears *out of the nothingness,* and now it is *impossible* to make him disappear. The eye that has once seen him now always sees him with anxious necessity." We should be careful to distinguish the "necessity" spoken of in this text from the "necessity" most often associated with natural causes and effects, since it is precisely the natural, mimetic order that is being interrupted by the ironic nothingness in the engraving. Irony, as the empty space of nothingness, as the nonmimetic inscription of a name on the tomb, seems to be what makes the subjective appearance of Napoleon possible while at the same time preventing it from ever managing to get itself (or its image) under control, since now it is "impossible" for it to relate to itself on anything other than conditions of necessity that remain entirely foreign to it. It is, therefore, not the freedom or caprice of the self-conscious subject that makes it look for and find itself again and again in the space of irony. Within the logic of this text, the self would be as powerless to generate the Napoleonic image as it is subsequently to be rid of it, and the "necessity" that makes the self look for itself again is the same *ironic* "necessity" that made the self see itself in the first place. What is this strange power of irony to produce a deluded subjectivity that can then be made to believe that it sees itself whenever it stares into the blank space of inscription, that affirms its absolute subjective freedom at the very moment it falls into the mechanical repetition of a blind necessity?

To answer this question fully would require a more extended discussion than is possible within the limited context of an introduction, but it is still possible to point in the direction such a discussion would have to take. Few readers of *The Concept of Irony* will forget the highly dramatic moment when Kierkegaard must finally ask about the limits of Socrates' irony. The question crystallizes around the element of negativity at the core of the Socratic method. What was the true status of the claim to ignorance that made all of Socrates' questioning possible in the first place? Were the assurances of Socrates that he knew nothing given in earnest, or was he merely being ironic? How far was Socrates *serious* about his ignorance? What hangs in the balance of such questions, of course, is nothing less than the possibility of philosophy itself being able to take irony "seriously," of being able to determine whether irony as a philosophical category is "serious" or hopelessly "ironic." Socrates, it seems, was not wholly ignorant, for he knew at least *that* he was ignorant, as is amply clear from the fact that he went to such great length to say as much. Such a knowledge, however, is not a knowledge of something, it has no positive content, and for this reason it cannot be taken entirely seriously. "To this extent," Kierkegaard concludes, "his ignorance is both to be taken seriously and not to be taken seriously, and upon this point Socrates is to be maintained" (*C.I.* 286).

What accounts for this aporia between seriousness and nonseriousness on which Socrates is to be kept suspended turns out to be a further extension of the linguistic complication between the subject as grammar and the subject as meaning (or proposition, thesis) that makes all language indirect in Kierkegaard's sense and that we were able to discover earlier thanks to Agacinski's reading. This time, though, the discrepancy turns out to be the slightly different one between language as *meaning* (a thesis) and language as *act* (a positing power). "The difficulty here encountered," says Kierkegaard on the same page, "is essentially that irony in a strict sense can never set forth a *thesis*"; nonetheless, he is quick to add, "the ironist must always *posit* something, but what he posits in this way is nothingness." The ironist speaks, then, but not in the language of meaning or of the thesis. Rather, he speaks the language of force or imposition, the "positing" of language as an arbitrary act of power prior to its determined meaning. What the ironist posits in this way is nothingness, or since irony *is* nothingness, what irony posits when it posits nothingness is itself *as* nothingness. But what must be kept in mind here is that since the language of positing is radically discontinuous with the language of meaning, the necessary gesture on the part of the self to understand the meaning of such a positing of itself will have to be aberrant. This moment, which is the necessary moment of (self)-reading that allows any text to come into being as text, occurs in Kierkegaard's own text when Socrates—as irony—says, "I am ignorant," which amounts to his trying to *say* that the language he speaks is not *saying* something, either positive or negative, but saying *nothing*, that is, *positing*. And since this "nothing" of positing is in no way symmetrical to the affirmations or negations of saying, it is precisely when Socrates (ironically) says that he is saying nothing that we (mistakenly) believe we know "what" he is saying. The irony here is the blind positing of the self as nothingness that necessarily ends up taking on the appearance of the self as something positive. In the mimetic imagery of the engraving of Napoleon, this occurs when the nothingness of positing the name on the grave actually *produces* the aberrant thesis or image of Napoleonic subjectivity, albeit in the negative though still symmetrical form of its natural death.[6]

Irony, then, is neither the empirical nor the ideal self but rather a purely linguistic self; it is the wholly arbitrary positing of the self as an empty inscription or name. Kierkegaard himself, at any rate, could not be clearer on this score when he later compares the Christian to the ironist. The scenario resembles in an uncanny way the earlier image of the engraving and the distinction in it between the ironic inscription of the tomb and the mimetic and subjective figure of Napoleon that suddenly appears out of this blank of nothingness. This time, though, it is the Christian— whose life can become meaningful only in the sacrificial space left by Christ's own empty tomb—who assumes the shape of Napoleonic subjectivity, since he is the one who finally takes the nothingness of irony "seriously," thus despairing of himself in order to allow himself to be produced poetically by God.

What is it that determines this poetic production of the Christian's subjective individuality, or what Kierkegaard refers to in other terms as "a plastic shape culminating in itself"? It is nothing other than the power to confer meaning upon words, to allow them to assume shape and figure by suppressing the knowledge

---

6. For a similar formulation of the nonsymmetrical distinction between positing and meaning, and one that goes a long way toward suggesting the place Kierkegaard would occupy in a wider examination of the period from Kant to Marx, see Paul de Man's "Sign and Symbol in Hegel's *Aesthetics*": "The philosophical I is not only self-effacing, as Aristotle demanded, in the sense of being humble and inconspicuous, it is also self-effacing in the much more radical sense that the position of the I, which is the condition for thought, implies its eradication, not, as in Fichte, as the symmetrical position of its negation, but as the undoing, the erasure of any relationship, logical or otherwise, that could be conceived between what the I is and what it says it is" (*Critical Inquiry* 8, no. 1 [Summer 1982]: 769).

that they are originally and potentially the dismembered and dismembering letters of (ironic) inscription: "The man who allows himself to be poetically produced also has a specific given context to which he must accommodate himself, and hence is not a word without meaning for having been divested of connection and context. But for the ironist this context or hanging together (this 'hang-up' or 'hanger-on' he would say) has no validity . . . he not only poetically produces himself but his environment as well. The ironist is reserved and stands aloof; he lets mankind pass before him, as did Adam the animals, and finds no companionship for himself" (*C.I.* 299–300). The scene, whether it be political (Napoleon returning from exile) or religious (the seriousness of the New Testament vs. Adam's ironic aloofness), is always a scene that covers over the grave of language by producing meaningful connections or figures where there may in fact be none. Irony, the positing power that belongs originally to all language and that is preserved in the figure of Adam imposing names on himself as well as on the animals, is the inscription of a word, "without meaning for having been divested of connection and context." What is free, arbitrary, and powerful in irony, and what Kierkegaard will refer to in the same section as irony's "sheer possibility," is therefore not some sort of *subject* or subjective will—man, or "Adam," being merely a personified example of what is fundamentally an impersonal language power—but rather the random coming apart, the chance disconnections of *words* and letters from any semantically determined context.

Kierkegaard's own text performs such a random coming apart of a word precisely when it names "irony" as the arbitrary power to undo all meaningful "contexts." The way that it undoes this particular "context" (*Sammenhaeng,* or hanging together) is by disconnecting what "hangs" *together* in the very word *Sammenhaeng* so that all that is left is the tangle of letters in which the serious meaning of the Christian threatens to get "hung" *up* when irony has its say in the word *Paahaeng.* Playing on its accidental proximity to *Sammenhaeng,* the Danish word *Paahaeng* (which means "accessory" or "encumbrance," or idiomatically, a "hanger-on") is also a kind of "hanging." But the hanging of *Paahaeng,* unlike the Christian's meaningful context or *Sammenhaeng,* gets ironically suspended "on" or "up" rather than "together with." What always remains, however, and what this example also goes on to illustrate, is how the "sheer possibility" of irony's disconnections are necessarily suppressed by a subjective consciousness that can survive only by recontextualizing them as moments in a sequential narrative rather than as absolute interruptions. One place where this occurs in the passage in question is when the ironist is further compared to Adam's attaching names to the animals, itself a constitutive moment of the biblical narrative of creation, fall, and redemption in which the mediating role of Christ's "hanging on" the cross promises among other things to "hang together" in a meaningful way all the accidents and interruptions of the salvation story.

The surprise here, of course, is that by taking such wholly arbitrary acts of imposition "seriously," by reconnecting in this way the gratuitous play of irony to "specific given contexts," the discourses of philosophy and religion can actually give themselves the impression of being "meaningful." A more complete reading of this chapter would have to show precisely how this occurs in the crucial distinction Kierkegaard makes when he describes the "twofold" nature of subjectivity's actuality as both a "gift" and a "task" to be realized (*C.I.* 293–97). For it should be obvious that the movement from "gift" to "task," which unquestionably constitutes the main burden of establishing the argument of historical continuity here, is something like the move that takes us from the arbitrary play of ironic imposition (a kind of gift) to the serious responsibility (or task) of philosophical or religious theses. What makes such a move possible, however, and what remains occulted in the English translation of the passage, has nothing to do with either philosophy or religion considered as meaningful and meaning-producing discourses.

What relates "gift" to "task" in Danish, and what therefore allows the freedom or gratuitousness of the gift to shade into the necessity of the task, or in slightly different terms, what allows the spontaneous and nontemporal sprites of irony to be reconnected to the gradual mediations of the historical task, is itself due to or made "necessary" by the arbitrary breaking loose of words and letters from their specific, i.e., determinate, meanings or contexts. The move from irony to history, or irony to philosophy, or irony to religion, is itself thoroughly *ironic* here since it takes place in Kierkegaard's text on the basis of the arbitrary play between *Gave* (gift) and *Opgave* (task), where the necessary link between the two crucial concepts is made thanks to an effect of the *letter* rather than of *meaning*. Such a play remains entirely foreign to the meaning of the two words in their specific, i.e., semantic, contexts, as is made amply clear by their translation into the wholly unrelated pair of English words "gift" and "task," and it takes place only by means of pulling the words *apart* into their constitutive letters.[7] In short, in order for the dialectical and recuperative process of history to begin to function effectively here, the gratuitous nature of irony (the gift) has to be sacrificed. But the meaning of the word that makes such a sacrifice necessary, "task," also has a particular syntax, *Opgave,* that makes this same sacrifice impossible. Irony thus reenters the system at the very moment the seriousness of the task of meaning was supposed to do away with it, since such a task (*Opgave*) can always be read quite literally as the arbitrary imposition of a sacrifice, that is, as a "giving up" (*give op*) of the arbitrariness of the gift (*Gave*). However, it is logically inconsistent to sacrifice arbitrariness in such a wholly arbitrary manner. Like the aporia between Socrates' seriousness and unseriousness, then, it remains forever impossible to mediate the aporia between *Opgave* as meaningful thesis (task) and *Opgave* as arbitrary positing (*give op Gaven:* "give up the gift," or what would amount to almost the same thing, "*give Op-gaven*": "*give* the task"). Nonetheless, like the engraving of Napoleon, such an aporia cannot prevent itself from taking on the (necessarily aberrant) figure of meaningfulness.

What Kierkegaard does when he actually goes on to trace the movement that leads from *Gave* to *Opgave* as though it were a form of mediation, as though it were a question of a temporal "upbringing or education" that progresses gradually from past

---

7. To the other more or less legitimate translations of *aparté*, we might as well add this more or less "ironic" one. Translating the French word *aparté* into English as "taking (words) apart" is "abusive" in the sense Philip Lewis has given the term, and it could also be called ironic in this case since it simultaneously names and repeats the *aparté* "of" irony; as such, it is an interruption of determinate meaning operated on the level of the syntax rather than semantics, or on the level of the letter rather than the word. The "specific context" of *aparté* as theatrical "aside" or parabasis is already a (scenic) translation of the radically nonscenic, nonrepresentative, nonmimetic element in irony.

(gift) to future (task) or what we do when we read such a story as a temporal unfolding, is to *impose* in turn a meaningful narrative on an ironic structure that in and by itself is devoid of any sequence or meaning whatsoever. The technical term Paul de Man has given to such narratives is, of course, allegory, and the real story and interest of *Aparté* begin at the point where Kierkegaard's entire authorship can be read as an intricate network of just such allegorical narratives of irony or allegories of Kierkegaard's theory of language as indirect communication. Some of the more important of these ironic allegories constitute the main narrative frame for Agacinski's own text, and they include the widely misunderstood erotic, politico-economical, and religious dimensions of Kierkegaard's thought. In each case, though, and whether it be in her exemplary treatment of *The Concept of Irony, Philosophical Fragments, The Concept of Anxiety, Repetition, Prefaces,* or the *Journal*, Agacinski's subtle and comprehensive reading is always careful to reinscribe the existential categories as aberrant narratives of the originally linguistic *apartés* from which they issue. From the opening ironization of sexual difference to a linguistic phenomenon of seduction (due to the arbitrary "gender" distinction present in the French pronoun "it") to the closing ambiguity that turns a racy psychoanalytical detective story of conscious or unconscious "recollection" into an allegory of impersonal "notation" (once again due to the "gender" distinction between "la mémoire" and "le mémoire"), Agacinski is virtually unsurpassed in following these erotic, philosophical, and religious narratives out to a point at which they can once again be taken apart. In so doing, she puts herself among the very few who have managed to set aside in the task of reading Kierkegaard a place for the gift.

CONCEPTIONS AND DEATHS OF SØREN KIERKEGAARD

ON A THESIS

IRONY AS A SUBJECT?[1]

Not in any case that it is subject *to* anyone, rather it subjects (but whom?) because it seduces, at the risk of sweeping away the ironist himself.

Irony, then, seems rather to be a withdrawal of the subject, indeed a void. But it is a void so vain and disquieting that it immediately calls for some kind of positivity—perhaps philosophy—to unmask, or manifest itself. What thus appears afterwards rushes in to master retrospectively a certain vertigo and to reappropriate this nothingness for itself in the form of *its* beginning. Socrates, since he's going to be this subject of irony, becomes a founder for philosophy.

But is it possible, even at the beginning, to *place* irony, which is perhaps displacement "itself"? And if philosophy claims to have no other beginning than *itself,* allowing for no preamble, then Socrates risks ending up in a position of instability (as is evident in Hegel)—should we even be able to speak of such a

---

1. Of Kierkegaard's thesis, for instance: *The Concept of Irony with Constant Reference to Socrates.* Copenhagen, 1841. *TN.* Since French personal pronouns have gender, Agacinski's immediate substitution of the feminine noun *ironie* by the pronoun *elle* makes the following paragraphs into a complicated but easily recognizable scene of seduction. Such a scene inevitably calls to mind the already ironic first paragraph of *The Concept of Irony,* where a trusting damsel (sensuous appearance) is treated first courteously, then sadistically, by the philosophical "knight."

subject in terms of "position." For from the Hegelian perspective, it is not yet a question of philosophy with Socrates, nor even of some "need for philosophy," but merely a question of what "aims at bringing forth" this necessity by means of a certain dialectical practice: one that allows the internal contradictions of the (still absent) Idea to appear, that allows its manifold determinations to develop and cancel one another in their reciprocal opposition. Socrates would have had the idea of the dialectic, but not the dialectic of the Idea. His dialectic leads to nothing, it only stirs up consciousness and destroys certitudes—so it is only negative. But this is not yet the negativity that is posited as such at the heart of dialectical movement. Socrates never makes it as far as speculation. For this reason his "position" will remain constantly ambiguous, in particular within the Hegelian interpretation to which Kierkegaard is inextricably bound by a debate that is sometimes complicitous, sometimes critical.[2]

If Hegel can be said to have perfectly understood Socrates' negativity (Kierkegaard borrows most of his analyses from him), he also wanted to find a "positive aspect" in Socrates that would have made him assimilable to the history of philosophy. This leads Hegel to "divide" Socrates and finally to relegate irony, or the "questioning attitude," to a secondary status by distinguishing it from its *goal:* the positing by subjectivity of the Idea as such. But this goal itself *is not* reached by Socrates. Since the Idea is "still" entirely abstract, it has no content whatsoever.

In brief: Kierkegaard refuses to grant Socrates any kind of positivity; Socrates has no point of view outside of irony, his attitude is infinitely subjective and infinitely negative regarding every positivity; he is incapable of "positing" anything, at least as long as he sees his *point de vue* to the bitter end.[3] Socrates himself is thus (nothing but) this infinitely ironic point of view. On the other hand, the Kierkegaardian interpretation is not for all that an *objection* to Hegel's: all the negativity of Socrates' di-

---

2. *Lectures on the Philosophy of History.* (*TN.* References to the German text will follow those to the English translation.)

3. *TN.* Agacinski plays here on an equivocation in the French word "point"; from a locus that allows vision to take place (*un endroit*), it becomes a grammatical negation (*ne . . . point*); from a "point of view," it slides ironically toward a "blind spot."

alectic, when pushed to its limit, can already be found in Hegel.

But who do we mean when we say "Socrates"? The interpretation is bound to be ambiguous given the diversity of the texts in which "Socrates" appears: Xenophon, Aristophanes, Plato. And under this last name, how many "Socrates" are there? In this regard, Hegel is a bit lax since he picks things out willy-nilly from the various texts. On the contrary, Kierkegaard isolates the specifically "Socratic" dialogues in Plato (the so-called "aporetic" dialogues), and he unhesitatingly dismisses Xenophon for having portrayed Socrates with a "shopkeeper's mentality," devoid of even the slightest trace of irony. Xenophon, for instance, sees in Socrates' death the "advantage of having escaped from the woes and worries of old age" (*Memorabilia*, 4:8,8). Xenophon is much too *dull* to have understood the least little thing about irony. For this reason we can expect nothing from him. Hegel, who had not thought of this argument, makes reference to Xenophon whenever he wants to illustrate the "positive side" of Socrates.

(We can assume that the plurality of Socratic figures is an effect of Socratic irony. Only a Socrates of negativity, of dissimulation, could have engendered so many doubles. There were several "conceptions" of Socrates for the reason that Socrates himself did not have any. The gods, he liked to say, had failed to grant him "the power to beget.")

Is irony a fit subject for a *thesis*? Is it possible to set something up on the basis of that which pokes fun at every tenable position? What position is to be taken with respect to (that) which posits nothing? Does an ironist write a "thesis"—did Kierkegaard?

*
* *

> He was not like a philosopher lecturing upon his views, wherein precisely the lecture constitutes the presence of the Idea itself (*selve Ideens Tilstedevaerelse*), on the contrary, what Socrates said meant something "other". (*CI*, 50)

Irony is an "interrogation" (*eirônia*). In reference to Socrates it would have also had the connotation of a *feigned* ignorance and indeed even a jesting, "in which what is said is the opposite of what is to be understood." Socrates is supposed to have questioned his listeners so that by *pretending* to be ignorant he showed just how real their own ignorance was. Socrates *knew*, but he simulated or played at being ignorant. Such is the traditional conception of simulation or ruse as dissemblance, indeed as deception. Irony would thus border on hypocrisy in the sense that *hypocritès* has always had: at once "actor" and "hypocrite." This conception is as traditional as it is reductive: if Socrates "knew," then his method would be nothing more than a pedagogical tool (still recommended to teachers today). For philosophy properly speaking, then, it becomes a most curious prelude to speculation. Such a method is useless for speculation *per se*, from whose point of view it could hardly ever have had any use.

This is not Kierkegaard's point of departure, though, and when he speaks of simulation it is in another sense. In fact, if irony is not a simple "pretending," then it consists in the interrogation itself, in the questioning—provided we make a distinction here between two forms of questioning (*CI*, 73). In the first case, the question takes place in view of an answer that will complete the question with its own (meaning)fulness—in the second, it is only a matter of letting the question draw out the apparent and contradictory contents of the "answers," letting it hollow them out and leaving behind "a void." It is in this second form of interrogation that we recognize the celebrated Socratic method, which has no other aim, or in any event, no other result, than to let in a "slight draught" well-suited to clearing out the clutter of opinions (*CI*, 74). But if this is the case, then Socratic dialectic is purely negative. It has no conclusion but is merely satisfied with negating (neither-nor). To any given question the answer is *neither* this, *nor* that. If, by means of negation, this method is able to indicate the Idea itself, it is only in the form of *allusion*. This negative dialectic at work in certain Platonic dialogues would thus be a dialectic devoid of syntheses and progress, unless we can speak of progress with reference to an Idea or an essence indicated in an allusive way but also completely "hollowed out" or evaporated. Such is the case in the *Protagoras*: "Socrates' argumentation essentially aims at reducing the relative dissimilarity among the various virtues in order to preserve their unity . . . But what I must call particular attention to is the fact that this unity of virtue becomes so abstract, so egotistically terminated in itself, that it becomes the very crag upon which all the individual virtues are stranded and torn asunder like heavily laden vessels" (*CI*, 94–95). The Idea appears only in its withdrawal, hollowed out.

The Idea would thus be related to the words of Socrates as the image of Napoleon is to the picture of his tomb: "There is an engraving that portrays the grave of Napoleon. Two large trees overshadow the grave. There is nothing else to be seen in the picture, and the immediate spectator will see no more. Between these two trees, however, is an empty space, and as the eye traces out its contours Napoleon himself suddenly appears out of the nothingness . . . It is the same with Socrates' replies. As one sees the trees, so one hears his discourse; his words mean exactly what they sound like . . . just as there is not a single brush stroke to suggest Napoleon. Yet it is this empty space, this nothingness, that conceals what is most important" (*CI*, 56–57).

We should ask ourselves about the pertinence of such an "image": why is an ironic practice of discourse compared to an empty picture? Why this strange painting—unless it is because the metaphor of painting (though only its metaphor) has always been used to depict the imitation essential to "thought" itself? Unless it is because this *logos* has always been "the faithful image of the *eidos* of what is," producing it as "a sort of primary painting, profound and invisible."[4] "Whether one conceives it in its 'Cartesian' or its 'Hegelian' modification, the Idea is the presence of what is" (Jacques Derrida's *Dissemination*, 194).

According to the metaphysical conception of the Idea as the presence of what is, Napoleon should have been in the picture, a true likeness, truly painted and truly present. Metaphysics, just as painting in principle, has no use for "allusions"—in every sense of the word.[5] Now Kierkegaard had already pointed out in his introduction that "he was not like a philosopher lecturing upon his views, wherein precisely the lecture constitutes the presence of the Idea itself" (*CI*, 50). So Socrates would have

---

4. The analysis and citations can be found in Jacques Derrida's "The Double Session" (189). (*TN.* This essay is published in *Dissemination.*)

5. *TN.* The now obsolete usage of *allusion* as "word play," or "pun," remains somewhat more discernable in the French word *allusion* than in its English equivalent.

posited nothing, exposed nothing. He would have engaged in an only *allusive* discourse, never expressing the Idea as such, never claiming to coincide with it. For this reason, the possibility of a painting which would itself be allusive (something which for metaphysics would perhaps be either repugnant or inconceivable) is decisive. Painting no longer functions here as an image, or in other words, as a faithful imitation of what is. This painting no longer makes *visible,* just as the discourse of Socrates does not express "the presence of the Idea itself," but only hints at it. Could it be, then, that the Socratic practice of interrogation, its allusive link to the Idea, does not belong to metaphysics? Yes and no. If we have recourse to those texts of Plato in which a Socratic conception of "the true" is worked out (the last pages of the *Cratylus,* for example), then it is obvious that Socrates defines as true that which resembles the thing in itself, even if such a resemblance occurs in a nonsensory mode. For the thing in itself is endowed with the status of an ultimate model to which both thought and word ought to align themselves and toward whose recovered presence they ought to strive. Thus, there can be no question here of seeing anything but a metaphysical definition of the Idea. Recalling this definition forces Socrates' metaphysics out into the open, and certain passages would justify such a procedure. But with respect to the *Cratylus* as a whole, the ending seems scanty and rather negative. We should not start out from names but rather from things . . . at which point the dialogue breaks off; there is nothing more to be learned from it. Socratic metaphysics is always failed or aborted—it is hardly a program. It is more common for Socrates to indicate where truth is *not* than it is for him to *tell* us where it is. He indicates where we have to start out from, but as Kierkegaard puts it, "where the inquiry should begin, there he stops" (*CI,* 83). Socrates did away with nontruths in the name of a certain idea of Truth (the thing in itself, what *is* originally). He does *not* pronounce the truth, even less so in the *Cratylus* than elsewhere, since it is there that he is so wary of words and shows how they can be made to say contradictory things. In other words, even if he refers his listener to the Idea, conceived metaphysically as the presence of what is, he himself is never able to make the Idea *present* in his discourse: whence a practice that remains ironic. He always says "something other" than what he says; he does not pronounce "Truth" as such. From this point of view it could be said that irony does not simply belong to metaphysics. Kierkegaard does not put the question precisely in these terms. Nonetheless, as someone who is so obviously preoccupied by Hegelianism, he gives his reader ample notice when he declares that Socrates does *not* expose his views within a discourse that constitutes "the presence of the Idea itself": Don't think that irony can be understood, or accommodated by philosophy; there is "something 'other' " at issue here— not, of course, another content or truth—perhaps another mode of discourse, another manner of speaking.

This whole interpretation is made possible only by isolating the specifically Socratic dialogues in Plato. Moreover, Hegel admits, but only in passing and without really paying much attention to it, that such dialogues do exist. They are characterized by a lack of dialectical progress, or synthesis. Kierkegaard, for instance, refers to the *Symposium*, where the various speeches are in no way moments that could coalesce in a final conception. It is not even possible to speak of any final "conception" here; Socrates has simply shown that Eros possesses none of those things he seeks (neither the beautiful nor the good): "Hence we see how Socrates gets at the nut not by peeling off the shell but by hollowing out the kernel" (*CI*, 82). Still, we should remember that it was necessary to have had the idea of the "kernel" in the first place, in other words, the Idea. For it is only possible to hollow it out insofar as we go looking for it.

Socrates thus liberates empirical determinations from the contingency of concrete existence (and in so doing he undermines the empirical), but he does this merely to indicate the Idea in its "most abstract determination" (*CI*, 83). As a result, love becomes nothing but pure longing, or pure desire. This is something like a delivery without the birth. An interminable dialectic leads only to an indeterminate Idea.

Socratic dialectic can therefore be considered doubly negative: it negates without positing anything. "In its overall effort," it destroys and negates concrete positivity (Socrates as the one who "delivers Greece," "purifies the temple," etc.), *and* it does *not* go beyond this negativity, this pure polemic, unless by indicating abstract, in other words, hollow, Ideas, like the engraving of the grave. But by assimilating the abstract to the negative, are we not already within the Hegelian critique of the abstract, already considering the abstract part of the category of the *not yet* ("still abstract," Kierkegaard says somewhere)?

Hegel can get Socrates into philosophy (in a way that remains ambiguous, in the mode of the *not yet*) only by separating irony, or the *via negativa*, from a positing of the Idea, no matter how abstract. If, following Kierkegaard, we interpret Socrates from the standpoint of infinite irony alone, then no basis, no positivity whatsoever can be attributed to it. Conversely, if Socrates is to *posit* something, then he will have to *go beyond* irony. Hegel hesitates, then, and is forced to make a distinction between two dialectics, or two interrogations, in Socratic *eirônia*. On the one hand, irony is simulation or ruse—Socrates asks questions in an "apparently naive manner"—this irony being merely "a way of getting along with others." So much for the subjective aspect of the dialectic. On the other hand, there is dialectic properly speaking, which "deals with the ultimate reasons for things . . . Out of every determinate proposition or out of its development, he developed the opposite of what the proposition stated: he did not affirm it against the proposition or definition in question, rather he took up this or that determination and showed how, even in itself, it contained its own opposite" (*Hist. Phil.*, 1:398; *Gesch. Phil.*, 18:458).

These two aspects of dialectic, sometimes simple simulation, sometimes manifestation of the dialectic *of* the Idea, are not easily reconciled with what Hegel goes on to say in these same lectures. Socrates actually knew nothing ("It may actually be said that Socrates knew nothing, for he did not reach the scientific construction of a systematic philosophy" [*Hist. Phil.*, 1:399/18:458]). Socrates' results were purely formal and unsatisfactory; all he did was throw consciousness into a state of confusion. From this perspective, the Hegelian distinction between an irony that simulates and a dialectic properly speaking becomes rather tenuous. Otherwise, it would have been necessary to distinguish two Socrateses—something Hegel does not do—as a function of the particular dialogue in question. Kierkegaard will "retain" only the negative Socrates, but is this any more legitimate, since to do so he will have to dismiss numerous other texts?

SOCRATIC IRONY—PURE NEGATIVITY

Kierkegaard's dissertation was preceded by fifteen "theses" written in Latin. The ninth declared: "Socrates drove all his contemporaries out of substantiality as if naked from a shipwreck, undermined actuality, envisaged ideality in the distance, touched it but did not acquire it" (*CI*, 349).

Socrates does not beget, nor does Theaetetus.

Were it a question of substantiating Kierkegaard's thesis, I would cite the ending of the *Theaetetus,* where, once the "pregnancy" has come to term, there is nothing to be known about knowledge except perhaps what it is *not*. No (philosophical) conception has taken place. "Socrates: So then, all those fruits which we have borne here today, doesn't our midwife's skill pronounce them to be mere wind and not worth the rearing?——Theaetetus: Why yes, it's just as you say" (20, c). A negative dialectic is an abortive dialectic. And yet, something does happen in it, something that provides irony with its double valorization: "For irony is a healthiness inasmuch as it rescues the soul from the snares of relativity: and it is an illness inasmuch as it is not able to maintain the absolute except in the form of nothingness" (*CI*, 113).

THE DOUBLE VALORIZATION OF NEGATIVE DIALECTICS

Negatively, irony prompts thought to "cut loose from the purely empirical sand banks and to set sail for the open sea" (*CI*, 153). Therefore, it is "liberating." It would seem that there is no image violent enough to express the destructive character of Socrates, and Kierkegaard depicts him by turns as an underminer, a warrior, a cannibal. First, he is the quiet underminer of the Sophists; he unmasks and confounds them by opposing their loquaciousness and pedantry with the silence of his own ignorance. He seems to efface himself before them, thus allowing their contradictory propositions to develop and cancel one another. At this point he rises above them, and in the deliberately ambiguous formula of Aristophanes, he becomes their *master* (*maître:* master, schoolmaster, mentor). The formula is remarkable for the very reason of its own profound irony: "For it certainly would be an irony worthy of Aristophanes to conceive Socrates, the Sophists' most spiteful enemy, not as their antagonist, but rather as their schoolmaster (*laeremester*), which in one sense he certainly was. And the *curious confusion* that one who combats a particular movement may himself be conceived as its representative . . . conceals in itself so much intentional or unintentional irony that it should *not entirely* be lost sight of" (*CI*, 168). Socrates brings sophistry to its term, so to speak, to the point where it exhausts and dissolves itself. He alone is "equipped and fitted out to do battle with the Sophists." He is also a warrior, then, who "in the infinite exaltation of his freedom" wielded irony like a brand or a sword: "the two-edged sword which he wielded over Hellas like a destroying angel" (*CI*, 232–34). Isn't it in the *Apology* (30, e) that Socrates compares himself to a gadfly or a goad sent by the gods to stimulate the Greek state?

The ironist talks—at least this one did not write—but he is not for all that a *voice;* he carries on a battle in which silence is both the means and the end of the combat. Even when he talks, the ironist does not *say* anything; he effaces himself in the questioning and allows the answers to become manifest in their apparent positivity. He is pure solicitation, provocation, although he himself remains hidden. And when at last all the answers have canceled themselves out, the ironist imposes silence on his distraught and befuddled interlocutors. Socrates is without a voice because he is not, or is not yet, the voice of Truth ("there's just nothing to be heard; a profound silence reigns . . ."). Irony is nothing but pause or suspense: "Truth demanded silence before lifting up its voice, and it was Socrates who had to impose this silence. Thus he was *exclusively negative.* Had he possessed a positivity of his own, he would never have been so unmerciful, never so cannibalistic as he was" (*CI*, 232–33). A strange image; the extreme case will crop up later, when the ironist gets swept away by his own negativity, as though he were in the process of devouring himself . . . One last image to show irony "opening up a vacuum," delivering its disciples of their fragile certitudes: the ironist not only strips his student clean, he actually skins him alive. For in *The Clouds,* Socrates is able to talk Strepsiades right out of the coat on his back. This is an apt way of symbolizing, according to Kierkegaard, that the disciple is also relieved of his now antiquated thought processes. Strepsiades, speaking of his vanished cloak, is thus fully justified when he says: "I haven't really lost it, I've just become dis-pensive about it."[6] Socrates does not give anything, he only disencumbers, and just as Charon, "divesting his passengers of the manifold determinations of concrete existence," he leads only into a void. "*Actuality became nothingness* by means of the absolute; but this *absolute* was in turn a *nothingness*" (CI, 255).

This "nothingness" is the *abstract* universal. Socrates brings to light the universality that, in Hegel's words, was "sunken in materiality." But for Hegel, it is a *moment*, necessary but unique, and it will not have to be repeated; it is a *moment* (in a sense which Kierkegaard will later take up without ever fully admitting it as such). After having considered the Sophists, Hegel begins his lecture on Socrates in the following way: "Consciousness had reached this point in Greece when Socrates appeared in Athens—the great figure of Socrates" (*Hist. Phil.*, 1:384/18:481). At that point, consciousness is able to separate the universal from the concrete and to understand that whatever is, "is mediated by thought." This moment *will have been* necessary, but at a given time and once and for all. We no longer need Socrates, neither his method nor his irony, nor even *his* dialectic. As far as Hegel is concerned, what manifested itself in Socrates (the interiorization of consciousness) "would later become a matter of habit" (*Hist. Phil.*, 1:391/18:449). Today, *we* are already "trained in representing to ourselves what is abstract," "*our* reflection is already accustomed to the universal." For *us*, then, "the Socratic method of so-called deference, the development of the universal from out of so many particulars, that verbosity of exemplification, all this has something about it that is often tiresome, boring (*taediositas*)" (*Hist. Phil.*, 1:404/18:465, emphasis added). In other words, the Socratic point of view and method are totally *outmoded*.

---

6. *TN.* In order not to lose altogether the French, *Je ne l'ai pas perdu, je l'ai dé . . . pensé* (I spent it, I thought it away)—which is itself an ironic twist on Strepsiades' original desire to get something for nothing, it has been necessary to dispense with the more literal translation, "I have cogitated it away" (*Clouds*, 857).

This is where Kierkegaard's resistance is located. We could put this in a somewhat programmatic way by saying that for Kierkegaard irony will always be what eludes Hegelian sublation (*Aufhebung*), to the extent that irony—and this may seem paradoxical—also represents, in a perhaps inevitable fashion, the writer's point of view. "Perhaps"—since the question remains whether Kierkegaard was ever able to get beyond what he called the author's ironic relation to his work. In his thesis and well afterward, Kierkegaard "re-works" the Hegelian concepts of moment, stage, station, and development. But just as in the conclusion to his thesis, it is in order to resituate them on the level of "private life," of "individual existence." Now irony turns out to be necessary from the start as a *moment* in poetic creativity: "the poet must maintain an ironic relation with his work." In fact, the author is able to conceive only finite works; every "conception" depends on a certain point of view and remains particular. An author thus gives free rein in his work, in each of his works, to this "positive element," but without ever identifying himself with this positivity (just as Socrates let the Sophists go on talking)—all this with profound irony. An author is thus always, and in advance, detached from the work with which he entertains a merely indirect relationship. Should he go further, should he become a philosopher, he will discover in each of his works a "moment" in his own development. Were this only possible, it would imply some final recuperation by the author, after the fact and outside every work, of his entire production . . .

Kierkegaard's thesis seeks to elaborate an interpretation of Socrates on the basis of irony as a negative dialectic. For this reason he must criticize the Hegelian reading, which attributes to Socrates a "positive aspect." But the arguments Hegel uses to distinguish a positive Socrates and a negative Socrates are not clear. On the one hand, it should be recalled that Hegel pushes the analysis of Socratic negativity just about as far as it will go. The result of the "dialectical" method is to throw "consciousness into a state of commotion," to startle it, surprise it, unsettle it, bewilder it, and finally to arrive at this point: "what we used to know has refuted itself." And again: "The main tendency of the dialogues was to provoke bewilderment" (*Hist. Phil.*, 1:404/18:465). Such a result really isn't one for Hegel. On the basis of the *Meno* and the *Lysis*, he shows that "in reference to the result (the content) the dialogues leave us totally unsatisfied" (*Hist. Phil.*, 1:406/ 18:466). But "this negative side is what is essential." It is of no use for Hegel to admit at first that such is the "essence" of Socratic dialectic; it is immediately apparent that such is *not* the essence for him, G. W. F. Hegel. What is essential is what Socrates makes possible, the beginning that he is (without really being this beginning, though, since neither philosophy nor the need to philosophize is actually there yet, it's just that now they *could* come into being). "Whence *ought to arise* the *need* for a *more strenuous effort after* knowledge" (*Hist. Phil.*, 1:405/18:465, emphasis added). The vexation apparent earlier, due to the tiresome "loquaciousness" of the dialogues, returns here in the form of a "more strenuous" effort. It would seem, then, that at the moment Hegel asserts the purely negative character of the Socratic dialectic, he dismisses it philosophically and relegates it to a point *short of* the beginning properly speaking. Nonetheless, Socrates remains a "founder," but for another reason and only to the extent, "on the other hand," as it were, that he has been constructive. The constructive element here is the idea of the Good posited as a universal. This is only the idea of some abstract good, and yet it is "no longer quite as abstract," says Hegel, since it is "produced by thought." Morality—the only real interest of Socrates—took the form of "the conviction of the individual in his own unique consciousness." Immediacy no longer has its own validity; rather, it must justify itself in the eyes of thought. This is the "return into oneself" and the isolation of the individual—who also separates himself from the State (*Hist. Phil.*, 1:406–9/18:467–70).

However, when Hegel wants to show in what manner Socrates at once represents the "two sides" of the universal—the negative that undercuts the particular, and the positive—he calls on Xenophon. In the *Memorabilia*, Socrates had been depicted "with much more precision and fidelity than in Plato." How could Xenophon have been more accurate? We can judge from the following passage: "In the fourth book (4:2,40), Xenophon wants partly to show how Socrates had attracted the youth to him and had led them to the realization that they *needed instruction* (*Bildung*)—something which we have already discussed—*on the other hand,* though, he *also* recounts how Socrates himself actually did instruct them and what they learned by frequenting him, 'who no longer bewildered (tortured) them through subtleties, but rather taught them the Good in a clear and open (unequivocal) manner. He showed them the Good and the True in concrete determinations, which he always came back to so as not to stay in the merely abstract'" (*Hist. Phil.*, 1:415/18:477–78, emphasis added). In order to confirm the interpretation of this Socrates who left behind the "subtleties" of his dialectic and led his auditors onto firmer ground (a Socrates, that is, who finally gives up his irony), Hegel makes reference to the conversation with Hippias recorded by Xenophon (*Memorabilia*, 4:4, 12–16, 25). Socrates asserts there that the just person obeys the laws even if individual laws change, thereby making them seem contingent. Why is this obedience necessary? For the simple reason that "the best and happiest state is that in which the citizens are of one mind and obey the laws." Hegel: "Thus, Socrates closes his eyes to the contradiction and lets stand the law and its institutions, just as they are conceived by the man on the street. Here we can see an affirmative (constructive) content" (*Hist. Phil.*, 1:416/18:478). Undoubtedly so, but does it have anything to do with the Socratic dialectic? Hegel explains this positive aspect in two ways: Socrates has understood the necessary movement in which laws are *sometimes* valid "just as they are to be found in the State," and "sometimes susceptible to being revoked inasmuch as they are particular laws." Socrates himself asks, "Aren't those who wage war the same ones who contract peace once again?" In this case, Socrates would not only be the one who brings to light contradictions and undercuts certitudes, but also the one who *already* comprehends the dialectic of the Concept. That is why, faced with the contradiction, he "looks the other way" and recommends obedience. The second argument, already referred to, occurs thanks to an unexpected coalition: "In a word, Socrates says that the best and happiest State is that in which the citizens are of one mind and obey the laws." If Kierkegaard remains puzzled by this interpretation, it is not without reason, then, and it is precisely because it completely drops the "negative" dialectic to which Hegel himself will return in the following pages. If "Socrates exhibits something positive here," remarks Kierkegaard, "it is because he *does not carry through his standpoint (son point de vue)* . . . hence it is not a positivity following upon his infinite negation but a positivity *preceding it*" (*CI*, 252, emphasis added).

This whole discussion shows how Hegel tried to rescue Socrates from what he called the "dangerous side" of abstraction and purely negative upheaval. Still, chances are that no one has done more to reveal this negative risk than Hegel himself, no one pushed so far the analysis of negativity, an analysis that at this point leaves the "moral" and positive Socrates of Xenophon in order to outdo even the portrait left by Aristophanes. It is in this oscillation between Xenophon and Aristophanes that the ambiguity of the Hegelian interpretation can be read.

But Hegel couldn't agree with us more. No one understood Socratic negativity better than Aristophanes: "he was perfectly right in his *Clouds*" (*Hist. Phil.*, 1:427/18:482). He was able to capture Socrates' philosophy with "precision," and the profundity of *The Clouds* lies precisely in its capacity to show how the Socratic method ends up suppressing whatever truth may be in naive consciousness and affirming in its stead the freedom—without content—of Spirit. In other words, and nearer the play itself, this dialectic allows a son, Phidippides, to behave most insolently toward his father, Strepsiades, and finally to give him a drubbing! Strepsiades, not having gotten much profit from the time he himself had spent with Socrates, decides to send his son to him. He regrets it, of course, and eventually curses dialectics and burns down Socrates' residence, the "Thoughtery." "We must admire," says Hegel, "the depth of Aristophanes in having recognized the dialectical side in Socrates as being something negative" (*Hist. Phil.*, 1:430/18:485). Even if they don't come right out and say so, it seems that for Hegel, just as for Kierkegaard, the image of a son beating his father is both a subtle and accurate representation for the liberation of Spirit. Having once learned his p's and q's from Socrates, Phidippides not only succeeds in getting rid of the creditors who pester his father by demanding payment for debts run up by Phidippides himself, but beyond that, "*filial respect* and obedience to his father fare no better than the due date under this dialectic" (*CI*, 171). The comic side of dialectics is at the same time its healthiness.

For Kierkegaard, the Aristophanic reading of the Socratic dialectic goes even further; its every detail becomes significant. As such, the clouds themselves (the chorus) become a symbol of vacuousness, a reflection of Socrates' vacuous interior. Here the irony belongs to Aristophanes, and it consists in having shown the absence of content that is specific to Socratic irony by putting it in the form of the clouds invoked by Socrates in the play. The clouds ("haze," "fog," "mist," "smoke") represent the end, the "result" of negative dialectics. Aristophanes would have thus hinted at an analogical link between Socrates and the clouds on the one hand, and Socrates and the Idea on the other. The Socratic Idea would be nothing but haze and smoke, "which have fallen silent before the splendor of the Idea." As Kierkegaard puts it: "For what remains when one allows the various shapes assumed by the clouds to disappear is nebulosity itself, which is an excellent description of the Socratic Idea" (*CI*, 166).

The fickle shapes in which actual clouds appear are related to the "essence" of clouds in the same way that every predicate is related to the Idea. Like clouds, "the True never *is*." Clouds (nothingness) and an eloquent tongue: that is all you have to believe in, according to Socrates (*Clouds*, 423ff.)—*Nothingness* and the tongue's *language*. Which is enough to imply that the tongue with which the dialectician speaks wags like the clapper in a bell and merely *resounds* like one: "Socrates impresses upon Strepsiades that instead of believing in the gods he must believe in nothing but wide empty space and the tongue, a condition describing perfectly all the obstreperous talk about nothing, and which reminds me of a passage in Grimm's *Irish Fairytales* where he speaks of people with an empty head and a tongue like the clapper in a church bell" (*CI*, 180. In Danish, *Tunge* means not only language and tongue, but also bell clapper). The basket in which Socrates is *suspended* is also an "excellent image." Like Mohammed's casket hovering between two magnets, Socrates' basket is balanced between the earth and the clouds. In more ways than one, the ironist incarnates a subjectivity that is left "hanging."

Finally, Aristophanes' projection is correct inasmuch as it is *comical*. If Socrates is entirely negative, if the ironist "is extremely lighthearted about the Idea . . . since for him the absolute is nothingness," then he achieves a high degree of the comical by means of this levity. "Aristophanes was wholly correct insofar as he was prompted to conceive [Socrates' activity] comically" (*CI*, 174). Hegel had already demonstrated the relevance of a comic representation of Socrates. "The comical," he said, "consists in showing how men or things bring about their own dissolution by making a show of themselves" (*Hist. Phil.*, 1:427–28/18:483).

In order for something to be comical it must contain its own contradiction; lacking this, the comical remains superficial. Socrates qualifies for the comical insofar as there is contradiction between the effort he expends and the result he achieves—"Socrates brings forth in his moral endeavor the opposite of what he intends" (*Hist. Phil.*, 1:428/18:483–84). This is not only true in *The Clouds*. It would be possible to suggest that Socrates is comical because he makes a habit of shortchanging us, and this would conform to an entirely negative conception of Socrates. Negativity and the comical go hand in hand, and when Hegel lends his approbation to Aristophanes, he necessarily gives up his positive conception of Socrates. Kant, to rely on those rather sorry "jokes" he tells on the only page of the *Third Critique* devoted to the comical, did not have much of an opinion of the comical and did not see much use for it in art (the fine arts). Nonetheless, he says enough to make us wonder about his apparent lack of appreciation of comedy, or the value of the comical—that of Aristophanes and/or Socrates, for instance. What he actually writes is: "Laughter is an affection arising from the sudden transformation of a strained expectation into nothing" (*Critique of Judgement*, 177/ *Kritik der Urteilskraft*, 273). The understanding, "which does not find what it was expecting, suddenly relaxes itself and the effect of this slackening is felt throughout the body." This is laughter. An expectation that is frustrated makes us laugh; not, of course, that it is pleasing, nor is it enjoyable in itself (to the first edition Kant adds, "as in the case of a man who gets the news of a great commercial success"), but merely because the play of representations brings about a kind of "equilibrium of the vital forces in the body." This sudden movement of body and mind has a beneficial influence upon the health . . . At this point, and leaving aside his "jokes" for a while, Kant would have been able to analyze the comical aspect in Socratic irony, unless this very aspect belongs to philosophy itself.

But if the act of shortchanging, i.e., producing an expectation that is forever deferred, engenders the comical, it is equally certain that it is also capable of arousing love. Socrates' negativity is at the same time his seduction. The erotic nature of the disturbance caused in his disciples seems to have escaped Hegel. On the contrary, Kierkegaard was to see in Socrates a demon of a seducer, a master eroticist. . .

Apology for a Seducer

Socrates' handsome boyfriend, Alcibiades, complains of having been one of the many victims of a seducer who lets himself be loved but who remains unapproachable, who takes without giving anything in return, who maintains himself at a distance and *keeps himself* from loving: "And he has fooled not only me, but Charmides, son of Glaucon, and Euthydemus, son of Diocles, and many others in the same way—he starts out as though he is the lover, but in fact he ends up being the beloved" (*Symposium*, 222, b). Socratic coyness is not derivative with respect to seduction, it is its cause. Alcibiades is thus "unable to tear himself away," says Kierkegaard (*CI*, 84). By "never expressing the Idea as such" (by never pronouncing the "Truth"), the ironist produces turmoil and makes a romantic attachment "not only possible but necessary." Irony is troubling, unsettling, disturbing; it has no other effect than to initiate a "love affair" between the ironist and his listener. That Kierkegaard qualifies this love affair as "intellectual" should not mislead us. What is at issue here is passion and the *erotic* relationship that, barring evidence to the contrary and no matter what form it takes, has always been of an "intellectual" order. "When I hear his voice," says Alcibiades, "my heart leaps within me more than that of any Corybantian reveller." "He is like one bitten by a serpent, yet bitten by something even more painful and in the most painful place: in the heart and soul" (*CI*, 85). This "power of seduction and enchantment" is irony's sole effect, inasmuch as it causes pure turmoil. In other words, irony does not produce the "third term" in which the lover could find appeasement. The ironist never comes out onto the field of exchange; no mediation intervenes in order to guarantee communication. After having been skinned alive and torn out of his immediate existence, the other is to receive nothing.

Giving away none of what he makes it seem as though he has, the ironist stays in control of things and continues to be an object of desire. Showing nothing, except by allusion, never expressing the Idea as such, he retains his mastery over the relationship— "it pertains to the essence of the Ironist . . . to possess the Idea as his personal property" (*CI*, 86). After having relieved the disciple of his cloak (*The Clouds*) and his certitudes, after having excited his curiosity and his desire, the ironist leaves him in the lurch.

The conveyance of a knowledge would never "have given rise to this kind of passionate turmoil . . . But as it pertains to the essence of irony never to unmask itself, and since it is equally essential for irony to change masks in Protean fashion, it follows that it must necessarily cause the infatuated youth much pain" (*CI*, 85).

Love is thus the effect of an indirect relation, or "communication," from afar, based on *allusion* . . . , which the disciple can *never* be certain of having understood. Prisoner of his own doubt, this is why he remains tied to the person of the ironist: "The disguise and mysteriousness which it entails, the telegraphic communication which it initiates, inasmuch as the ironist must always be understood at a distance, the infinite sympathy it assumes, the elusive and ineffable moment of understanding immediately displaced by the anxiety of misunderstanding—all this captivates with indissoluble bonds" (*CI*, 85).[7] The ironist, a moment ago an underminer, now becomes a *vampire*—the obvious delight which Kierkegaard finds in developing these images is a good indication that they are not meant to denigrate the seducer. Characterizing the seducer in such a way serves only to reinforce his power— "The ironist is a vampire who has sucked the blood out of the lover and fanned him with coolness, lulled him to sleep and tormented him with turbulent dreams" (*CI*, 86). If this seducer is able to get himself paid in the bargain (as in *The Clouds*), then his vampirism becomes total. All the same, there is no law that says that someone who pays to get himself seduced can't make a profit on it, even if he is not, as the saying goes, paid back in kind. The ironist, the questioner who keeps himself out of sight, who stays behind a mask, is thus all the more seductive insofar as *he does not respond*, and this in more ways than one. He leaves the question, the disciple, and even himself, "up in the air." Just as he admits in the *Apology*, Socrates is nothing but a goad sent to stimulate the Athenians. "An eroticist he certainly was to the fullest extent . . . in short, he possessed all the seductive gifts of the spirit. But communicate, fill, enrich, this he could not do. In

---

| 7. The same "erotic" dialectic can be found in Johannes the Seducer.

this sense one might possibly call him a *seducer*, for he deceived the youth and awakened *longings* which he *never satisfied*, allowed them to become inflamed by the subtle pleasures of anticipation, yet never gave them solid and nourishing food" (*CI*, 212–13). Then the youth which he "deceived"(?), "felt the deep pangs of unrequited love." Such is irony's mastery: it awakens desire just as it dominates and maintains it, all the while holding itself back— "Alcibiades' growing impetuosity always met its master in Socrates' irony" (*CI*, 214).

Now for Kierkegaard—and this will be verified elsewhere— there is no mastery other than that of seduction, never. This seduction, which he first finds in Socrates, also belongs to Johannes. Moreover, it is the seduction of God himself. Is it not true that one of the most excruciating dilemmas is always to have to choose between the pleasure of seducing and that of being seduced?

Such is the dilemma of the fiancé who also wants to be an "author" and of the author who also wants to be a Christian. For the fiancé or the "writer" (the "poet") chooses seduction, while the Christian chooses passion. *Philosophical Fragments* develops the theme of divine seduction (a veritable rapture), which it is necessary to distinguish from the simply human seduction of Socrates. Sent on a mission of divine inspiration, "a midwife subject to examination by the God himself," Socrates represents only an "occasion" for the disciple to discover his ignorance in a relationship "between man and man." But the God will not permit Socrates to beget: "Heaven has debarred me," he says, "from giving birth" (*Fragments*, 12–13). He who begets, for Kierkegaard, can only be the God himself. But this God, what does he do if not "teach" man all over again that he is a man, that is, a nontruth, and that the unknown something colliding with the passion of his reason is the God? By which, according to this teaching, God is master.[8] It is easy to see at what price, in what sort of panic, the mind is carried away. We need only recall Alcibiades.

---

8. *Fragments*, 48–49: "So let us call this unknown something: *the God*." Cf. also below, *Economies of Sacrifice*. "Passion, Panic." The God is "nothing"—if not difference itself insofar as it can never be conceived as such (except by interiorizing it, and thus missing it altogether).

The God ravishes the mind and deals it a mortal blow; such is love. This is God's irony with respect to human intelligence.

But the *thesis* hasn't gotten that far. Kierkegaard still believes in speculation and in speculative knowledge. It could be that his own understanding of irony has him a little frightened. Even though it seems to be only in passing, he still makes a point of limiting its effects. Alcibiades is a most inflammable tinder since he is "rash, sensuous, and highspirited . . .", but Plato, conversely, is strong enough to avoid getting taken in. "*Naturally,* for *more gifted* natures this realization [of the deceptive character of the ironist] could have been neither so noticeable nor so distressing" (*CI,* 213–14, emphasis added). Plato will learn to turn his gaze inward and to gain access to the Idea, though he also knows that, in a certain sense, he owes none of this directly to Socrates. Here is one of those numerous points where Kierkegaard joins Hegel and endeavors to go beyond irony. From this point of view, since he eludes the torments of love and moves toward authentic speculation, Plato is by far the best disciple. But it is not possible to say that Kierkegaard himself follows Plato. His model remains Socrates.

Indifference: such is the other name for ironic negativity. All the relations of the ironist—to his lovers, to the State, to death itself— are marked by indifference. This is what gives Socrates that haughty freedom, that attitude which could also seem "aristocratic."[9] The lofty "ironic freedom," which elevates Socrates above empirical facticity, which produces Alcibiades' torments, and which will eventually cause Socrates' death, is not without a certain sensuous enjoyment. The ironist *delights* in his indifference and in his infinite detachment. Hegel does not miss the opportunity to condemn this sensuous enjoyment of subjectivity, which indulges itself in a lamentable vanity at the very moment (which in itself is necessary) that it becomes conscious of itself as absolute: "I am the master of the law and the world alike, I simply play with them as befits my caprice. My consciously ironic attitude lets even the highest things perish, and I merely delight in myself at the thought" (*Phil. Right,* 102, para. 140). Kierkegaard

---

9. *CI,* 207. Kierkegaard specifies, "this of course in an intellectual sense."

does not pick up on this condemnation, but before returning to the Hegelian point of view on "authentic freedom" in the life of the State, he treats himself to a moment's pause over the link between the delight of ironic enjoyment and the delight of cynical enjoyment. In its own way, each is to be understood as "negative enjoyment." This curious notion obviously does not mean—contrary to what has sometimes been suggested—that Socrates (like Diogenes) would have simply liberated himself from sensuous enjoyment, supposing he could have done this in the first place. Diogenes seems actually to have enjoyed the specific pleasure (negative enjoyment) of finding satisfaction in a lack, without in any case having been unacquainted with desire: "[Cynicism] seeks its satisfaction *in not surrendering to* [*this desire*] . . . instead of issuing in desire it turns back into itself at every moment and *enjoys the lack of enjoyment*—an enjoyment vividly suggesting what ironic satisfaction is in the intellectual sphere" (*CI*, 207). How is it possible to enjoy the absence of enjoyment? It would be necessary here to distinguish between negative (ironic) enjoyment and *"happiness,"* "that enjoyment possessing absolute content" (*CI*, 176). This happiness—let's call it positive enjoyment—has to do with "possession." Obviously, the ironist possesses nothing; if he enjoys (it), it is perhaps because he knows that positive enjoyment can never quite be a sensuous enjoyment. Possession implies involvement and a dependence on the "content" in possession, something which always deprives the possessor of his mastery, therefore of his possession, and at the same time of his enjoyment. There is no such thing as a simple positive enjoyment. The desire to possess always hands itself over for possession. The ironist, thanks to the distance he maintains with respect to his own sensuous enjoyment (his hovering, the suspension of his desire, his detachment), is free to *not* enjoy sensuously; in which he delights. "Whereas the Sophist runs about like a harassed merchant, the ironist moves proudly as one terminated in himself—enjoying" (*CI*, 176).[10]

> 10. In a note inserted here, Kierkegaard refers to what the chorus in *The Clouds* says about the difference between Socratic seduction and the seduction of the learned Prodicus: "For to none other would we be inclined to listen, unless it be Prodicus; to him for his wisdom and knowledge; to you for the grandness of your demeanor in the streets, your sideways glance . . . your imposing air."

POLITICALLY BLAMEWORTHY IRONY

It remains to connect Socrates' politically negative attitude, a negativity that is in no way separable from negative dialectics in general, to the pure negativity of Socrates' irony. Insofar as dialectics is without a result here (except a "negative" one) and that it leads to indetermination, insofar as it is pure emancipation with respect to every positivity and that it denies every "established order" without ever establishing anything of its own, it is emancipation with respect to stability *par excellence*—that is, to the Institution of institutions, to the State. Corresponding to the nonpositing of the Idea would be the Socratic wariness of any position, in particular a political position. There is neither Idea, nor stability, nor establishment, nor institution, without posit(ion)ing. Now irony "establishes nothing"; even more importantly, it "leaves nothing standing." Irony does not oppose itself to the State; rather, it is not capable of entering into a relationship with the State: "for [Socrates] *was incapable* of contracting *any real relation* to the established order" (*CI*, 203).

Socrates is in *ignorance* of the State; therein lies his irony. And his crime. The irony is double: there is the private individual's simple ignorance, and then there is the (ironic) claim that is made upon this ignorance before the people's tribunal. Socrates *boasts* of having never bothered about "acquiring money, nor about the management of his household, about military, civic, or other offices . . ." (*CI*, 205). "Now this can scarcely be regarded as so praiseworthy from the standpoint of the State," remarks Kierkegaard judiciously. If, when it comes to particular instances, Socrates can excuse himself on the basis of his ignorance, he is not able to do this with respect to the overall issue, for it is precisely this ignorance that renders him guilty in the eyes of the State, and of the people.[11] "This non-acceptance of the gods of the State stems essentially from his whole standpoint theoretically designated by himself as ignorance" (*CI*, 195).

Whoever is not with the State is against it; the death sentence

---

11. Hegel: "He was condemned to death because he refused to recognize the competency and majesty of the people as regards the accused" (*Hist. Phil.*, 1:431/18:498).

will quite aptly label the ironist a "revolutionary" in spite of himself, negatively. "World history must adjudicate the case. But if it is to judge fairly, it must also admit that the State was within its rights in condemning Socrates. In a certain sense he was revolutionary, yet not so much by what he did as by what he omitted to do" (*CI*, 206–7).[12]

Ironic negativity, both in its reserve and its nonposition, is interpreted by the State *ipso facto* as opposition. Whether we call it revolutionary or counter-revolutionary, we are equally correct. In its subjective vanity, irony is always a threat to institutions, established order, and to the power of the State. Persecution, indeed the death sentence itself, is its destiny: Antigone, Socrates, Christ. By this means irony is not destroyed, but rather fulfilled.

Christianity, for Kierkegaard, can never have anything but an ironic relationship with the political order. The *extremely* ironic religious attitude, carried far enough, would consist in *defending* the powers that be, *no matter which ones,* out of indifference.

The Nontragic Death of Socrates

The death of Socrates is neither an unfortunate accident nor the result of a tragic confrontation; irony necessarily ends up by getting carried away with itself. The ironist seduces (himself) and holds (himself) back according to the logic of his point of view. Ironic negativity runs amuck: "totally, in its complete infinity . . . it finally swept away even Socrates himself" (*CI*, 240). Death, that "next to nothing," was undoubtedly well-suited to the ironist's taste. Once again, though, it is especially his ignorance concerning death that makes death the one punishment that is possible for the ironist, since *it really isn't one.* Socrates chooses his own sentence: "whatever is no punishment at all" (*CI,* 220). For he is ignorant of whether it will turn out to be a good or an evil.

---

12. "His accusers ought to have accused him of this very ignorance, since there is an ignorance which, to a certain extent in every State but especially in the Greek State, must be regarded as a felony" (*CI*, 195).

Socrates is in ignorance about death, and this last ignorance sweeps him away. To the ironist, death would be what the "negative result" was to his questioning: self-destruction. "Whereas even scepticism always posits something, irony, like the old witch, constantly makes the tantalizing attempt first to devour everything in sight, then to devour itself too, or as in the case of the old witch, her own stomach" (*CI*, 92). A witch has nothing of the hero about her. If, faced with death, Socrates maintains his point of view right up to the bitter end, this is not because he is a hero—for the hero always posits or defends something. Kierkegaard does not say exactly why he refuses to see in Socrates a hero. Quite simply, he does not bother to find out if the verdict of guilty is "fair" or "unfair." He gives short shrift to the "erudite mourners, that insipid host of tearful philanthropists, whose weeping and wailing over the fact that such a noble creature, such an honorable man, a paragon of virtue . . . became a sacrifice to the meanest of envies" (*CI*, 194). Then he also dismisses in passing "recent philosophic investigators"—by which we are to understand Hegel—who sketch Socrates as a "tragic hero." All of that with no further explanation: "these things we need not discuss further here."

What prevents Kierkegaard from following Hegel at this point? For the thesis easily concedes that *from the point of view of the State and the Greek populus*, "Socrates actually perpetrated evil," just as it also concedes that the Socratic point of view is different from that of the State; it is one of subjectivity, of an interiority that reflects itself into itself. So far, nothing would prohibit seeing in the death of Socrates the effect of a confrontation between two equally justified claims, in other words, the very condition for the appearance of tragic destiny, according to the Hegelian analysis. Nothing, that is, but the structure of opposition and the reference to a historical necessity according to which, at a certain *moment*, two prerogatives *oppose* one another. Hegel says, "They were right, but so was he." How could Socrates have been *right*, and how could he have opposed himself to the State, since he is ignorant of it and *posits* nothing? In order for there to be tragedy, in the Hegelian sense, it is necessary for the negative to posit itself and oppose itself to something: "Tragedy consists, then, in the fact that within such a conflict, each of the opposed sides has *justification:* while each can establish the true and positive content of its own aim and character only by denying and infringing the equally justified power of the other. The consequence is that in its ethical life, and because of it, each nevertheless becomes guilty" (*Aesthetics*, 2:1196/*Ästhetik*, 15:523). The interpretation of tragedy is part and parcel of the dialectical "System." It is less the notion of the "hero" that is being rejected here than the system that posits it only in order more effectively to do away with it. As tragic hero, the ironist would become a combatant and join in the dialectic. Once irony is sublated, it disappears. "Ordinarily," writes Kierkegaard, "irony is made into an ideal concept; its place in the system becomes that of a moment which vanishes." "Doubt, too, effaces itself within the system." The question, for Kierkegaard, will always be to find out whether subjectivity's and irony's point of view, as an existential category, can ever be surpassed, whether it is true that subjectivity never gets beyond itself and thus always remains *the* particular point of view of an empirical existence. Kierkegaard could have said that there is no point of view of all the points of view. That is why he could never understand Hegel and why, for instance, he wrote in his thesis: "in the System . . . but in reality," always conceiving "reality" as existential subjectivity. Ironic subjectivity (was Kierkegaard ever able to get beyond that?) is defined as an oscillation "between the ideal self and the empirical self."

Socrates has no philosophy; he only has a point of view. For Kierkegaard—but for Nietzsche too—this is what resists philosophy, in other words, the System. Obviously, we have to say "resists" and not "opposes."

IRONY: NONDIALECTIZABLE NEGATIVITY

The system, to put it quite simply, if that's even possible, consists in internalizing every negativity, in making it immanent to some positivity. Hegel: "We have to think this absolute concept of difference in its radicality as an immanent difference (*als innerer Unterschied*)" (*Phenomenology*, 99/ *Phänomenologie*, 130). "But *who*," Kierkegaard would ask, "can do such thinking?" Can simple infinity, or that absolute concept which Hegel also calls "the simple essence of life," "the universal blood, whose omnipresence is neither disturbed nor interrupted by any difference" (*Phen.*, 100/ 132)—can this simple infinity ever be "thought" by a living, existing subjectivity, insofar as such a subjectivity never has more than just one point of view? Is it not a paradox to speak of a "point of view" of the absolute, or infinity? The system actually ought to *lose* all the particular points of view, all the differences, and that is perhaps why it must give the absolute all those names which designate difference: Subjectivity, Interiority, Life—marking them off at the same time, as is evident in their translation, with a capital letter.

But what resists the system does not oppose it from the *outside*. Between Hegel and Kierkegaard what we have is not contradiction. What resists the system is found inside it without disturbing it, without upsetting it. More specifically, this also means that it is to be found in Hegel's text. But does that which is in the text necessarily belong to the system? There is no need to insist further on the nature of that which resists systematization, or the Hegelian *Aufhebung:* it is clear that what is at stake here is existence in its singularity, its difference, etc. What is remarkable, though, is the mode in which this resistance is expressed, we might say its *style*. Kierkegaard does not put his criticism in the form of opposition but in what is perhaps the only form left open to him, irony, taken here as a rhetorical figure and described in the chapter of the thesis called "For Orientation." With this figure, the ironist "goes along with" what he actually considers a foolishly inflated wisdom and *outdoes* the very thing he is belittling: "In relation to an insipid and inane enthusiasm it is ironically correct to *outdo* this with ever more and more elated exultation and praise, although the ironist is himself aware that this enthusiasm is the greatest foolishness in the world" (*CI*, 266). Such is Kierkegaard's own method. He seems to relate the Hegelian "oversights" to the system's grandeur and the haughty superiority of its perspective. It is as though the cogency of the Hegelian interpretation depended on the very thing that makes it suspect: as such, his lack of attention to "details" and also the way Hegel, for instance, "doesn't bother himself" about "the difficulty involved in obtaining certainty regarding the phenomenal aspect of the existence of Socrates" (*CI*, 243). Can we ever know who Socrates really was?

This question would constitute a critical problem that "does not disturb Hegel in the least." He seems to do a leapfrog over the questions concerning Socrates' existence that would be raised by a comparison of the texts of Plato, Xenophon, and Aristophanes, just as they would be raised in Plato alone by the confrontation of those dialogues more properly "Socratic" with the others—a distinction to which Hegel alludes, moreover, but only "in passing." Now according to the needs of the demonstration, Hegel picks and chooses indifferently among the texts. To tell the truth, "such *trifles* are wholly unknown to him." Even the critical work of someone like Schleiermacher cannot match up to the *elevated* aims of Hegelianism: "All such investigations are wasted energy on Hegel, and when the phenomena are presented on parade he is in too much haste and too aware of his role as commanding general in world history to have time for anything more than the regal glance he sweeps over them" (*CI*, 244).

Hegel, then, gets right to the point and neglects what Kierkegaard is content to call *details* or *trifles*—though not without having what is "repressed" by his regal glance and military bearing come back in his text as "isolated remarks" or "observations" made in passing, so much so that we could look for the symptoms of what remains refractory to the System in Hegel's own writings, in the remarks strewn about here and there, in the whole package of accessories that comes along with the Hegelian text. Kierkegaard took advantage of this opportunity, moreover, in his thesis: " 'Many dialogues [Hegel had pointed out "in passing"] contain merely negative dialectic, and this is the Socratic conversation.' These particular statements are in complete agreement with what I have advanced in the first part of this essay . . ." (*CI*, 245).

Anticipating just a bit, let's say that the thesis is ironic, at least in one sense, since it treats Hegel with irony. And if it does "treat" him in this way, this is perhaps because irony represents a means of criticizing or resisting the "System" in a noncontradictory, thus in principle, in a nondialectizable way—perhaps one of the only means of "contesting" speculative dialectics without immediately becoming part of it. By not stepping onto the field of its oppositions, irony exasperates dialectical thought: it displaces without opposing, it contests without contradicting. As a result, dialectics cannot figure out what to do with irony: neither how to get hold of it nor how to get rid of it. The reductive gestures made by dialectics bear this out, just as, from another perspective, it is borne out by a certain *tone*, a certain *pathos* which accompanies the Hegelian discourse as soon as it broaches the question of irony. And this did not escape Kierkegaard's reading, either—a reading that is less trusting and respectful than it might sometimes appear in its attempt to slip past a Danish university wholly won over to Hegelianism. Hegel never mentions irony without a certain exasperation, especially when it involves its modern representatives. Furthermore, he has been so blinded by his hatred of the romantics and their (informed or uninformed) appropriation of irony for themselves that he cannot even allude to irony without immediately launching into a diatribe against Schlegel. (Such is the case right in the middle of his *Lecture* on Socrates [*Hist. Phil.*, 1:400–2/18:460–61]). Hegel does not like irony. Before returning to the tone he assumes when speaking of it, though, we ought to recall what efforts were expended to dismiss it philosophically in his *Lectures on the History of Philosophy* as well as in paragraph 140 of *The Philosophy of Right*, where we read: "Irony is only a manner of conducting oneself with others in conversation." It has nothing to do with the Idea itself. In the same way in the *Lectures:* "Irony is a particular way of getting along with others . . ." what [Socrates] wished to effect thereby was to make others express themselves . . ." (*Hist. Phil.*, 1:399–400/18:458). Here it is nothing but a pedagogical tool that makes use of a ruse, and it has nothing to do with speculation, nor with dialectics.

However, Hegel admits at the same time that Socrates knew nothing, which seems to contradict the thesis of a ruse. What is even more surprising is that this "conversational nuance" will be joined later on in the *Lectures* by two other meanings that are apparently incompatible with each other as well as with this earlier meaning. At times, irony has the effect of *disengaging* the *abstract* Idea from its empirical determinations—at others (a most unexpected reversal), it allows abstract representations to become *explicit* and *developed* by making them *concrete*. "The irony of Socrates has this great quality of showing how to make abstract Ideas concrete and how to effect their development . . . it is a matter of developing what was mere representation, and for this reason, something abstract" (*Hist. Phil.*, 1:400/18:459). Here, then, irony accomplishes the task of modern speculation, and this by *starting out* from the abstract in order to make it determinate.[13] That Hegel ends up "by confusing everything" (*CI*, 284) is clear enough, and Kierkegaard is more than happy to point this out. We might even go so far as to notice at least a certain perplexity on the part of Hegel. So much for Socrates.

How do things stand with romantic irony? Hegel makes a violent and merciless attack on it, *but* he takes care in so doing not to aim at irony itself; the only thing at issue here is that movement which, along with Schlegel or Solger, has arbitrary pretensions to irony. "The arbitrary name 'irony' is of little or no importance," Hegel adds in a note devoted to Solger and attached to paragraph 140 of *The Philosophy of Right*. Likewise, the *History of Philosophy* disputes the right of the romantics to have any pretensions to irony: "In recent times, too, much has been said about Socratic irony" (*Hist. Phil.*, 1:400/18:460). (Hegel goes on to characterize all dialectic by its capacity to allow any given thing to accomplish its own self-dissolution.) However, "men have tried to make this irony of Socrates into something quite different, for they extended it to a universal principle." This "something," which comes from Fichtean philosophy by way of Schlegel, is nothing other than "a trifling with everything": "to this subjectivity nothing is serious any more." Let us recall that the Socratic moment represented the prelude to "a *more strenuous* effort after knowledge." Actually, what the romantics call irony is only a matter of hypocrisy, of subjective caprice, of vanity. All the supposed profundity of their inmost being is merely the profundity of an emptiness—"as may be seen from the ancient comedies of Aristophanes." We should remember *The Clouds* in this context. But didn't Hegel himself show us how profoundly Aristophanes had understood and recorded Socratic negativity? The truth cannot be so simple since "From this irony of our times, the irony of Socrates is far removed" (*Hist. Phil.*, 1:401–2/18:461).

---

13. In this respect, we could compare the way in which Hegel distinguishes between the starting point of Socrates (the concrete) and that of modern philosophy (the universal) [26, above]. On Hegel and Schlegel, see Philippe Lacoue-Labarthe's "L'imprésentable," *Poétique*, 21 (1975).

In those pages of the introduction of the *Aesthetics* that are devoted to irony, the "romantic" use of the word is not challenged. The Schlegel brothers are introduced there as critics whose philosophical baggage is on the meager side. As the inheritors of Fichtean philosophy, they conceive irony as an exaltation of the infinite freedom of the Self, posited as the principle of all cognition. This Self of the living individual is lord and master of everything; everything, every determination, every content loses itself in its liberty. Left to the caprice of the Self, the world is reduced to the appearances it receives from that Self. Armed with this principle, the ironic artist adopts the point of view of a Self "which posits and destroys everything," wholly at its own pleasure. Once all bonds have been snapped, there is nothing left to "take seriously." How close the results of such a point of view come to those of the Socratic method of questioning, as it is delineated in its negative aspect by Hegel himself, remains to be seen. Concrete values are repudiated; neither justice, nor morality, nor truth is taken seriously anymore. But you don't just give up taking things seriously with impunity. The Self is not able not to aspire to truth and objectivity. Hegel is exuberant and now feigns pity; the ironist inevitably pays for his levity—he suffers. Unable to tear himself out of his isolation, the unfortunate ironist cannot help falling prey to "a yearning which we have also seen proceeding from Fichtean philosophy" (*Aesthetics,* 1:66/13:96). The repudiation of objectivity is unhealthy—the argument is not without its merit—there is something debilitating about it. Dissatisfaction, the feeling of his own emptiness, plunges the beautiful soul into a *morbid* state full of nostalgia. *Beautiful soul* is to be understood ironically here, for Hegel adds immediately afterward, "A *truly* beautiful soul acts and is actual." It should be remarked in passing that irony must be distinguished from the comical, since "the comical must be restricted to showing that what it destroys is itself something inherently null, a false and contradictory phenomenon, a whim, e.g., an oddity, a particular caprice in comparison with a mighty passion, or even a *supposedly* tenable principle and firm maxim" (*Aesthetics,* 1:67/13:97). How can we classify the *genre* of Aristophanes' *Clouds?* A large number of highly scornful epithets completes the analysis of the ironist: "null in character and contemptible," "weakness and lack of character," "impotence," "vanity," "wishy-washy," "moral inferiority," "worthless yearning character," "bad useless people," etc.

Solger is granted a special indulgence. He died prematurely and thus did not have the chance to go beyond the dialectical moment of the Idea represented by infinite absolute negativity. This he surely would have done, had he but lived.

Did Hegel ever talk about irony?

Two hypotheses:

1) Hegel "overlooked" irony, blinded as he was by his contempt for Schlegel. Such is Kierkegaard's opinion in the matter, though he is just Hegelian enough to accept Hegel's scorn for the romantics as his own. "In one-sidedly focusing on post-Fichtean irony, Hegel has overlooked the truth of irony . . ." (*CI*, 282). In the meantime, the question of "style" surfaces: "I shall first attempt to illuminate . . . a weakness from which Hegel's entire conception of the concept of irony seems to suffer. Hegel always discusses irony in a most contemptuous fashion, indeed irony is an abomination in his sight. Now concurrent with the appearance of Hegel occurred Schlegel's most brilliant period" (*CI*, 282). Furthermore, "The fact that Hegel lets the form of irony that is closest to him *get under his skin* has naturally distorted his conception of the concept. And if the reader seldom gets a discussion, Schlegel, on the other hand, always gets a drubbing. But this does not mean that Hegel was wrong regarding the Schlegels . . . This does mean, on the other hand, that Hegel has *overlooked the truth of irony* . . ." And finally, "As soon as Hegel pronounces the word 'irony' he immediately thinks of Schlegel and Tieck, and his style instantly takes on the features of a certain indignation."[14]

2) Second hypothesis: the fact that Schlegel and Tieck have pretensions to irony is not simply fortuitous. The romantics repeat in their own way a moment in subjectivity's exaltation, a moment of absolute freedom in which subjectivity "posits nothing" and "leaves nothing standing." Kierkegaard uses both expressions with reference to Socrates *as well as* to the romantics. In the

---

14. *CI*, 282–83, emphasis in the text. If Kierkegaard pokes fun at Hegel's impatience, he also concedes that romantic irony, which boasts of "creating a world of its own" at the expense of all historical reality, is "unjustifiable."

romantics we find once again the haughty bearing, the elusiveness, the wariness, the vanity, the consciousness that maintains its distance from all empirical actuality, the sensuous enjoyment, the withdrawal into itself, the exemption from established morality, and all that negativity which is associated with Socrates. But especially this: wherever it is to be found, irony is the mark of displacement. If these romantics have something in common with Socrates (and Kierkegaard), it is a mode of discourse that is *indirect* (allusive or poetic, for instance). And it is perhaps that which cannot help "getting under Hegel's skin." This form of discourse that, positing nothing, represents a negativity that is not manifest, that is not dialectically sublatable. (Socrates is never overtly negative, and that is why he is infinitely negative.) Socrates sneaks off and lays no claim to having anything more to say about his own questions. Irony, or the ironist, is always missing from its place, and it is this gap (*cet écart*) with which Hegelian phenomenology can do nothing. "So then, Socrates is not allowed to stand there (*à l'écart*) like a *Ding an sich*, but must come forth whether he likes it or not" (*CI*, 243). Whence the Hegelian need for a "positive" Socrates. One way of reappropriating—in order better to be rid of it—this sort of operation that both displaces and is displaced would be to assign it a permanent place, to make it a "moment" that is both dispensable and dispensed with once and for all: let's say by doing justice to it (Socrates *will have been* necessary) while depriving it of any future relevance (irony can no longer be possible). "Finally, irony here met its master in Hegel."[15] Whereas the first form of irony [Socrates] was not combated but *pacified* by doing *justice* to subjectivity, the second form of irony [the romantics] was both combated and *annihilated*, for since it was unjustified, doing it *justice* could only mean sublating it" (*CI*, 260).

All the same, without deciding on a definition for irony, Hegel denounces the lack of *earnestness*, provisional or definitive, of everything that is in any way connected with it. Socrates was *not yet* able to be earnest, that is, to gain access to speculative philos-

---

15. Is Kierkegaard thinking here of what he has already said (p. 12) regarding the highly ironic technique of calling the archenemy of a given school's representatives their "master"?

ophy. He can be excused for having waited on the doorstep of philosophy, for that was his place. But that modern thinkers should allow themselves, in a regressive fashion, to adopt the point of view of subjectivity, to affirm its infinite freedom in defiance of all earnestness, borders on scandal.

Kierkegaard could not have been expected to take the side of the "romantics." Rather, he goes the Hegelian critique one better, in earnest it would seem, and reproaches the Schlegels for having wanted to "create a world of their own," for having wanted to deny all historical reality—thereby transforming the historical character of myth in the twinkling of an eye—finally and above all, for having wanted to free themselves from all morality and virtue. He could not read *Lucinde* without becoming indignant, and just like Hegel, he mixes both moral and aesthetic complaints together in the same critique and refuses to grant the novel any ironic value whatsoever. If Schlegel's text borders on impudence, it is not only because it signals the suppression of objective values: "*Lucinde* has a most doctrinaire character." It *suppresses* all virtue in order to end up in sensuality. The sensuous enjoyment of irony is not like this; rather, it fulfills itself only in despair, and then turns religious.

The thesis won't be able to end without a certain ambiguity. For irony has at least two fates: either it is expunged, overcome at last (Hegel as its master), or else it turns into madness. It is engulfed by philosophy or religion.

Apparently, it is philosophy that carries the day: the conclusion of the thesis is Hegelian, or just about. But in a sort of digression, the chapter entitled "For Orientation" seems to indicate quite a different outcome, by means of which the ironist already has been able to make off, or do away with himself. This curious aside (*aparté*), which is not taken into account by the conclusion, will prevent the thesis from coming to a smooth stop.

But let's start at the end: irony mastered in conclusion. For the conclusion necessarily puts an end to irony, by exclusion, foreclusion (foreclosure), or inclusion. If conclusion there be, then irony has to appear there in the end. The truth *of* irony has to show up there, has to be recognized there. In so doing, it has at last found its place, by assuming the aspect of a *moment*. Everything turns out all right in the end, though not without Kierkegaard's having subverted the notion of *moment* along the way by making a stage or moment of *personal existence* out of it. It is a moment of consciousness, but it is now a matter of individual consciousness, and it is indispensable—as moment—to every "human life" (*CI*, 338). "Irony is like the negative way, not the truth but the way. Everyone who has a result merely as such does not possess it, for he has not the way" (*CI*, 340). For the benefit of those unconditional partisans of the "system," who are in a hurry to have the results, Kierkegaard points out that there is no way of getting around irony: "There is an *impatience* that would reap *before* it has sown. By all means let irony chasten it."

Since irony names the moment of a necessary detachment, going beyond it entails recuperation, reconciliation, reappropriation. *For example,* an author discovers his identity by seeing in each of his works "a moment in his own development" (*CI*, 337).

Insofar as he is productive, "the writer" will always have been an ironist, he will always have maintained an "ironic relation" with each of his productions. Considered in itself, every work is fragmentary, partial, finite; an author's irony is his awareness of this finitude. As if detached and absent, he "lets the objective prevail" in his work (*CI*, 336). Kierkegaard had already detailed this conception in the preceding chapter, which was consecrated to Solger. For Solger, God's existence has been turned into irony: "God posits himself constantly over into nothingness, takes himself back again, then posits himself over once more, etc." (*CI*, 331). But as "philosophical spokesman for romanticism and romantic irony . . . it is in art and poetry that Solger seems to find the 'highest' actuality that becomes visible through the negation of finite actuality" (*CI*, 331, 332).

Such is not the case, remarks Kierkegaard, from the point of view of the romantics themselves: "[romantic poetry] strives essentially to bring to consciousness the fact that the given actuality is the imperfect, while the higher actuality only allows itself to be envisaged in the infinite approximation of presentiment and intimation (*Ahnung*): so it seems necessary once more to relate oneself ironically to every particular production inasmuch as each individual product is but an approximation" (*CI*, 332). Like all finite actuality, the work requires ironic reserve. A reserve that is wholly provisional here, for the higher actuality *becomes* what it is: "this *higher actuality,* which is to become visible in poetry, *is nevertheless not in poetry,* but constantly becoming." The romantics won't have been able to understand this actuality of the work as a *moment:* "For the romanticist the particular poetic production is either a darling with which he is wholly infatuated and which he is unable to explain how it has been possible for him to call to life, or it is an object which awakens disgust. Both alternatives are naturally untrue. The truth is that the particular poetic production is simply a moment" (*CI*, 337).

There is a dream of sublation, then, in this conclusion. In it the ironic distance of the poet regarding his "production" would finally be blotted out. Once irony has been subdued, it makes room for identity, in any case the identity of the author who is then reconciled with himself in the dialectical reappropriation of his works. Such is the advent of the work's truth in the totality of its meaning: an end to the gaps, the disguises, the asides, the ruses—to hell with irony! It will have been *mastered,* in other words, reduced to a mere moment, like all detachment (division, remoteness, withdrawal, suspension, separation, negation). The subjective is reunited with the objective, the inside measures up to the outside.

But where? Obviously not in the work, which remains always—*a parte.* It would be necessary to stop writing. Speak, maybe—but Kierkegaard will always give up on it, saying instead how impossible it would be. What "Point of View [of my Work as an Author]" would bring to light the ultimate coincidence?

If this conclusion is not able to bring the thesis to a definitive close, this is not because we know that Kierkegaard will later accuse himself of having been a "mad Hegelian" at the time that he wrote the dissertation. Rather it is because the text, as we have seen, remains constantly ambiguous, zig-zagging continuously, continuously reserved or signaling abruptly in a different direction, toward "something other." It is time, then, to take hold of the text short of its ending.

*
* *

The lone chapter entitled "For Orientation" marks a change in point of view. It is a question there of the various uses of irony in the current sense of the term, in other words, in the sense of a *stylistic figure* in which (as the dictionaries still tell us) one says "the opposite of what is meant." The irony so described is only an inferior kind. But already present here is the decisive possibility of play, gap, inadequation, which Kierkegaard will identify as the possibility of a certain sensuous enjoyment.

By means of this stylistic figure known as "irony," the speaking subject affords himself the possibility of breaking free of the bonds that, when he is expressing "his thought" adequately, tie him to it and thus to himself. Should the ironist have accomplices who are in on the joke, however, the figure cancels itself out immediately. The irony that is savored in isolation is of another kind, and otherwise provocative. For instance, the ironist outdoes an absurdity, or, on the contrary, does not seem to know what appears to be the most common knowledge, feigning candor and giving himself out to be sillier than he actually is. This is still deception, but of a secret kind: pure provocation. The ironist conceals himself so that another will come out of concealment.

Finally, irony is also a simple matter of *pulling a fast one* (*donner le change*). It is not a question of "cheating" with a view toward realizing any particular gain from it, for it is hardly misleading. Or else we should use the word "cheat" in the sense that we say that someone temporarily "cheats death" or an author "cheats" his reader of an expectation, a hope, etc. As such, it is a means of escape, thanks to a subterfuge, from a given audience avid of information, dying of curiosity: a kind of slipping off, thanks to a diversion, from the diverse forms of supervision and power that insist that everyone declare his position and then stick to it. Irony is less a true provocation or challenge, then, than it is a means of resistance. If it pulls a fast one, or *changes* the tempo (donne *le change*), it is not out of any concern for "contradiction," it is for the fun of it, and in order to retain control (off on the side) over the play of substitutions.

If irony "makes its appearance through a relation of opposition," though, this is not in order to affirm this relation, but in order to liberate itself from it. The ironist confuses the opponents and does not take the contradiction between them seriously. True and false; serious and laughable; as far as he is concerned, they are all on the same team. Irony actually is involved with opposition, but less in the form of opposition than of complicity. The ironist is thus able to perceive in nature herself an unconscious irony; for instance, in the way she "strangely conjoins mirth with lament, joy with sorrow" (*CI*, 271). But this is merely a perspective *on* nature, for nature herself is without malice.

Every manifestation that is not simply what it is, but that always appears to be accompanied at the same time by its opposite, is related to irony: like nature's voice in the music of Ceylan that "sings frightfully merry minuets in tones of a deep, wailing, heartrending voice" (*CI*, 271).

Sometimes as point of view, sometimes as style, what is always at stake in irony is the subjective freedom that liberates itself from apparently contradictory finite determinations and established values. It is well known that no institution is above making occasional use of irony's dangerous point of view so as to neutralize it better. All that is needed here is to regulate closely those times at which irony is allowed. So it was during the Middle Ages when the Church instituted, or at least tolerated, the Feast of the Ass, a feast during which the "Ass's Prose" was sung after the animal itself had been led into the church.

Irony, then, prefers duplicity to contradiction. It is at home in *discord*, and almost all those words beginning with "dis" could serve to characterize it. Inadequation: that is the only rule. The ironic style, always *allusive*, works like a "play on words." It has always already extracted or distracted, diverted or perverted the meaning of its discourse, of its own discourse.

This means that irony is highly diverting. It is not without a certain interest to note here that words that indicate a turning aside, or a separation, for example "distraction," or "diversion," are words that also have connotations of amusement and pleasure. The ironist distracts (himself from) the thing (itself), diverts (himself) by turning (himself) aside, by making light of everything. But this game is amusing not because there is "distraction" (in the sense of *dis-tractio*, separation) or opposition in it, but rather because the oppositions in it all turn out to be the same thing. In this game, what seems to get away always ends up by coming back. Compromise or substitution: that's where the player finds his distraction.

But that is also where his madness lies. In play, the ironic consciousness flees from the anxiety of its alienation, though this is an infinite flight in which, by means of a generalized diversion or displacement, it finds a merely negative freedom. The other solution, the earnest one, would consist in preserving its equality with itself in alienation, in order to achieve—in knowledge—the mastered difference of consciousness. Irony's subject "is constantly in retreat"; he maintains a negative independence with respect to everything. This infinite skittering is one way of not stopping at any particular moment, and yet it neither reconciles nor unites them all in anything but a playful manner. The ambiguity of ironic expression would thus be more closely related to the symptomatic formation of a compromise than to a dialectical synthesis. It is not the Hegelian who is "mad" but the ironist: "This is what might be called irony's attempt to mediate the discrete moments, not in a higher unity but in a higher madness" (*CI*, 274).

Once irony finally turns "against the whole of existence," once everything has become nothingness before irony, then it approaches religious devotion, it takes on the *appearance* of piety—something that also affirms that "all is vanity": "[Irony] thereby expresses the same proposition as the pious attitude" (*CI*, 274). There is no way to tell them apart; but this is in appearance only, since piety obliterates even itself in order to offer itself up to religious devotion, while the ironist has not yet learned to see his own vanity. All the same, are we so far removed here from the Socratic irony, which sweeps itself away into death? Isn't faith another name for death, the ultimate form of obliteration? Irony might thus represent the point of view nearest the religious point of view; it would be the prelude, not so much to speculation, as to religiousness. One more step, and ironic scepticism opens onto religious humor.

Did Kierkegaard take this step? When did he do it? How are we to get our bearings here if the ironist, like the man of faith, always travels *incognito?* Nothing sets them apart from others, nothing sets them apart from one another, either.

Ordinarily, we only get to know pseudo-ironists, the ones who let you in on everything—but do we really know just how far? The weakness of the romantics, from the point of view of irony, was to have laid claim to it. If the ironist flees from (positive) determinations, it is not so that he will get pigeonholed as an ironist. He must, then, look serious and refrain from offering an apology for irony. Irony is thus always possible; it does not attract attention to itself. Shouldn't a real ironist, moreover, go out of his way to repudiate irony and to make known in a loud voice just how little he thinks of it? Hegel himself could very well have been the real "master of irony." His entire philosophy could have been written as a diversion in order to pull a fast one on us. Nor would it be any less likely that, having made us accomplices to his irony, such an ironist would suddenly, without warning, start speaking in earnest.

Someone else then might write a thesis *on* irony, treat it in all seriousness as though it were a concept, describe its mechanisms and develop its critique, its apology, or its historical significance with an entirely scientific objectivity. Should this doctor of philosophy later produce a work in which there gleamed the slightest hint of irony, we might be inclined to regard his meaning with suspicion, to be wary of whatever he might say in a fictitious mode or under pseudonyms. We would always be ready to give irony its due. Should he at last claim to give up all indirect forms of discourse and to speak in the first person, we might be inclined to believe him, glad to know just how things had finally turned out.

The Serious Side of the Thesis: The Defense

"Irony as a subject?" was the question we were asking. Add to it, as a subject for a *thesis,* and we have one style of discourse getting hold of another.

The thesis is to be declarative; it affirms or negates, it is true *or* false. It posits, places, establishes, even institutes; it fixes or decides something, it marks out a pause. An institutional form of discourse, the thesis defines, determines, expounds. Irony is of a different style. If it is the Socratic operation that Kierkegaard (and even Hegel) describes, then "it establishes nothing." In other words, "irony in a strict sense can never put forth a proposition [*Satz* proposition, thesis]" (*CI,* 286). Like prayer, it belongs to nonthematic discourse. For a thesis to make a ruling on irony would amount to determining it, assigning it a place, establishing it in some way—even if that had to be in spite of itself. And this is always possible. But irony is not to be found in this or that particular statement, it is the more or less apparent reserve of a speaker, or it is in the noncontradictory opposition of his statements. The thesis itself, then, could always be infected by irony . . .

But the thesis is also an instrument of the institution. More than just institutive, it is institutional and inscribes its author in the institution. If the basis for the thesis has been firmly established and adequately defended, then the thesis will be happy to establish the author who defends it; it will give him a university title. Such is the end of all theses.

The manuscript of *The Concept of Irony* is preceded by two riders: the fifteen theses presented as:

THESES
attached to
THE DANISH DISSERTATION ON THE CONCEPT OF IRONY
which
SØREN AABYE KIERKEGAARD
theological candidate
WILL ENDEAVOR TO DEFEND PUBLICLY
on 29 September
at ten o'clock
in order to obtain in the usual manner
THE DEGREE OF MASTER OF ARTS
in the University of Copenhagen
1841
————and this certification:

The Faculty of Philosophy in the University of Copenhagen has declared this inaugural dissertation as worthy of securing the author the degree of Master of Arts, after it, together with the accompanying theses, has been defended in the usual manner.

16 July 1841
F.C. Sibbern
Dean of the Faculty of Philosophy

(*CI*, 347).

Obviously, this certification did not appear when the dissertation was published commercially; but then the fifteen theses, along with their presentation, were not included there either. In a gesture that is by no means rare, the author seems to have wanted to efface the institutional finality (*la finalité*) of his text, and in so doing, would have equally demonstrated that, once removed from their context, the exposition of the theses had in fact no other purpose (*n'avait pas d'autre fin*). Nonetheless, the theses remain embedded in the text, they are to be found there, along with several others. Theses are something that are never in short supply. Set off from the text and given a prominent position, they are not simply offered to the reader's attention: they prescribe a mode of reading, in this case, by a jury and "in the usual manner."

With the theses, the text lays claim to *occasional* discourse (the defense of 29 September 1841 at ten o'clock). It is in itself an indication of the place it holds in an institutional ritual and is a reminder, insofar as it makes mention of the occasion in question, that it was meant "seriously" and taken "seriously." Thus, by virtue of the fact that it indicates its own institutional nature through the adoption of the forms traditionally prescribed for it, its discourse will have *laid claim* to circumventing what certain contemporary philosophers of speech act theory have tried to dismiss as "parasitical" uses of language (for instance, fiction, theater, etc.).

To take another example: irony. It could be argued, then, that the elimination of the prefatory material and its "theses," by uprooting the "thesis" from its occasional circumstances, sets the text free, sets it adrift. Cut off from the institutional requirement, the thesis is nothing more than a text destined, like all other texts, to an absence of speaker and "context," destined, in other words, to a (possible) "nonearnestness." If, that is, one accepts the curious distinction—held to dearly by speech act theorists (such as Austin or Searle)—between "normal" and serious discourse, and "parasitical" discourse.

According to this distinction, evident in Austin for example, a "normal" (or "ordinary") speech act is an act of communication. In order to function in an effective way, this communication implies: 1) that the speech act expresses the conscious intention of the speaker; 2) that the speech act occurs within an appropriate "total context." It is only by fulfilling these conditions that linguistic usage can be considered "serious." Beyond these "ordinary" circumstances, the use of language becomes "parasitical," even "aberrant," as in the case of soliloquy, or fiction, etc. It is no longer necessary to enter into the details of a critique of this distinction.[16] The risk of parasitical use does not come from outside, by accident, to corrupt ordinary usage, since every speech act—serious or not—has to be first of all identifiable, repeatable, coded; in other words, it must be capable of *citation*. That is why, while recognizing the relative specificity of ordinary usage for a given speech act in "communication," it is always possible to show that the parasitical element is structural and that successful communication—to say things somewhat quickly—constitutes something of an exception, a special case of "citation" inside a general economy of "citationality."

Irony, as it applies to equivocal and dissonant language, cut off in various ways from the intention of its speaker, is obviously a kind of "parasitical" use (as this is understood by Austin) and will be the object of the same kind of philosophical exclusion that is exercised on all "aberrant" forms of discourse, for example, writing in its most common acceptation. Furthermore, this exclusion of writing is based on an unverifiable complicity that is always possible between irony and the written word. Insofar as it is always already cut off from the moment and the context of its inscription, just as it is from the intention that presided over that inscription, the written word can always be suspected of irony, or nonearnestness. Let's take the question that is raised by Kierkegaard's thesis itself—the question of its own earnestness. Could *The Concept of Irony* have been an ironic thesis?

Two answers are possible.

——Insofar as it was addressed to a jury whose responsibility it was to ascertain its relevance, insofar as it was *defended* by its author in the prescribed manner and respecting the appropriate rites, the thesis belongs to occasional discourse and is placed within a conventional context capable of ensuring the conditions necessary for serious communication. The socio-historical setting of the 1841 dissertation, the presence of the candidate and the jury, the mutual effort to agree on the meaning of the statements that were advanced, would seem to exclude, in conformity with the conventions or the rules of the game, the possibility that the

---

16. For instance, see Jacques Derrida, "Signature, Event, Context," in *Margins of Philosophy*.

subject would not be thinking whatever it is he is arguing, that the thesis would have been conceived by somebody else or that it would be fictitious, that the jury would possess none of those qualities required to understand the communication, etc. It is never possible, though, to prevent such accidents from happening, to prevent the earnestness of the procedure from being thereby encroached upon.

——Insofar as the text is written, the dissertation is deprived of the context and the situation that made it work as communication; it is no longer addressed to such and such a particular jury, here present, promising to supervise and verify the effectiveness of the communication (the exclusion of equivocations, the reparation of any deterioration of meaning between what the speaker is conscious of wanting to say and what the listener understands him to say, etc.); it is no longer defended or defensible by its author here present to answer for his own discourse. It has been left on its own, cut off from its source as from its end, left running all by itself, unsupervised. As for the author, he has washed his hands of it, just like Pontius Pilate when he said, "What is written, is written." The phrase is quoted in Kierkegaard's *Journal*.

From this point on, the *earnestness* of the thesis is no longer "vouched for"; nothing prevents the signatory from being an ironist, a poet, or a practical joker who does not believe or no longer believes in the theses which he himself(?) advanced, who entertains that *indirect* relation with his work which is described in the work itself.

The possibility of writing is also the possibility of irony: it is the possibility of detachment.

But the two answers do not exclude one another; a given discourse can be (functioning as though it were) serious because it can also *not* be serious. What is true for the written word (its potential for detachment) is also true for every oral expression, inasmuch as it is conventional, as it can always be said unseriously, as it must be capable of repetition, citation, etc. This possibility—which has always been rejected on the grounds that it is an exceptional and parasitical instance with respect to the "normal" functioning of language and which is also the condition for irony's possibility—is the condition for every locution and is not some accidental deviation from it.

In *The Concept of Irony,* philosophical discourse shows that even it runs a risk which it has always tried to hold at bay.

At this point, there is no question of demonstrating that Kierkegaard was sometimes earnest, sometimes ironic—earnest in defending his thesis, ironic in publishing it. It might be tempting to do this by saying that, since he erased the traces of the text's connection to the defense, he *"wanted"* to change the meaning or destination of his text. In effect, that does change the text, but the reference to Kierkegaard's own intention is unnecessary. For he would have been able (without ever having submitted any thesis whatsoever) to write a fictitious thesis that included, in the form of prefatory material, the (fictitious) certification of some Faculty of Philosophy, a number of theses attached in the customary fashion to the dissertation, and the reference to a (fictitious) date of defense . . .

The defense itself, the one on 29 September 1841 at ten o'clock, does not prove that Kierkegaard was speaking seriously that day. Earnestness does not speak for itself, does not go without saying. The discourse that is meant to be serious must be defended against its natural propensity for drifting. In nautical terms, we might say that it is necessary to maintain course by *defending* against the drifts and currents of dis-course. Rites and ceremonies are created—by tightening up and adding to the existing conventions—in order to reduce the ambiguities and alleviate the drift. It is not by means of the speech act itself but thanks to what is there to lend it social approbation that the channels of meaning can be kept clear and that the supervision of communication is ensured. The defense of a thesis, for instance, has as its end the social approbation of a given discourse, and this approbation implies the existence of representatives who are invested with a certain authority. But during the same ceremony, it is also a matter of establishing a text and eliminating the potential drifting of its meaning. The two operations are necessarily related. It could be argued that it is in response to social, ethical, and political exigencies that we tend to privilege discourse that is serious and univocal and for the same reason that we call it "normal." A commitment, a promise, a contract cannot take place without excluding every "parasitical" use of language—for instance, irony or fiction.

However, in view of the general "citationality" referred to earlier, there is no precautionary measure—ever—that is capable of guaranteeing in an absolute sense the earnestness of a given discourse. Rather, all the rites, all the paraphernalia used to attach a speaker to his discourse indicate that he is primordially detachable.

A reading of *The Concept of Irony*, for instance, discloses fifteen theses, more or less present in Kierkegaard's text, more or less compatible with each other. They could be formulated in the following manner:

1. The ironist does not expound his views in a discourse that is the presence itself of the Idea.
2. Philosophy can't stand irony.
3. The ironist has no voice.
4. The ironist is seductive because he falls short.
5. The ironist is comical because he falls short.
6. The ironist gets negative sensuous enjoyment.
7. The State is always in the right when it condemns irony.
8. Irony gets swept away all by itself.
9. Hegel let irony get under his skin.
10. The mastered form of irony is a moment of individual consciousness.
11. The master form of irony unites the discrete moments of consciousness in a higher madness.
12. The ironic point of view resembles the religious point of view.
13. The possibility of writing is also the possibility of irony.
14. The earnestness of a discourse can never be taken for granted.
15. A thesis can always be haunted by irony.

Economies of Sacrifice

Copenhagen, 1846: a first *Glance at a Contemporary Effort in Danish Literature.*

Suppose we now let some of the deflections of this glance *glance off* one another.[17] Suppose we take a number of looks at, multiply the points of view on, several works which, taken together, do not form a single canvas. But at the same time, moving through several scenes, suppose we retrace the unity of a proceeding that continues to go on even today.

We will reread, then, some of the texts in a body of literature that undertakes to bring suit against speculative dialectics, to wit, against Hegel, more or less openly accused of fraud.

> *And yet no manacled robber of Churches is so despicable a criminal as the one who swindles holiness in this way, and not even Judas, who sold his Lord for thirty pieces of silver, is more contemptible than someone who peddles greatness in this way.* (F&T,63–64)

More than just a simple traitor, Hegel seems to have been the inventor of an infamous machine, a vending machine, capable of wiping out instantaneously the risk of death, of loss, of sacrifice.

Speculative dialectics would end up by allowing us to make light of this risk.

---

17. TN. "Répercuter maintenant ce coup du *coup d'oeil*." The glance in question here occurs in the first of several appendices in *Concluding Unscientific Postscript* (225–66).

Every criminal is a thief. Peddler and secondhand dealer, the philosopher buys up everything in sight, doing his reckoning only at the end, posting figures, doing business even with unscrupulous middlemen.

> *Theology sits all rouged and powdered in the window and courts philosophy's favor, offers its charms to philosophy.* (F&T, 32)

Johannes de Silentio refuses to take part in this scene of complicity between theology and philosophy, in which incommensurable values are nonetheless exchanged indiscriminately:

> *Our generation does not stop with faith, does not stop with the miracle of faith, turning water into wine—it goes further and turns wine into water.* (F&T, 37)

Where is this voice coming from?

In distinction to Nietzsche or to Bataille, this voice speaks in a discourse intended to be religious, and it says as much.[18] We cannot simply bypass this profession of faith without taking notice of it. Furthermore, this discourse also addresses itself to philosophy and speaks in its language. A restricted complicity, perhaps, but it is an inevitable one and in keeping with the tactics of subversion. However, if Silentio calls Hegel "to account"—during the course of which S. tries to liberate from the *Aufhebung* what it had presumed to wear down and enclose within its economy—can this accounting do any more than whittle away at the philosopher, and wear down his machine in turn? Undoubtedly not, but this, in any case, is not what is intended. To what end

---

18. The texts of S. are not religious by virtue of affirming the autonomy of religious discourse as such, but rather because they deny this same autonomy to philosophy—which does lay claim to it—and because they make an attempt to disclose the figure of philosophy in its dark aspect, blind and silent. The style of S. is neither philosophical nor mystical, but rather *dialectical-lyrical* (the sub-title for *Fear and Trembling*)—not a mixture of styles, which would already suppose the purity and autonomy of its components, but a collapse of styles, due to a kind of trampling down of the discourse that gives up on presenting itself in a form of knowledge and that then undertakes a commentary on this surrender.

liberate the excess if it is only to stick it back into another *system*? S. is able only to notice what—perhaps—resists dialectics: flights, losses, leftovers.

A risk has no meaning for Hegel, unless you can be sure to come away from it a winner. S. affirms the *value* of risk in its moment of uncertainty, the value of death itself, without the reappropriation of consciousness, in blindness and madness. If "meaning" is what involves reappropriation, then "value" is what involves loss, the one loss that consciousness is unable to "sublate": the loss of self. Self-sacrifice, in fact, brings down the last safeguard of consciousness, the difference between sacrificer and sacrificed, between priest and that "danger zone" referred to by Georges Bataille,[19] between active and passive, which the grammar of the word *sacrifice* leaves undecided: "the word is sometimes passive: the sacrifice of Isaac, Isaac is sacrificed; sometimes active: the sacrifice of Abraham, Abraham does the sacrificing." It is possible, then, to speak of the sacrifice of the father or the sacrifice of the son. Who sacrifices (himself)?

In the "religious" discourse of S., the name of *God* designates less a trinity than a double reality: the name of the father and of the son. God the Father is the name for absolute excess, the name of the Other or of difference. God the Son is the name for the model sacrificial victim, the Crucified one who, by his death, annihilates the difference Father/Son.

Passion, Panic

How is it possible to prevent dialectics from incorporating the sacred, from plugging up the difference which religion tries to think as such, or at least to preserve, even if that means to *not* think it? Through positing an "absolute" contradiction, without

---

19. "At any rate, in ritual forms of communal sacrifice an animal becomes the sorry replacement for the sacrificer. It is only a pathetic intermediary-victim that, according to Hubert and Mauss, 'penetrates the danger zone of sacrifice. The victim succumbs, and that is what it's there for. The sacrificer stays at a safe distance' " ("Sacrificial Mutilation," 69).

any possible synthesis, in other words, an *alternative:* either reason/or faith. How is it possible to posit an alternative, on what grounds? Insofar as it is an alternative, an absolute disjunction, the *either . . . or* has no ground to stand on, it cannot posit itself, it is not a *question*, it is not a "problem"—in other words, a *philosophical* question. In this alternative it is not a matter of what *sense* there is to religion, nor even, of course, of its non-sense, short of a return to philosophical interpretation.

Nonetheless, Johannes Climacus, author of *Philosophical Fragments*, calls himself a "subtle dialectician." He would presume less to deny all dialectics than to uncover *another* dialectic, a dialectic that would go beyond—but can we even use that word here?—the dialectic of consciousness; another game, and one which consciousness would no longer master.

If *God* is the name for the *absolutely different*, the question of a *relation* to the god is paradoxical right from the start. Reason's other cannot be reached by speculation's mediations. And *there is no speculation without mediation.* If it is necessary to seek something like the abolition of difference, it will not be an effect of reason in its own activity, but this abolition of difference will rather constitute, through an abandoning of cognition, the moment when the passion of reason leads to *its own undoing.* In this way, the paradox of reason is analogous to the paradox of love: both have as their basis something that is destined to perish when they become inspired by "passion." The self-love that presides over all love loses itself in passion and, beyond the knowledge which it at first seeks, reason "collides" with the unknown, its other, which J.C. names *God.*

> *But what is this unknown something with which reason collides when inspired by its paradoxical passion, with the result of unsettling man's knowledge of himself? It is the unknown. It is not a human being, insofar as we know what man is; nor is it any other known thing. So let us call this unknown something* the God. (*Fragments*, 49)

The relation of reason to its other will always be played out in a game with its own limit, an impossible game in which difference is inevitably but also fatally rounded up and then disappears as such.

> What then is this unknown? It is the limit to which reason repeatedly comes; and as such, when it substitutes a static determination for the dynamic, it is the different, the absolutely different. But because it is the absolutely different, there is no mark by which it could be distinguished. When qualified as absolutely different it seems on the verge of disclosure, but this is not the case; for reason cannot even think this absolute difference. Reason cannot negate itself absolutely, but must rely on itself for that purpose, and thus conceives only such difference within itself as it can think by means of itself. It cannot absolutely transcend itself, and hence conceives only such sublimity [den Ophøiethed, die Erhabenheit] beyond itself as it can think by means of itself. Unless the unknown (God) remains a mere limit, the single idea of difference will be thrown into a state of confusion by the many ideas of difference. (Fragments, 55–56)

As soon as it "thinks," reason distinguishes; it thinks what has been differentiated, and not difference as such. As soon as it attempts to think this difference, it assimilates it to what it (difference) is different from. Reason would thus only be able to think difference within itself, or rather would never be able to think it. In other words, by itself thought does not get outside of itself and cannot play on, off, around with, or at its own limit. God becomes the name for the limit that is unthinkable, insuperable. Difference remains outside—even if imagination does its best to give it some sort of representation, which is always arbitrary—and *"deep down in the fear of God cowers in distraction the arbitrary caprice which knows that it has itself produced the God"* (Fragments, 56).

But if reason can neither confine nor "produce" difference, it will have at least been necessary to "encounter" it in some way: reason must have been solicited by difference, in other words, by the God who alone is able to reveal (himself as) difference.

> . . . if man is to have any true knowledge about the unknown (the God) he must be made to know that it is different from him, absolutely different from him. By itself, reason cannot possibly come to know this; we have already seen that this would be a self-contradiction. It will therefore have to obtain this knowledge from the God. But even if it obtains such knowledge it cannot understand it, and thus is quite unable to possess such knowledge. For

> *how should the understanding be able to comprehend what is absolutely different from itself? If this is not immediately clear, it will become so in light of its consequence; for if the God is absolutely different from man, then man is absolutely different from the God; but how could the understanding comprehend this? Here we seem to be confronted with a paradox.* (Fragments, 57–58)

In the same way, then, it is its *own* difference which the understanding cannot comprehend; at the most, it can learn of it (from the other, the God), but it cannot comprehend it. To the extent, though, that this difference is its *own*, it is not something for which the understanding could hold God responsible. No, "man" *has only himself to thank for this difference.* He himself is what differs . . . and through a faulty, that is, sinful difference:

> *But what can this difference be? Aye, what can it be but sin; since difference, absolute difference, is something for which man himself must be guilty.* (Fragments, 58)

Difference is a sin—or rather: the sin is to differ, man is *guilty of difference*.

Regarding this sin which man is guilty of, though, *"it would be too much to expect of man that he should find this out for himself."* He has to learn of it, then; someone has to teach him about it. This instruction is not without its own mystery: how is it possible to *teach* what has *no distinctive mark?* How is it possible to recognize a difference which does not distinguish itself?

> *. . . it is with difference and equality as it is with all such dialectical contraries: they are identical.* (Fragments, 56)

This paradox leaves the door open to all kinds of confusion: nothing distinguishes the man-god from all other men, and thus those who have seen him enjoy no special privilege—unless the God himself has provided the *condition* (Fragments, 85). Difference must therefore be its own teacher, the God must also be a (school)master, but already a curious and close relation is established among mastery, difference, and teaching. For if, by right, difference precedes instruction, then mastery takes place only *through* the teaching of this difference. God is master only *inas-*

much as he teaches, and he teaches *because* he wants to be a (school)master. Climacus writes, "*the consciousness of sin . . . which only the God could teach to him—should he want to be a (school)master (en Laerer)*" (*Fragments*, 58). This is a relation that is complicated by a new paradox since the master also wants to be a savior, and since mastery is attained only by the teaching of a difference it claims at the same time to abolish. If "man" were to receive enough instruction so that he could absolutely understand his difference, this difference would by the same token be abolished.

> *Thus the paradox becomes still more terrifying, or the same paradox has the double aspect which shows it to be absolute: negatively by revealing the absolute difference of sin, positively by claiming to do away with the absolute difference in absolute equality.* (*Fragments*, 59)

But *abolition* can mean neither "reconciliation" nor reunification. The difference between man and God, between nontruth and truth, between the understanding and that which exceeds it, will not be removed in favor of a higher identity. On the contrary, the understanding is already aware that the "solution to the problem" *may well be its undoing*, that its undoing is undoubtedly the price to be paid for the abolition of difference, and that it is also its own undoing which the understanding *seeks* in its paradoxical passion.

Difference, should it carry the day, will be necessarily the undoing of the understanding, it will draw it far out to a point of eccentricity, to a point of no return, into an absolute departure. At this stage of passion, the understanding tumbles from its throne. Let's call this its *panic*.[20]

---

20. From the Greek *panikos* (an epithet of "terror") derived from the name Pan, a god who was thought to disturb the mind in a violent way. In a very "Climacusian" chapter of *L'Entretien infini*, entitled "Knowledge of the Unknown," Maurice Blanchot characterizes this panic as "a rapture of fright." If anything like a relation to the unknown can be experienced, it could only be in anxiety and ravishment: "I would add that, if we can have anything to do with this unknowable, it would be precisely in fear, or in anxiety, or in one of those ecstatic states to which you object on the grounds that they are

It goes without saying that for speculative dialectics such a panic makes no sense; it is like falling into a void, into nothingness. The consciousness that leaves itself with no hope of return merely gets stuck in what could be called either an empty representation or a representation of emptiness.

> *However, if such a consciousness [that has set aside its immediate unity] does not reflect itself, the intermediate position, or middle term, which it occupies is an unhappy void, since what should fill and fulfill it have been turned into a fixed extreme. So it is that this final stage of reason in its observational role is its worst; and that is why its reversal becomes a necessity.* (Phenomenology, 206/ Phän., 257–58)

An absolute departure makes no sense here since Spirit has no absolute opposite. By *nature*, it is always in its own element, its other is never altogether other, in other words, this other can always return to it, as its very own. That is why Christianity, insofar as it is a revealed religion in which God makes himself manifest, is the only authentic religion of speculation, while Judaism would be a cult of the void, a cult of a God absolutely separated, absolutely other. Cult of the void because this alterity cannot be actually thought but only represented. The God of Christianity is infinitely *familiar*. The "character" of this familiarity is generally expressed by the affirmation of a new bond (with respect to that of Judaism) between God and the Christians: a bond of love, a filial relation, a relation of proximity. So J. C. both is and *is not* Christian. For, although the relation Father/Son, which is proper to Christianity, is essential to the faith of Jo-

---

non-philosophical. Out there, we get some premonition of the Other; it gets hold of us, jostles us, ravishes us, carrying us far away from ourselves.

"—But precisely in order to turn us into the Other. If, within knowledge—even if it is dialectical and with ever so many mediations—there is appropriation of the object by the subject, and therefore, in the end, reduction of the unknown to the already known, then in the rapture of fright there is something worse. For here it is the self that is lost and sameness that alters itself, shamelessly transformed into something 'other' than the self" (*L'Entretien infini*, 74).

hannes, it signifies less a proximity than a profound split that seems to reopen a pre-Christian abyss.

Of course, God is a real father. The comparison Climacus draws between divine instruction and Socratic instruction, for instance, bears witness to this. God reveals sin as difference and thereby teaches the disciple to remember that he is nontruth and that this is his own fault; but this recollection constitutes a passage from nonbeing to being for the disciple, a *new birth* whose only *father* is God. The disciple, knowing himself to be a son and recognizing his father, in other words, his progenitor, contracts an eternal debt toward him. It is as though the debt would thus reopen an infinite difference, for the son will never be able to make good on it. The image of the father takes the form of an infinite gap here, and not a proximity, between the God as father and his "sons." Generation becomes an irreducible rift, even if it signifies *at the same time* the proximity of an origin.

The father is master. The son, eternal debtor, will be able to pay his debt off only by *handing himself over* to the father who gave him life. This is the only means for him to liberate himself, which is perhaps also to say, to get out from under the father's mastery. Religious love is a filial love insofar as it entails self-renunciation. Either mastery or renunciation: either philosophy or religion, in which case "*intellectual reflection gives up the game.*" Renunciation, then, is not the *opposite* of mastery: it leaves contradiction behind, along with all the games of speculation. It says, "I won't play anymore." How is it possible to just pick up and leave like that? Is this just another ruse of the understanding—but then how could the understanding still be thinking about what *it is* doing when it renounces *itself*? Can reason itself be responsible for its own renunciation?

Since it is only appropriate that reason try to *be reasonable,* or since reason has an innate right to *be right*—haven't philosophers always done what was necessary to achieve this? We shouldn't be overly surprised, then, if its renunciation is made in the form of a strange claim, that is, the possibility of wanting from now on to be in the *wrong*. Undoubtedly a curious twist for a form of reason that is at the very least somewhat twisted: for what was right about reason was so only insofar as it had no *other*, while what is *wrong* is wrong only in relation to an other, even if the claim of being wrong is not the result of a comparison but is rather affirmed *a priori*. Being wrong is thus what is appropriate to difference insofar as difference recognizes and declares itself as such. And negates itself. To want to be in the wrong is the claim of the son with regard to the father, of man with regard to God, of the lover with regard to the beloved, of the finite with regard to the infinite. Juxtaposing the following texts bears this out; the first was published by the Danish editor Victor Eremita, the other by the bookbinder Hilarius:

So, then, this thought that against the God you are always in the wrong is not a truth you are compelled to recognize, not a comfort which assuages your pain, not a compensation for the loss of something better, but it is a joy in which you triumph over yourself and over the world, it is your delight, your anthem of praise, your divine worship, a demonstration that your love is a happy one, as only that love can be wherewith one loves God . . . God I will love . . . He bestows upon the lover all things, He fulfills my dearest, my only wish, that against Him I must always be in the wrong. (Either/Or, "Ultimatum," 2:353, 352)

I believe that to owe life to another is the highest good, I believe that this debt can neither be settled nor fathomed by any reckoning, and hence I find that Cicero is right in saying that with regard to the father the son is always in the wrong, and it is filial piety precisely that teaches me to believe this, teaches me not even to wish to penetrate the hidden, but rather to remain hidden in the father . . . the son is most profoundly moved when he thinks of his relationship to the father . . . for then the thought is so dreadful that there is nothing on earth so dreadful as to be a father. (Stages on Life's Way, "In Vino Veritas," 57–58)

The young man at the banquet given by William Afham—where the guests drink Château Margaux while they listen to arias from *Don Giovanni*—says that he is only capable of maintaining his relationship with his father by giving up the possibility of his own paternity. The son cannot become a father in his turn; he has to stay a son *"hidden in the father."*[21] "What does it

---

21. Where can one hide in a father? What if this father were also a mother? We could then read: ". . . for then the thought is so dreadful that there is nothing on earth so dreadful as to be a *mother*." And also: "I may indeed smile to myself at the thought of being a *mother*."

mean to be a father? I may indeed smile to myself at the thought of being a father . . . here there is a contradiction, one fit both to laugh and to weep over" (*Stages*, 58).

Such is the contradiction of passion, which laughs 'til it cries because it knows that what it really wants is its own undoing or ruin. *"Is it not its own undoing that the understanding seeks in its paradoxical passion?"*

But according to Climacus, the understanding does not create the paradox. The paradox befalls it and subjects it to its own power. And in this collision either paradox and the understanding are able to come to some understanding with one another—in which case there is happy passion—or else they cannot arrive at any understanding—in which case there is offense. Happy or unhappy, the collision brings the paradox into existence, and along with it, difference.

> *However, one merit unquestionably belongs to the offense in that it shows off difference more clearly; for in that happy passion to which we have not yet given a name, difference and the understanding have come to an understanding with each other.* (*Fragments*, 67)

For the time being, let's keep the name of this happy passion a secret, so that we can first notice the ambivalence of the offense. The offense is a kind of *suffering* in a sense that is at once active and passive. It is just active enough so as *not to permit itself to be wholly annihilated*, though it is weak enough, passive enough, that it *cannot free itself from the cross to which it is nailed or tear the arrow from out of its wound*. Let's keep in mind the image of the crucifixion, and also this note:

> . . . *linguistic usage also supports the view that all offense is passive. We say: "to be offended," which primarily expresses only the state or condition; but we also say, in the same sense as the foregoing: "to take offense" (in which there is identity of the active and passive). The Greek word for this is* σκανδαλίζεσθαι. *This word comes from* σκάνδαλον *(offense or stumbling block) and hence means to take offense or to receive a shock. Here also the sense is clearly indicated: it is not the offense that does the shocking, but that receives the shock, and hence passively, although so*

far actively as itself to take offense. This is why the understanding has not of itself brought forth the offense. (*Fragments*, 62–63)

Offense, then, is the understanding's resistance to the paradox. Already wounded, and with the presentiment of rushing headlong into its ruin, the understanding tries to remove the arrow. To accept the mortal wound would be an act of faith, the name for happy passion. This would be a mortal wound, at least for reason, which loses its sight on account of it. For faith *is* blindness itself, and it is in the risk of *not seeing* that it becomes an act of faith.

> *Now faith is precisely of this character; for in the certainty of faith there is always present a sublated uncertainty* [det Ophaevede den Uvished] *in every way corresponding to the uncertainty of becoming. Thus, faith believes what it does not see.*
>
> *This also throws light on faith; when faith resolves to believe it runs the risk of committing itself to an error, but it wants nonetheless to believe. Otherwise, there is no faith involved; wanting to avoid this risk is like wanting to know with certainty that you can swim before you go into the water.* (*Fragments*, 101, 103)

In any case, there is uncertainty, you do not get away from the risk. But if faith here starts to look like the Pascalian wager, the sacrifice of the understanding is in no way part of some sort of strategic calculation, of some kind of game. And how could the understanding still comprehend, moreover, a game in which it has itself been put up for stakes? Would it ever be able to master the rules of such a game?

If reason, though, no longer represents a principle of mastery and calculability, does this mean that there is no more calculating at all, no more economy? If, somewhere or other, there is still *some sort of* calculation, then reason and faith will at least not be able to watch it together.

> *Faith begins precisely where reason ends.* (*F&T*, 53)[22]

---

22. A certain reason, a certain type of thought. Are there other kinds? In reference to the *idea of the God who keeps himself hidden*, M. Blanchot

The Logic of the Hero

If it is in the nature of reason to pursue certain ends, then *right where reason ends* is right where the end(ing) or goal is missing. For reason to finish or come to an end—to be ended (finite) or finished—would be for it to lose sight of its end(ing) or goal. The end(ing) or goal is what reason has always wanted to see—beforehand or afterward. In this way, it has always believed itself capable of understanding faith thanks to the retrospective arguments of those "Monday-Morning Prophets," those result-experts. But the *result* will never ever be able to explain the *leap*:

> *Although the result may give joy to the entire world, it cannot help the hero, for he would not know the result until the whole thing was done and over, and he would not become a hero by that but by making a beginning.* (F&T, 63)

Heroism is not determined by the end(ing), but rather by beginnings. Johannes de Silentio develops at great length a logic of the hero in *Fear and Trembling*, not of course of the tragic hero of Greek antiquity, but of the hero or "knight" *of faith*.

This knight is first of all Abraham. Who is he? *Either a murderer, or a man of faith.*

This means, in any case, a lunatic (but J. de S. doesn't come out

> writes: "But what is such an idea? is it mystical? is it dialectical? is it tragic?" Then he adds in a note, "What form would be appropriate for the tragic idea? 'A paradoxical form,' as Lucien Goldmann says, and a form of expression which is at home only in the *fragment*. Paradoxical: which means that it always pushes to the extreme the opposing affirmations which it is supposed to maintain together. Even though it is not able to avoid the paradox, it is still not able to accept it, either, since what it aspires to is the accomplishment of the synthesis which it affirms absolutely, but as absolutely absent . . . The fragment: if the *Pensées* of Pascal remain scattered thought for Goldmann, this is because the fragment is the sole form of expression appropriate for a paradoxical work . . ." This note ends with a question which it would be well to repeat here: "But if such is the tragic work, what is tragic art? Is there only one tragic *work*?" (Blanchot, "La Pensée tragique," in *L'Entretien infini*, 152).

and say this). His sacrifice made no sense. Abraham was, and will always be, secret, silent, incomprehensible. It is not a matter of making him more comprehensible, but rather of letting *"the incomprehensibility go 'round and 'round"* (F&T, 112).

Agamemnon can be understood; he sacrificed his daughter *in the general interest*. He observed a moral code and remains comprehensible within the teleological sphere. Abraham, though, is beyond this sphere. He did not act in view of any end—his act, that is, his decision to sacrifice Isaac, could not be read, already, from within the perspective of some sort of master text, susceptible to being totalized in the truth of its meaning.

The *moral* virtue of the (tragic) hero consists in his sacrificing himself in the general interest (to the populus, to the State, or even to the Church). The religious virtue of the believer is a private affair; faith is this private relation which the believer has the strength to maintain with the divinity, in an absolute solitude. In contrast to the paradox of the hero whose particular sacrifice is brought back into contact with the general by means of mediation, J. de S. proposes the paradox of faith, which involves having recourse to a *new category* capable of accounting for an absolute and absolutely private relation with God. The relation to God is a *secret* link, and it is opposed to the religious order and to the Church, just as the *private thinker* is opposed to the *publicly certified professor*. The relation to God that takes place in silence and darkness is *the most difficult attachment*. The valorization of individuality and singularity is a valorization of difficulty.

Of course, the individual who is capable of sacrificing himself in the general interest does overcome one difficulty, but this is the simplest one, for "he knows the consolation of becoming understandable to himself in the general." Faith does not understand itself.

In sacrifice and renunciation, reason cuts itself off from itself—the sacrifice is *its* sacrifice, but reason cannot understand it.

A question of values. Who is Abraham?

> There was one who was great by virtue of his power, and one who was great by virtue of his hope, and one who was great by virtue of his love, but Abraham was the greatest of all, great by that power whose strength is powerlessness, great by that wisdom whose

secret is foolishness, great by that hope whose form is madness, great by the love that is self-hatred.

By faith Abraham emigrated from the land of his fathers and became a stranger in the promised land. (F&T, 16–17)

These "contradictions" could be understood in Hegelian fashion—something that is *always* possible when we speak of contradiction, provided we are already working within dialectics and we deny the difference between "absolute" difference and *immanent or localized* difference. J. Climacus speaks of a "true" difference, an unsettling, anxious difference, while Hegel writes:

This simple infinity, or the absolute concept, may be called the simple essence of life, the soul of the world, the universal blood, whose omnipresence is neither disturbed nor interrupted by any difference; but rather it is itself every difference, as also their sublation [ihr Aufgehobensein]; *it pulsates within itself but does not move, inwardly vibrates, yet is at rest. It is self-identical, for the differences are tautological; they are differences that are none.* (*Phen.*, 100/Phän., 132)

Hegel could always, and without being much bothered by it, interpret Climacus as the spokesman for what *vibrates* in the *depths* of *simple infinity.*

Considered from within this simple infinity, Abraham would have been only a privileged example of the "Judaic spirit": in other words, of an *alien* spirit, separated from the God who enslaves it, not even enjoying the right to its body as its own. He would have been the "true progenitor of the Jews," starting his life out from a split, leaving his family and country behind in order to live as a nomad:

With his herds Abraham wandered hither and thither over a boundless territory without bringing parts of it any nearer to him by cultivating and improving them . . . He was a stranger on earth, a stranger to the soil and to men alike. Among men he always was and remained a stranger . . . He steadily persisted in cutting himself off from others, and he made this conspicuous by a physical peculiarity imposed on himself and his posterity. (*The Spirit of Christianity*, 186/*Der Geist des Christentums*, 278)

Believing himself to be the favorite of a jealous God, he would thus be *capable* of renouncing his paternal love and of sacrificing his son Isaac. The contract concluded with a God who promises him everything and robs him of everything would make Abraham "capable" of every severance, of every sacrifice—even of the most terrible and especially, as Hegel sees it, of the most absurd sacrifice, since God had *promised* to Abraham the *renown of his race*. But isn't a son the very condition of this progeny? (From which it becomes evident just how little Hegel and his rationalism will be impressed by faith.) For Hegel, then, Abraham would end up by being terribly gullible.

> *On account of his faith in the Totality he sacrifices every particularity, he tears himself away from them. In respect to this Totality even its very condition, that is, his only son, appears to him at certain moments as something heterogeneous, as something that disturbs the pure unity of his relation to the Totality and that causes him to be unfaithful to it through his fatherly love. And so he is also capable of breaking even this tie.* (*Entwürfe zum Geist des Judentums*, 369)

(The "at certain moments" here is somewhat mysterious, to say the least.) True, from the point of view of the Absolute, jealousy makes no sense; in order to be jealous, it would be necessary to believe in difference. But the God of Abraham does believe in it. Faith, which is to say faithfulness, is necessary because there is difference. And the relation father/son is one of difference rather than a relation to oneself through the mediation of a son.

Hegel and Johannes actually see Abraham in the same way: he is the figure of the stranger, but this figure is necessarily valorized by them in inverse proportion to each other. For the same reason, "Danish" Christianity would have seemed Judaic to Hegel had he been able to read the following *Journal* entry of a certain K.

> *Judaism is a godliness which is at home in this world; Christianity is alienation from this world.* (*Journal*, 2:506)

The affirmation of (absolute) difference is also repudiated by Hegel in the name of morality, inasmuch as it is an affirmation of singularity. Abraham, according to Hegel, "lived only for himself. He existed for himself alone, and so he had to have a God all to himself who would lead and direct him" (*Entwürfe,* 369). There is no contradiction here between this and the story in Genesis, where it is written that Abraham follows Yahweh's orders after being promised a magnificent destiny and the renown of his race: "And I will make thee exceedingly fruitful, and I will make nations of thee, and kings shall come out of thee" (Genesis, 17:6). Abraham may be gullible, but he is not for all that any the less calculating. In the end, it would be to himself, to his own unity that he sacrifices (himself). For himself, when all is said and done, but by virtue of a curious misunderstanding, since the divinity he enters into contract with is nothing but *the projection of his own unity.*[23] Everything seems to take place between one singularity and another, with no mediation whatsoever between the two absolutes.[24] This strength or virtue of singularity is not particularly moral. But Silentio himself says pretty much the same thing:

> *Therefore, while the tragic hero is great because of his moral virtue, Abraham is great because of a purely personal virtue . . . [Abraham does it] for God's sake and—the two are wholly identical—for his own sake . . . Faith is namely this paradox that the Individual is higher than the universal in such a way that the Individual stands in an absolute relation to the absolute. This position cannot be mediated, for all mediation takes place only by virtue of the universal.* (F&T, 59, 55, 56)

Whereas for Hegel a contractual relationship that leads to a form of enslavement is the worst possible, Silentio valorizes just such a relationship in an absolute manner since it is the most

---

23. Hegel writes that ". . . he must have projected this oneness from himself outwards . . ." (*Entwürfe,* 369).

24. Singularity is in essence what is evil. See *The Phenomenology,* "The Law of the Heart and the Frenzy of Self-Conceit," 221ff./*Phän.,* 275ff.

difficult, since it allows taking up both blindness and enslavement, since it allows taking up murder itself.

It wasn't *easy* to put the son up on that mule, to travel slowly for three days and three nights, to climb Mt. Moriah, to chop the wood, to tie Isaac up, and to *sharpen the knife.*

Not to mention the blade which would have served to sign the covenant by leaving its mark on the body. Silentio passes over this side of the story, but can it really be a question of anything else here? It might just be that it all hangs on circumcision. On circumscission, or on castrascission. An incomprehensible, admirable castration, which S. cannot comprehend, of course, just as he cannot comprehend Abraham: "for, as I said before, I cannot understand Abraham—I can only admire him" (*F&T*, 112). Just like Abraham—who seems to accept it—this castration will only let us watch *the incomprehensibility go 'round and 'round.*

Phantasmatics

Castration saves. Renunciation constitutes the only salvation. What does it save from? At the other end of this chain that leads to a wish for blindness, there is another "fall": one which the God had inculcated *because he wanted to be master:* difference.

But if the "logic" of faith is a-teleological, a reading of the phantasmatic projections at work in the writings of Climacus—as well as in those of Vigilius—will also show that such a logic is without basis. Reason without end(ing) turns out to be a reason without origins.

Man has no one *but himself* to thank for his difference; it is by differing that he sins. But this difference cannot be referred to an opposition. The word sin—so outmoded that we come close to committing one just by still daring to write it—is something that, according to *The Concept of Anxiety,* we must already know how *not* to understand. And to start with, of course, *original sin.* The first thing to know about original sin is that it is not the *first* sin; for there is no first sin in any numerical sense of the word.

Sin came into the world by a sin. (*CA*, 32)

No sinfulness whatsoever preceded it. "Before" sin, there was neither sinfulness nor innocence.

"*Thus sin came into the world as the sudden, i.e., by a leap.*" It is the leap that posits sinfulness and not the other way around: sinfulness already presupposes the leap—but the understanding will have none of that. For philosophy (in other words, the faculties of the intellect, the understanding, and reason), the leap is a blank. And philosophy has always worked hard at filling it in. Leibniz, for instance:

> *Nothing takes place suddenly, and it is one of my great and best confirmed maxims that* nature *never makes leaps. I called this the Law of Continuity when I discussed it formerly in the* Nouvelles de la république des lettres. (*New Essays on Human Understanding*, 56)

There are perhaps *imperceptible* changes, but no leaps. And this becomes a target for Vigilius' irony:

> *All the pretty speeches of the understanding may on this occasion be compared with the counting rhyme in which children delight: one-nis-ball, two-nis-balls, etc., up to nine-nis-balls and tennis balls.* (CA, 32)[25]

---

25. Allowances should be made here for the role of the translator with respect to the choice of this rhyme . . . (*Il faut faire la part du traducteur dans le choix de cette ronde* . . .). In general, reading all these texts in translation is already tantamount to not reading them, even though certain aspects of their style make it through translation (sentence rhythm, leitmotiv effects, staging various voices, imitations of tone or of Biblical formulae . . .). But the attention to language as such, the numerous word plays, the constant search for sonorous effects; all these are untranslatable, as they say. In this respect, we shouldn't forget Kierkegaard's own request: "An urgent plea to the reader: Please read out loud if you're able to." And then there is that fragment in the *Journal:* "Everything ends with hearing—the rules of grammar end with hearing—the command of the law with hearing—the figured bass ends with hearing—the philosophical system ends with hearing—therefore the next life is also represented as pure music, as a great harmony" (*Journal*, 5:74).

Between innocence and guilt, then, philosophy would have tried to slip in, surreptitiously, a sinfulness capable of introducing sin.

> *But if this were true in the sense that sinfulness has come into the world by something other than sin, the concept would be canceled. But if it comes in by sin, then sin is prior to sinfulness.* (CA, 32)

Sinfulness, then, would have occurred only afterward; as such, it belongs to those concepts which Vigilius Haufniensis characterizes as *retrogressive*. It is the same with innocence, which never appears until after it has already been lost.

> *Innocence, unlike immediacy, is not something that must be annulled, something whose quality is to be annulled, something that properly does not exist, but rather, when it is annulled, and* only *as a result* of being annulled, *it for the first time comes into existence as that which it was before being annulled and which now is annulled.* (CA, 36–37, emphasis added)

Without exactly being *nothing*, innocence is still not there before sin, which itself did not just come out of the blue to put an end to innocence. For innocence has no present, even though it is not nothing, which is to say, an immediacy of the Hegelian type: "the most correct expression for immediacy is that which Hegel uses about pure being: it is nothing . . ." (CA, 37). Immediacy, in fact, is never given as anything other than the "to-be-annulled," the "ought-to-be-annulled" of *logical haste*. A haste by means of which logic sweeps up ethics. To say that innocence *ought* to be annulled is to *hurry* ethics . . . into logic. This is a kind of haste that is as misguided as it is useless:

> *The concept of immediacy belongs in logic; the concept of innocence, on the other hand, belongs in ethics. Every concept must be dealt with by the science to which it belongs . . . in logic, it should*

> *try to hurry a little more, for in logic it always comes too late, even when it hurries.*[26] (*CA*, 35, 37).

In this sense, innocence is merely dead and gone. It is always missing, and we cannot help but always miss it by wanting to have it or by wanting to have it come back to us.

> *As soon as one wishes for it, it is lost, and then it is new guilt to waste one's time on wishes.* (*CA*, 37)

To ask at this point how the fall occurs—on what shores of innocence—or of ignorance—the fall—or knowledge—can land—is to miss the point.

The fall is neither a passage, nor a beginning, nor an end; it does not designate a limit where innocence would stop and where culpability would begin. Rather, it would be a gap or an opening (*ouverture*). (Perhaps it would be useful here to read and listen to all the texts of J. C., J. de S., V. H., as so many *overtures*. The overture to *Don Giovanni* to start with, where we already hear resonances of his fall, which is also a cleft, a separation or hole that can never be closed up and that resists philosophical remedies. A kind of wound.)

But the word *fall* marks still other openings and differences: it is the name for a general principle of derivation that does *not* explain difference, since nothing seems to have preceded it, but which is difference, just as much as it is the opening or the condition of history—and not its origin. The fall is the name for the possibility *of* differences, for the possibility of the alterity thanks to which the son is different from the father, man something other than "the God," woman something other than man.

---

26. *TN*. The editors of the English translation point out that the antecedent of this "it" is ambiguous even in Kierkegaard's text (*CA*, 234), though the only choice seems to be between reading either "innocence" or "immediacy." The French translation, by actually moving farther away from a literal rendering, may perhaps come closer to Kierkegaard: in French, the "it" is replaced by a person (*on*); the "haste" that arrives too late to catch either "immediacy" or "innocence" thus becomes a necessary precipitate of (one's) *reading*.

We could note here how a certain form of religious thought is able both to be and to avoid being simply metaphysical.

The analysis by Vigilius H. of this "concept," myth, or phantasmatic projection of the *fall* is *not* metaphysical since it points up the division of the origin, of the present, of the original presence that in (metaphysical) principle oversees all derivation and all difference.

However, the concept of the fall remains metaphysical—and essentially Christian—insofar as it also signifies the nostalgia and the desire for a *primordial* presence that is always valorized over difference.

The "misfortune" for such a form of religious thought would thus consist in being confronted with the impossibility of metaphysical thought while it nonetheless continues to maintain its values.

> . . . *without sin there is not sexuality, and without sexuality, no history. A perfect spirit has neither the one nor the other.*
>
> . . . *Attention has been called to the fact that the creation of Eve outwardly prefigures the consequences of the relationship of generation. In a sense, she signifies that which is derived* . . .
>
> *The difference common to all subsequent individuals is derivation* . . .
>
> What is derived is never as perfect as the original. (CA, 49, 63, emphasis added)

This is why the fall also causes both anxiety and dizziness. Difference makes us anxious. Nothing to be surprised about, then, should we now learn that woman, the very image of derivation itself, is *more anxious than man.*[27]

---

27. If woman is more prone to anxiety than man is, this is also because she is *more sensuous* than he is. On the nature of sensuousness, though, Vigilius gives a somewhat skimpy explanation: "The derivation of woman also contains an explanation of the sense in which she is weaker than man, something that in all times has been assumed, whether it is a pasha speaking or a romantic knight. Nevertheless, the difference is not such that man and woman are not essentially alike despite the dissimilarity. The expression for the difference is that anxiety is reflected more in Eve than in Adam. This

And yet, to call it a myth or a phantasy of the fall deserves some explanation. We could ask, in fact, on what basis the name *phantasy* can be given to what V. H. treats as a "concept," and whether a passage to the level of psychic reality is not an unwarranted reduction. No doubt it is, if by phantasy we understand a simply imaginary, illusory projection that is opposed to "reality." The same objection would apply were we to insist on an absolute distinction between "religious" truth and psychological "truth." But Vigilius' originality might well consist in his not making this distinction and in his speaking as much from the "psychologist's" point of view as from the "believer's." *The Concept of Anxiety* starts with the following heading: "The sense in which the subject of our deliberation is a task of psychological interest . . ." (CA, 9). The author never makes the claim to *possess* faith but only to describe it and to point out in what way Christianity is irreducible,

> is because woman is more sensuous than man . . . At this point the investigation already shows that the proportion of sensuousness corresponds to that of anxiety . . . *That woman is more sensuous than man* appears at once in her physical structure. To deal more particularly with this is not my concern but is a task for physiology. However, I shall introduce her aesthetically under her ideal aspect, which is beauty. To call attention to the circumstance that this is her ideal aspect indicates precisely that she is more sensuous than man."
>
> In the end, it is because beauty excludes Spirit that there is in her *a profound unexplained sorrow*. At this point, it is beauty which draws out sensuousness and anxiety: *feminine* beauty which culminates in the absence of Spirit. The beautifully written analysis that follows deserves to be cited here: "To develop this further is not my task, but I shall indicate the dissimilarity with a single suggestion. Venus is essentially just as beautiful when she is represented as sleeping, possibly more so, yet the sleeping state is the expression for the absence of Spirit. For this reason, the older and more spiritually developed the individuality is, the less beautiful it is in sleep, whereas the child is more beautiful in sleep. Venus arises from the sea and is represented in a position of repose, a position that reduces the expression of the face to the nonessential. If, on the other hand, Apollo is to be represented, it would no more be appropriate to have him sleep than it would to have Jupiter do so. Apollo would thereby become ugly and Jupiter ridiculous. One might make an exception of Bacchus, because in Greek art he represents the similarity between manly and womanly beauty, as a consequence of which his forms are also feminine . . ." (CA, 64–66).

which is why, even if V. H. does not speak of phantasies, he is not afraid of myths. In reference to the "prohibition" and the "sentence of judgment," for instance, he writes:

> Even though one may call this a myth, it neither disturbs thought nor confuses the concept . . . The myth allows something that is inward to take place outwardly. (CA, 46–47)

All that makes it so difficult for us to read V. nowadays, and sometimes even painfully confusing, comes from his not making the distinction between the mythical—or the religious—and the psychical. He works directly from the myths. But that is also why we should not read the analyses of "concepts" belonging to Christian mythology (the fall, sin, etc.) as though they formed some sort of haphazard discourse that would be naively pre-psychoanalytical. Granted, V. H. never provides explanations of a psychoanalytical type; he never brings anything like a mechanism of the unconscious directly into play. But in these texts it is as though Vigilius had recognized an identical function shared by both myths and what he calls "something that is inward," which perhaps refers to nothing other than *primal phantasies*. Such would be the case for the phantasies of castration and its various manifestations. These texts seem to be organized around a core of myth-concepts that constitute a kind of phantasmatics, which is to say, not just a collection of phantasies, but their organization into a kind of logic as well. This logic, though, resembles no other, and if Vigilius calls it "dialectical" and gives himself out for a "subtle dialectician," it is not because such a dialectic would have anything to do with the oppositions of conscious thought, in other words, with philosophy. Should we be so surprised, then, if this *other* dialectic, which would not be played out on the scene of philosophy, were to offer, even unbeknownst to it, some sort of analogy with the logic of the unconscious?

Which is why, without either analyzing Vigilius or turning him into an analyst, we can try to see how, in these texts, analysis takes place all by itself. The hypothesis of a scene on which instinctual phantasies would play themselves out in the guise of "concepts" or Christian myths raises in its own way the question of the truth of religion.

If, in fact, we speak of *primal* phantasies in reference to V.'s

Christianity, it is partly because he considers the fall as a psychical or mythical reality (*something that is inward*), and partly because this reality has no other source than itself—neither material nor historical. Furthermore, the fall is the condition for history. The myth of the origin—which here in fact is the expression for an absence of origin—is neither an object of knowledge nor something produced by the imagination, which would, of course, *explain nothing*, but which has all the characteristics of an *a priori concept*. (Such is the concept of an original sin that would not be the first sin.) If it is a question of phantasies, then, they would have to be *a priori*, in other words, instinctual. This kind of interpretation of religion, which is by no means Freudian, would raise the question of the truth of religion. For, as an expression for phantasies that are at the same time *a priori* and universal, would it not be expressing "the truth," in at least one sense? The character of these "phantasies," moreover, would account for the fact that speculative dialectics is not able to reduce them to one of its "moments." It would be possible, therefore, to invoke these analytical concepts in order to protect those myths from the "sublating" operations of Hegelian dialectics. But the type of truth that is granted to religion in this way would be no less *reductive* than that granted to Christianity by Hegel.

In fact, speculative dialectics actually does acknowledge the truth of Christianity, but it turns out to be a truth of the interpretation of Christianity, exactly like the type of truth we've just been looking at. Climacus analyzes it with irritation:

> *So that it is not Christianity which is and was and remains the truth, and what the speculative philosopher understands is not that Christianity is the truth; no, it is the philosopher's understanding of Christianity that constitutes the truth of Christianity. The understanding is thus to be distinguished from the truth . . .*
> (*Postscript*, 200)

That Christianity could have *represented* the truth, as is the case for an Hegelian reading, does not mean that it *is* the truth. The hypothesis of V.'s phantasmatics remains on the level of "an understanding" of his text. And not of a truth.

If we now try, with the help of Freud, once again to watch the possibility or the impossibility of *understanding* Vigilius or Johannes *go 'round and 'round*, we notice that the psychoanalytical interpretation, inasmuch as it is an *interpretation*, both is and is not reductive with respect to the myth of original sin as it is outlined by V.

It is reductive since it makes original sin into a substitute for a murder:

> *The unnameable crime was replaced by the hypothesis of what must be described as a shadowy "original sin."* (*Moses and Monotheism*, 135)

The murder is of a God, who is himself the substitute for a father. Not only is the individual's God more or less the substitute for the actual, flesh and blood father,[28] but the collective god, the God of religion, also has to have an origin in the (actual) historical past. The phantasies of expiation to which the believers are still susceptible would thus have their probable *source* in the actual murder of a chieftain of the *primitive horde*. And even if the causal links of the expiation phantasies could in the end be explained

---

28. To this extent, it would be necessary to undertake an analysis of the author, to study his relationship with his own father, etc. Freud himself writes, "The psychoanalysis of individual human beings, however, teaches us with quite special insistence that the god of each of them is formed in the likeness of his father, that his personal relation to his father in the flesh oscillates and changes along with that relation, and that at bottom God is nothing other than an exalted father. As in the case of totemism, psycho-analysis recommends us to have faith in the believers who call God their father, just as the totem was called the tribal ancestor" (*Totem and Taboo*, 13:147). But we ought to be even more attentive to something else that Freud draws our attention to: trans-individual phantasies, schema that are no longer dependent on "individual experience": "wherever experiences fail to fit in with the hereditary schema, they become remodelled in the imagination . . . It is precisely such cases that are calculated to convince us of the independent existence of the schema. We are often able to see the schema triumphing over the experience of the individual; as when in our present case (the Wolf-Man), the boy's father became the castrator and the menace of his infantile sexuality in spite of what was in other respects an inverted Oedipus complex . . . The contradictions between experience and the schema seem to supply the conflicts of childhood with an abundance of material" (*From the History of an Infantile Neurosis*, 17:119–20).

by psychical reality alone—by dropping the hypothesis of an actual "heinous crime"—this psychical reality would still have to have an actual origin in the *hostile instincts* toward an (actual) father and in the *imaginary wish* to kill him (*Totem and Taboo,* 13:159–60).

The reductiveness here thus consists in retracing, step by step and from one substitution to another, the path of an originary reality and in unmasking the illusion of the religious phantasies still at work. But it could also be said that this interpretation is not reductive with respect to the myth of original sin *as it is outlined by V.* And this insofar as Freud—at least here—remains within an investigation of the origin, an investigation V. actually means to stop short of when he speaks of original sin as a kind of difference prior to the (historical) origin, a kind of difference prior to (particular) differences: the very difference of the father with respect to the son. Whereas Freud is looking for the origin of a myth here, V. H. is able to say *in a myth* that the origin *is* itself the illusion. Substitutions always point to some kind of presence, whereas sin or the fall would signify that such a presence has already been snatched away. Whether he revolts or not, every "man" is *already* a son.

THE CUT

> *Circumcision is the symbolic substitute for the castration which the primal father once inflicted upon his sons in the plenitude of his absolute power, and whoever accepted that symbol was showing by it that he was prepared to submit to the father's will, even if it imposed the most painful sacrifice on him.*
> Moses and Monotheism

The descriptions of the acts of faith included in these texts are such that they cannot help looking as though they are "symbolic substitutes for castration"—(self-sacrifice, absolute submission, blindness, etc.)—signs or simulacra for castration, *therefore,* one might say, of submission to the paternal will. It is this *therefore,* though, that must be examined. Or more precisely, it is the meaning of this submission attributed in this way to whoever agrees to castrate *himself.* For what is at stake here, among other interpretations, is the meaning of two religions often separated by the very sign of separation: Judaism and Christianity.

In the New Testament, in fact, it is written that Christ had come to liberate mankind from its submission to the Father, from its bondage. This liberation is essential for the Hegelian interpretation of Christianity:

> *In contrast to the Jewish reversion to obedience, reconciliation in love is a liberation; in contrast to the further recognition of mastery, it is the sublation of mastery in the restoration of the living bond, of that spirit of love and mutual faith which, considered in relation to mastery, is the highest freedom; a situation which is the incomprehensible opposite of the Jewish spirit.* (The Spirit of Christianity, 241/1:357)

The role of the apostle Paul in liberating mankind from the submission to the (Jewish) law of the Father—which is also a liberation with respect to the Father himself—seems to have been essential. The fact that he rejected circumcision can thus be understood not only as the result of his critique of an overly formal submission to God, but also as a sign of his revolt against the Father and his rejection of his authority.[29] But this liberation

---

29. See the Epistle to the Galatians, where the institution of a filial relationship actually takes on the appearance of a liberation with respect to the previous bondage imposed by the father: "Stand fast therefore in the liberty wherewith Christ has made us free, and be not entangled again with the yoke of bondage. Behold, I Paul say unto you, that if ye be circumcised, Christ shall profit you nothing" (Galatians, 5:1–4).

Just as the acceptance of circumcision would signify submission to the paternal will, its rejection would have to be related to a revolt against this will. Such is the argument of Herman Nunberg in an essay entitled "Attempts to Reject the Circumcision," where he writes, "St. Paul did not accept this symbol demanded by the one and only God. He rejected circumcision and also renounced a great part of the Judaic law, attributed to Moses, the powerful father figure who introduced monotheism to the Jews, and, according to Freud, also circumcision. By the removal of the sign of man's submissiveness to God, he essentially undermined God's authority . . . The external signs of the revolt were the rejection of circumcision, of the ceremonial laws of the Torah and of the dietary laws. Since circumcision

is possible thanks only to that definitive sacrifice, that *once and for all* castration which was Christ's death. The foundation of Pauline instruction is thus redemption through the death and resurrection of Christ, and it is this redemption that has to be believed in. From this point on, the object of faith is not so much God as it is salvation itself. Luther will repeat the same thing later on. Faith in God was indicated by the acceptance of castration. But this cowering faith and the mark of its submission are taken off the books through a *unique* castration that is a substitute for all the others and that thus represents liberation. This second faith is itself indicated by a new simulacrum of castration: baptism. In place of circumcision, a sign of alliance and submission (Freud calls it an attenuated castration, a substitute for death), a new alliance is substituted. This time, though, it is a liberating one and is sealed in the simulation of a highly attenuated death that in fact signifies a *new birth*.

> *John's habit (nothing of the sort is known to have been practiced by Jesus) of baptizing by immerging in water those drawn to his spirit is an important and symbolical one. No feeling is so homogeneous with the desire for the infinite* (dem Verlangen nach dem Unendlichen) . . . *as the desire to bury oneself in a body of water* (sich in einen Wasserfülle zu begraben). *He who plunges into it is confronted by an alien element which suddenly flows around him on every side and which is felt at every point of the body; he is*

> is a symbol of submission to the father's will, the rejection of circumcision is a flight from the father's authority . . . Thus the rejection of circumcision and the Torah means essentially the same: renunciation of the father" ("Attempts to Reject the Circumcision," 85, 89).
> Whoever is willing to take the risk, in order to "explain" the nature of the phantasies at work in a given text, of analyzing its author, should no doubt also take the following passage into account: "These contrasting reactions [to circumcision] are the consequence of a basic conflict which, intensified by circumcision or the mere idea thereof, drives toward consciousness. The biological basis of this conflict seems to be formed by the homosexual attachment to the father. Man has always rebelled against this attachment . . . Christianity abandoned circumcision and loosened the homosexual relationship to God-Father; but the adulation of the Woman, the Mother, and the Son was re-instated" (Nunberg, 90, 91).

> *taken out of this world* (er ist der Welt genommen) *and the world out of him. He is nothing but the feeling of the water that touches him where he is, and he is only where he feels it* . . . *He who has just plunged in climbs up into the air again, divides himself from the body of water, is already separated from it, and yet it still drips from him at every point. As soon as it is gone, the world around him regains its determinateness, and he steps back into the manifold play of consciousness* (in die Mannigfaltigkeit des Bewusstseins zurück). (Hegel, *The Spirit of Christianity*, 275/1:390–91)

Baptism, then, is a sort of momentary submergence in the tomb; it is a baptism of death out of which consciousness rises up alive. This is precisely how St. Paul understands it:

> *Know ye not, that so many of us were baptized into Jesus Christ were baptized into his death? Therefore we are buried with him by baptism into death; that like as Christ was raised up from the dead by the glory of the Father, even so we also should walk in newness of life.* (Romans, 6:3–4)

In place of a death that cut (things) off for real, an appearance of death is substituted: a "cut" which forestalls being cut off, a death which forestalls death itself. The simulacrum of death, or of castration, assumes here the value of a conjuration and an exorcism, whence its liberating effect. Through the death of Christ and through its representation in baptism a threat seems to have been forestalled. The father just might have been "had."

If it actually *was* a victory over death, then Christianity seems to have been "truly" comprehended by Hegel. And this would be so even if, in religion, truth is only posited "in the element of representation (*in dem Elemente des Vorstellens gesetzt*)."[30] Along

---

30. In *The Phenomenology of Spirit*, the life and death of Christ are in fact merely symbols or *representations*. They provide an image of the union between human and divine nature but are not yet "the self-consciousness of Spirit which has arrived at the concept as concept."

The *content* is the true content, but all its moments, when placed in the medium of representation, have the character of not being fully conceived, but rather of appearing as completely independent

with St. Paul, Christianity says: you are free, you no longer need to sacrifice yourself—to castrate yourself, to circumcise yourself. You can renounce renunciation and its outward signs, since the sacrifice has taken place *once and for all*. But this is not the way Climacus sees things, nor Haufniensis, nor K. For them, faith remains a form of blindness. If Hegel had read these authors, he would have understood them in the same way that he understood Abraham and his Judaism, which is to say, as a form of thought incapable of rising as high as freedom and subjugated to an exterior God. It is as though the culpability were also imposing the necessity of *repeating* the expiation here. But why this repetition, since through the new alliance the necessity for this kind of submission should have been removed? Why submit oneself any more, since the reconciliation has already taken place, since difference has been abolished?

There *should* no longer be any difference: God has become a father, the slave has become a son, *adopted* by the Father who sacrificed his only Son.

> *But after that faith is come, we are no longer under a schoolmaster. For ye are all the children of God by faith in Christ Jesus. For as many of you as have been baptized into Christ have put on Christ. There is neither Jew nor Greek, there is neither bond nor free, there*

> sides which are *externally* connected with one another (*Phen.*, 463/ 3:556). Christ projects only the *figure* of truth. The truth of Spirit, though, is to become an effective Self, "to reflect itself by itself in itself and to be a Subject." What is still missing from religion is the auto-conception of the Self in relation to which representation is merely a loss and a schism. It is well known that, for Hegel, representation is to the concept what urine is to sperm. "*The* depth *which Spirit brings forth from within—but only as far as the* representational consciousness *where it lets it stay—and the* ignorance of *this consciousness about what it is really saying, are the same conjunction of high and low which, in living beings, Nature expresses in a naive manner by conjoining the organ of its highest fulfillment, the organ of procreation, with the organ of urination. Infinite judgment, qua infinite, would be the self-fulfillment of self-comprehending life; the consciousness of infinite judgment that remains in representation, though, carries on like urination*" (*Phen.*, 210/ 3:262).

> *is neither male nor female; for ye are all one in Christ Jesus.*
> (Galatians, 3:25–28)
> *. . . Therefore you are no longer slave but rather son.*

That was called a *liberation* . . . Filial love replaces fear and bridges the gulf: the son is no longer afraid, he *loves*. Could it be that Johannes and the others were able to see things more clearly? It seems, in fact, that they couldn't at all see in what way a son would be any less castrated than a slave, that they didn't understand how a son could not be *other* than his father. The metaphor of filiation is therefore ambiguous: it is able to signify identity as well as irreducible difference. Actually, it is not able to represent oneness, as in Hegel, except by already *presupposing* it, by already supposing an immanence through which the son has never left the father. Pushed far enough, it destroys itself all by itself, and says that there isn't even any son.

> *How could heterogeneity be unified . . .*
> *. . . Only a modification of the Godhead can know the Godhead*
> *. . . All thought of a difference in essence between Jesus and those in whom faith in him has become life, in whom the divine is present, must be removed.* (*The Spirit of Christianity,* 266, 268/ 1:382, 385)

For Hegel, filial love and faith are nothing but the *recognition* of God, the *return* to the divinity, the return to an *original oneness*. (It is seldom a question of adoption, which has the disagreeable smell of a contract and which really does presuppose a difference.) But if there is re-cognition, if there is no longer either difference or the unknown, why the need still to talk about faith? It would not make sense any more.

The oneness of unity, in any case, is undiscoverable. Either it was already there, and we can do no more than rediscover it, return to it; or else difference would not have been a passing event, and no higher identity could ever embrace it. Could it be, after all, a question of interpretation, of values, of caprice?

Whereas Hegel reproaches the Jews for their incapacity to draw near to their God, an incapacity that goes so far as to become the deliberate wish to keep themselves away from him:

> *How were they to recognize divinity in a man, poor things that they were, possessing only a consciousness of their misery, of the depth of their servitude, of the opposition to the divine, of an unbridgeable gulf between human and divine reality?*
>
> *. . . The manifestation in connection with the solemn lawgiving on Sinai had so stunned the Jews that they begged Moses to spare them, not to bring them near to God; let him speak with God alone and then transmit to them God's orders.* (*The Spirit of Christianity*, 265, 193/1:381, 285)

Johannes, on the contrary, identifies a sense of the sacred with a sense of distance and fear. In regard to Abraham, he writes:

> *One approaches him with a horror religiosus, as Israel approached Mount Sinai.* (F&T, 61)

How can anything be kept, unless it is kept at a distance? By trembling before him, by prohibiting themselves from looking at him, would the Jews have been any less religious than that overly zealous apostle who got close enough to kiss Christ?

It remains to be seen, by clarifying the question which is raised by the repetition of the sacrifice, in what way J. C. was much less Christian than Hegel. In what way, in fact, J. C. was perhaps not at all Christian, since he did not consider Christ a Savior but rather a *model*.

Christ, the crucified Son, the figure of renunciation, of blind submission and of the gift of self, is the figure of faith. Conversely, though, sacrifice becomes the sign of the son. If filiation does not signify the *natural* sign of oneness—since unity is not original— then sacrifice is the pact or the contract through which it is possible to *become* a son, which is to say, a slave. It is by offering oneself to the father that one becomes a son, which is to say that one consecrates the glory or the victory of the father through self-renunciation. Castration is the only way to "conciliate" God once difference has revealed itself to be irreducible.

At this point, then, shouldn't we oppose some kind of *contractual* and institutional relation of filiation to natural filiation? Through the sacrifice that seals the pact, man conciliates God and difference; he becomes his son and makes a father of him.

In this respect, we ought to recall the curious story of that painter, Christoph Haizmann, analyzed by Freud in *A Seventeenth-Century Demonological Neurosis*. The painter claimed to have signed two pacts with the devil: one written in ink, the other with blood. This devil, in fact, seems to have been a substitute and an "exaltation" of Haizmann's (real) father. Here are the texts of the two pacts:

Ich Christoph Haizmann vndterschreibe mich disen Herrn sein leibeigener Sohn auff 9 Jahr. 1669 Jahr.
Anno 1669
Christoph Haizmann. Ich verschreibe mich disen Satan ich sein leibeigener Sohn zu sein, und in 9 Jahr ihm mein Leib und Seel zuzugeheren.

Now in these pacts, the devil does not commit himself to anything, it is only the painter who "submits to him body and soul." But *leibeigener Sohn* is actually more than *his own son*, it is his son as slave or *serf* (*leibeigener* was the name given to a serf whose body belonged to the Lord).[31] Haizmann promises, then, to be *at one and the same time* son and slave; but how can we know here which qualification is reinforcing the other? It is as though, at bottom, son and slave meant the same thing. The serf who is wholly subjugated is like a son, and the best son is like a slave. The best slave is one who loves his master, and the best son (who loves his father the most) is one who submits to the father like a slave. At this point, how are we to interpret things? Wouldn't it be possible to say that the son is a *substitute* for the slave, as well as the other way around, and that the father is a *substitute* for the devil, for God, or for the Master?

---

31. The English translations for the two texts are: "I, Christoph Haizmann, subscribe myself to this Lord as his bounden son till the ninth year. Year 1669"; "Christoph Haizmann. I sign a bond with this Satan, to be his bounden son and in the ninth year to belong to him body and soul" (*A Seventeenth-Century Demonological Neurosis*, 19: 81–82).

And if the son is always already a slave, then the Christian will perhaps always still be a Jew. The alternative between the relation of enslavement and filiation, between fear, submission, and love, between Judaism and Christianity would thus be a fiction. Or a ruse. Better yet: wouldn't we have to say that Christianity only aggravates the gulf it claims to bridge? In fact, doesn't it substitute an even more profound difference for an expression of difference?

To *imitate* Christ: why *wouldn't* this be essentially to understand him? What is a model? There is an *argument of the model*. For the idea of a model implies the idea of a basis for measure, a basis for evaluation. If measure (*modus*) is based on the model, the model is something which can itself be neither measured nor evaluated. If Christ *is* truth, there can be no truth *of* Christ . . . therefore no comprehension, no interpretation of Christ, no Christian doctrine.

Which is why what we are calling the argument of the model here is always the argument advanced against a philosophy *of* religion and against philosophy in general insofar as it claims to be able to interpret; which is to say, to possess the mastery of meaning. But why should it be a question of preferring imitation to that particular "mastery"? Naturally, by raising this question, we would have already chosen to speak yet again of the meaning. Assuming there is a choice.

In the defense of the model there is an affirmation of the intellect's sacrifice and this entails a sacrifice of meaning. Reason sacrificed has this to say: "You can't—and I can't either—comprehend faith. You have no right to assign it a meaning (and) an end(ing), for truth comes before meaning." The speech we lend to faith here can also find other arguments. In numerous texts written about a certain "Christianity," for instance, there is a denunciation of the exegete's *power*. Behind the accusations aimed at meaning, behind those aimed at interpretation, there are the accusations aimed at the professor and the priest. However paradoxical, these accusations resemble those made by Nietzsche in the *Anti-Christ*.

The truth *of a unique meaning*, an effect of interpretation, appears as an instrument of domination and the foundation of a power structure. Christ as individual seems to have been exploited by a faction which consolidated its power thanks to him.

But on the one hand, he is Truth incarnate (the meaning of meaning?), and on the other, an *Idiot*.[32]

But ethically, religiously, especially religiously, there is no subject matter in the sense that it is the essential thing and the person the accidental; here imitation is the essential factor. What nonsense, then, that—instead of imitating Christ or the apostles and suffering as they suffered—that one becomes a professor instead, of what? Yes, of this—that Christ came to be crucified and the apostles were stoned. The only thing lacking at Golgotha was a professor, who promptly would have appointed himself as professor—of theology!

So it ended with the apostle's being crucified—and the professor became professor of the apostle's being crucified. After a while the professor departed this life in a quiet and peaceful death. (Journal, 3:640)

. . . I shall now show that the priests are cannibals, and in a far more odious way . . .

But what does the "priest" do? This educated man is far from being crazy. "To imitate him!" What a proposal to make to a shrewd man! First this shrewd man must have undergone a transformation, he must have become

To reduce being a Christian, Christianism, to a matter of considering something true, to a mere phenomenon of consciousness, is to negate Christianism. In fact there have been no Christians at all . . .

It is false to the point of nonsense to find the mark of the Christian in a "faith," for instance, in the faith in redemption through Christ: only Christian practice, *a life such as he* lived *who died on the cross, is Christian . . .*

The life, for example, the doctrine, the death, the meaning and the right of the entire evangel—nothing remained once this hate-inspired counterfeiter [the apostle Paul] realized what alone he could use . . .

His need was for power; in Paul the priest wanted power once again—he could use only concepts, doctrines, symbols with which one tyrannizes masses and forms herds. What was the one thing that Mohammed later borrowed from Christianity? Paul's invention, his means to priestly tyranny, to herd formation . . .

---

32. See *The Anti-Christ:* "Spoken with the precision of a physiologist, an entirely different word would be even more appropriate here—the word *idiot*" (p. 601, para. 29).

crazy, before it could occur to him to go in for such a thing. No, but might it not be feasible to describe the sufferings of these glorious ones, to preach their teaching as doctrine, and in such a way that it would yield so much profit that a man could live off it, marry on it, beget children who are fed on it? (The Instant, 268)

The "law," the "will of God," the "good book," "inspiration"— all mere words for the conditions under which the priest attains power . . . these concepts are found at the basis of all priestly organizations, of all forms of priestly or philosophic-priestly rule. (Nietzsche, *The Anti-Christ*, 613, 612, 617, 618, 641–42)

Of course, the analogy stops there: with the shared affirmation of a link between dogma, doctrine, and a power structure underwritten by doctrine. Nietzsche and K. oppose dogmas to a "practice," but this is by no means the same sort of practice. It is obvious, in fact, how Christ appears in *The Anti-Christ* as the innocent and joyous messenger who brings tidings of truly good news, tolling the death knell of sin and of culpability as well as of the Judaic church (*The Anti-Christ*, 592–99). The Christian *should have been* the one to distinguish himself through *another form of action*. Instead, though, St. Paul reintroduces the significance of sacrifice, invents the "Redemption," "Judgment Day," etc. Out of which comes a mighty second wind for dogma and all of Judaism. But even if the author of the *Journal* is no closer to a belief in doctrine, for him the Christly model is still a model of suffering. Nietzsche's Christ was a kind of simpleton, albeit a sympathetic one—which suggests that Nietzsche's interest in Christ's person was after all never anything more than a pose— whereas in his *Two Minor Ethico-Religious Treatises*, H. H. finds in Jesus a conscious desire for his own death, a willingness to die. He would have been, and is, Truth suffering:

He is the Truth. He wills his death. ("Has a Man the Right to Let Himself Be Put to Death for the Truth?" 98)

This intention must be understood in light of its consequences:

He wills his death; yet he is not guilty of his death, for it was the Jews who put him to death—and he wills to die the death of atonement, and it was with this intention that he came into the

> *world . . . In love he would die the death of atonement; but in order that he may die, the contemporary generation must become guilty of a murder . . .* ("Has a Man the Right?" 98, 97)

Whereas Hegel is constantly erasing it, here there is no dissimulating the terrible violence of sacrifice, the terrible power of castration. In fact, H. H. is so sensitive to this violence that he almost has to justify the god's right to sacrifice, as well as defend himself against the reproach he might actually incur by claiming to advocate such a right himself. His responses to the possible accusation of presumption almost always go hand in hand with the expression of his willingness to imitate Christ.

> *Once upon a time there was a man who, as a boy, was strictly brought up in the Christian religion . . . All the more frequently he had been shown the crucified one, so that this picture was the only one he had, the only impression he had of the Savior . . . For he had always felt it an impiety to venture to paint this picture and an impiety also to look with an artistic eye upon a picture so painted, to see if it bore a resemblance—instead of becoming oneself the picture which resembles him, and being driven by an inexplicable force to desire to resemble him, insofar indeed as a man can resemble him . . . But his willingness to suffer for the same cause, even unto death, in that* there was no presumption . . . ("Has a Man the Right?" 81–82)

An *inexplicable force* is required to dare to want to resemble Christ, in other words, to let oneself be persecuted—and indeed to provoke this persecution—to dare to make the persecutor *guilty of murder*. In the *Journal* entry of 16 August 1847, the author outlines the *Two Minor Treatises:*

> *The new book will be entitled: How did it happen that Jesus Christ could be crucified? Or: Has a man the right to sacrifice his life for the truth? . . . After all, one may be so conversant with the world and with men that simply by doing what is good and true he is saying very precisely: I want to be persecuted. Is this not being too hard on men?* (*Journal*, 5:405)

Just how much strength is necessary to sustain such toughness? But, then, what strength, what *glory,* is not to be expected from it? And what if it were equally necessary to take into account the possibility of a profit on one's death, a kind of posthumous gain? *Profit, gain,* horrible words to use in connection with the most generous, the most absolute of renunciations. Nonetheless, it is possible to find remarks on this very subject in the *Journal.*

> *Scrivner says that we can't help making a good deal with death—the advantage is always on our side* ("to die is gain," Philippians, 1:21). (*Journal,* 1:338)
>
> The Dying Paul
>
> *Legend tells us that when Paul was beheaded, his head still cried out the name of Christ three times. This signified that his preaching essentially began with his death. It is traditional to say that in death the beloved's image is found in the lover's heart . . .* (*Journal,* 3:468)

The deceased, as Freud put it, *became even more powerful than he had been during his lifetime.*

But if there is reason to suspect a hidden structure or economy here, how would the sacrificed consciousness be able to hope for any profit, unless it were by arranging (for) some ploy capable of permitting it to "survive the fact of its own suppression"? Once again, the contradiction lends itself *at one and the same time to laughter and to tears.* This is "Bataille's peal of laughter" and the suffering of the *wholly silent ones.* And how would it even be possible, with no hope of any gain, to withhold the sacrifice from every reappropriation, unless it were by suffering from or laughing at the simulacrum?

What did "Christian authors" *do?* They wrote about sacrifice, they wrote commentaries on an incomprehensible silence and an incomprehensible sacrifice. Through their writing, though, they did not die, they merely gave expression to the "insane" suffering of a risk which after all they may not have taken. What sort of writing is this? What does it mean, for a religious author, to write? We must at last interrogate the *author* about this kind of operation.

Sacrifice to the Letter

> *For the sake of form and the smooth running of things, I hereby acknowledge, what in fact hardly anyone can be interested in knowing, that I am the author, as they say, of* Either/Or *(Victor Eremita), Copenhagen, February, 1843;* Fear and Trembling *(Johannes de Silentio) 1843;* Repetition *(Constantine Constantius) 1843;* The Concept of Anxiety *(Vigilius Haufniensis) 1844;* Prefaces *(Nicholaus Notabene) 1844;* Philosophical Fragments *(Johannes Climacus) 1844;* Stages on Life's Way *(Hilarius Bookbinder: William Afham, the Judge, Frater Taciturnus) 1845;* Concluding Unscientific Postscript to the Philosophical Fragments *(Johannes Climacus) 1846; an article in* The Fatherland, *1843, No. 1168 (Victor Eremita); two articles in* The Fatherland, *January, 1846 (Frater Taciturnus) . . . My wish, my prayer, is that, if it might occur to anyone to quote a particular expression from the books, he would do me the favor to cite the name of the respective pseudonymous author and not mine, i.e., to distinguish between us in such a way that the expression belongs in a feminine manner to the pseudonym, and the responsibility, in a civil sense, to me.*
>
> S. Kierkegaard (*Postscript*, "A First and Last Declaration")

The author, as they say, is someone who, properly speaking, produces, which is to say he works, labors, operates, and draws up in his own hand. The signing or the signature is usually what provides the author's identity, from which we can tell that several works have been produced by the same hand. Through which we are given the identity of a *single* authorship with several titles. Something that in itself doesn't tell us anything about the supposed author's existence or his true identity. In this sense, it would matter little that the above signature were or were not the proper name of the author—actually the name of the author's father—provided only that it endowed the authorship with an identity, which is to say, a father. It is customary, though, to identify the signature of the author (the signatory) with the proper name of the actual citizen who is supposed to have done the work of the signatory, even if this were a pseudonym, indeed even if it were intentionally obliterated, as is the case in certain anonymous works.

We know that Kierkegaard found anonymity scandalous,[33] and that he always wanted to remain *civilly responsible* for his works.

> *My pseudonymity . . . was certainly not caused by a fear of legal penalty, for in this respect I am confident that I have committed no crimes, and at the time the books were published, not only the printer but also the Censor qua public functionary, was officially informed who the author was.* (*Postscript*, "A First and Last Declaration")

What are we to make, though, of a proper name that is at the same time one signature among others, a name more proper than others though still a signature and still to be distinguished from the name itself of the producer, and which then becomes "personally" the signatory of the signatures, including its own? Would this name be the seal of seals (*le seing des seings* the sign, seal, paraph, signature), the father of fathers?

This question now extends beyond a mere invitation to sacrifice. It is no longer simply concerned with sacrifice as a theme.

A question, then, addressed to writing as an operation—given its capacity to answer for itself—a play of forces in which the identity of an author with several (false) names, of which only one is revealed as proper name, is engaged in problematical fashion here.

Kierkegaard himself identified the question of the name with that of the work's paternity, regardless of whether he lay claim to this paternity retrospectively or whether, on the contrary, he marked out its irrevocable ambiguity, designating himself sometimes as the author of an operation strategically calculated from

---

33. See *The Point of View*, 44: "anonymity, as the most absolute expression for the impersonal, the irresponsible, the unrepentant, is a fundamental source of modern demoralization . . . But in our age, which reckons as wisdom that which is truly the mystery of unrighteousness, viz., that one need not inquire about the communicator but only about the communication, the objective only—in our age what is an author? An author is often merely an *x*, even when his name is signed, something quite impersonal, which addresses itself abstractly by the aid of printing to thousands and thousands of people . . ."

the outside, sometimes as the victim of an operation of pure loss, as though in the end he had been the sacrificial victim of his writing. But Kierkegaard knew that in order to break loose from this alternative, it would be necessary at the same time to break loose from writing and from the dialectical duplicity that works on behalf of a dialectical reappropriation.

In April 1848, Kierkegaard therefore decides to *speak:*

> *My whole nature is changed. My concealment and introversion are broken—I am free to speak. (Journal, 5:443)*
> *. . . the dialectical nets are rent asunder; now I dare to speak openly.*
> *Having finished (my work), I considered putting my pen down in order to speak in my own voice.*

He then draws up *The Point of View for My Work as an Author,* in which, assuming mastery over his entire authorship, he presents himself at the same time as both martyr and sacrificial victim. Implicitly or explicitly, Kierkegaard compares himself as an author to those who let themselves be sacrificed "for the Truth": Socrates and Jesus.

> *To take the highest example: the whole life of Christ on earth would have been mere play if he had been incognito to such a degree that he went through life totally unnoticed—and yet in a true sense he was incognito. (The Point of View, 16)*

Like them, he would have known duplicity, martyrdom, and persecution. Like them, he would have declined to write his own apology. He cannot help, though, defending himself for having wanted to defend himself. This virtuoso of the *mise en abyme* of his own discourse may in this way have left at least one foothold for reading. He does not miss a single opportunity to launch into the most blatant disavowal:

> *What I write here is for orientation. It is a public attestation; not a defense or an apology. In this respect, truly, if in no other, I believe that I have something in common with Socrates. For just as his demon—on whose account he stood accused and about to be judged*

> by the "crowd," he who knew that he was a kind of divine gift—forbade him to defend himself—indeed, if he had done that, how unseemly it would have been, and how self-contradictory!—likewise there is something in me, and in the dialectical position I occupy, which makes it impossible in itself, to conduct a "defense" for my work as an author. (*The Point of View,* 6–7).

Although he does not defend himself, and although the work speaks, at least indirectly, of itself, K. "*qua* man," thus wants to give *a direct assurance that the author has been and has remained a religious author.*

> *I was of the mind that I, who in my melancholy loved mankind, should be of succor to them, to find comfort for them, and above all clarity of thought, and that especially in regard to Christianity.* (*The Point of View,* 79)

The author here is no longer writing, then, nor is he speaking. But insofar as someone is an author, he does nothing but write. Once he *stops writing,* "someone else" speaks about the author and his work, and the one who does this speaking is neither Climacus nor V. Eremita nor Kierkegaard, signatory author of *The Edifying Discourses,* or "third-person prompter." With respect to the authors of the literary production, the one who draws up this *Point of View,* therefore, represents a third instance. Such an instance would at once go beyond the aesthetic author (the "poet"), behind whose manifestation the religious author hides, and even the religious author himself who, *qua* author, has to calculate the part of his discourse to be indirect (pseudonymous) as well as direct—but who *has to* do this only at the bidding of the religious man, who does not write (who does not yet write, or who no longer writes) but who watches himself write, who watches himself have the work done for which he has been chosen:

> *It seemed to me that I was designated for this role . . . The whole productivity has had in a certain sense an uninterruptedly even course, as if I had nothing else to do but to copy daily a definite portion out of a printed book.* (*The Point of View,* 72)

This third instance was not yet, or no longer, Kierkegaard the author, but merely a copier in the service of Providence. But if this diligent copier was already there at the beginning, sacrificing himself to his task, he does not understand himself, thanks to a rereading of his work, *until the end.*

> *For in case I were to affirm out and out that* from the very first instant *I had an overview of the whole dialectical structure of the whole authorship . . . it would be a denial of God and an act of disloyalty towards him . . . But what I cannot understand is that* now I can understand it *and yet cannot by any means say that at the instant of commencing it I understood it so precisely— though it is I who have carried it out and made every step with reflection.* (*The Point of View,* 72)

What exactly is this *I* that labors but does not understand itself until afterward, if not the result of a process of reappropriation in whose service the authors and the works have been only intermediate steps, mediations?

Even while it portrays the author as a sacrificial victim, *The Point of View* "sublates" or elevates him through an *understanding* of the dialectical structure of the authorship in which the last stage is also the final and essential stage.

> *The various stages taken together constitute the spontaneous stage, and it follows that each stage manifests a certain attribute, so that all the attributes are contained in the fulness of the final stage, since it is the essential one.*

Moment of reappropriation, the moment of *The Point of View* recalls the work's duplicity and the author's martyrdom and at the same time puts an end to this duplicity and martyrdom by an all-embracing recuperation of the meaning of both one and the other.

Nonetheless, the author seems to have been the victim of his own writing, and this because the indirect form of the "communication" corresponds to an effacement of the author who gives up on him-*self,* and because the dialectical structure of the authorship corresponds to a kind of strategy in which the author offers himself up for persecution. The poet, the ironist, starts out *incognito* in a "work of expectation," a "deception," a "necessary expurgation," behind the "mask of a scoundrel and a seducer." This is a first renunciation.

> *I started out as an author with an immense furror—that in private I was regarded as little more than a scoundrel—but of course for that reason alone was I all the more likeable . . . This was necessary in order to attract the "crowd" of Christians just a little. And even if one were a saint, to start out in a saintly manner would amount to giving up the whole thing.* (*The Point of View,* 94)

This beginning, then, corresponded to the necessity of holding off on the religious writing, of postponing any more direct action, "for in the age of reflection in which we live people are prompt to parry, and even the death of the saint is of no avail." Of course, it was also a question of postponing death; but then comes the moment of the second and true sacrifice:

> *And then I did something decisive that was just a little bit Christian . . . I cast myself as a sacrifice into the upheaval of riffraff—then I was regarded by the public as crazy and queer, almost condemned as criminal—but that goes without saying, for there was not the least trace of the scoundrel or the rascal in what I did.* (*The Point of View,* 94–95)

"And now I am no longer interesting." Having become serious and "moralizing," the author has stepped into the *"danger zone of laughter and mockery."*

> *If it is from the crowd that evil proceeds, the contemporary religious author must for God's sake see to it that he becomes the object of its persecutions and of its grinning laughter, and in this he should take care to receive special treatment.* (*The Point of View,* 60–61)

The risk of death which the religious man as such must incur is the death that might befall him in the midst of laughter and persecution *as author.*

> *And the essentially religious author has but one fulcrum for his lever, namely a miraculous syllogism. When anyone asks him on*

> *what he bases the claim that he is right and that it is the truth he utters, his answer is: I prove it by the fact that I am persecuted; this is the truth, and I can prove it by your jeers . . . Every religious writer or speaker or teacher who absents himself from danger and is not present where it is and where evil has its lair is a deceiver . . . Only one exception is made, and that is with reference to the man who in his lifetime has been a religious writer or teacher or speaker and has been so at his own risk and peril. (The Point of View, 59, 60)*

But the sacrifice here is not death itself: it is merely the "death" of the author. It is *as author* that K. claims to take his chances and offer himself up for sacrifice—for persecution. It is especially honor, praise, and success which he claims to be giving up. Later on, he will write in his Journal:

> *I have also been able to deceive myself about myself, never realizing to what extent I have been unable to prefer even death itself to the pursuit of something more tranquil.*

If K. freely sacrifices a chance for glory here on earth, it is, nonetheless, because this sacrifice is the price of an even more glorious summit: that of the true "religious teacher," an honor that will be bestowed on him by "the true religious teachers, who all of them so long as they lived were mocked." This is the price to be paid for a more distant profit, but in light of which an immediate renunciation becomes less frightful.

> *Having been a religious teacher, he will be judged by the true religious teachers, who all of them so long as they lived were mocked, persecuted, derided, scorned, and spat upon. Ah! how frightful it is for the natural man to stand here on earth and be derided, mocked, and spat upon! More frightful still to stand in eternity with this bundle [of praise, honor, and reputation] under his arm or attired in his . . . finery. (The Point of View, 60)*

That is why whoever lays claim to religious distinction does not just "let" himself be persecuted: he is *on the lookout* to become the *readiest butt of mockery*, and he moves heaven and earth in order to provoke his persecution. At various points, after having laid out the scenario necessary for his sacrifice, Kierkegaard congratulates himself on his success, even if, like Marcus Curtius, he had to *appear crazy.*

> *And even those who would not be scared by this would be upset by the next obstacle, by the thought that I had voluntarily exposed myself to all this, giving proof of a kind of madness. Ah yes! so did the contemporaries doubtless judge of the Roman knight who made the immortal leap to save his country! Ah yes, and yes again, a kind of lunacy, for it was dialectically precisely Christian self-denial—and I, poor old Magister of Irony, became the pitiable target for the laughter of a most highly respected and cultivated public. (The Point of View, 58–59)*

Even if he was a victim, the author would have at least wanted to show how much control he had always had of the operation whose conditions and effects he had minutely calculated. But Kierkegaard did not publish his *Point of View* . . . He gave up on speaking about himself.

> *N.B.-N.B.* The Point of View for my work as an Author *must not be published, no! no! (Journal, 6:108)*

After having considered "making it into something by a third party: A possible Explanation of Magister Kierkegaard's Authorship," K. put *The Point of View* back in a drawer.

> *No, one finishes a book like that, puts it away in a drawer, sealed and marked: To be opened after my death. (Journal, 6:109)*

Kierkegaard will not be able to get out of writing, at least not alive. He gives up on putting his books away again, on taking on the weight of their meaning, on standing in or standing up for them himself; he gives up on speaking.

> *The rest of the things written can very well be published. But not one word about myself . . . Suddenly to want to assume this enormous productivity as one single thought is too much—although I see very well that it is that. Yet I do not believe that I was motivated by vanity. (Journal, 6:144)*

But this new and final disappearance, this new effacement is not an ultimate sacrifice, or not exactly, for it is not a new suffering. *The Point of View* cannot be published because it does not speak the truth, because Kierkegaard did not, could not write the *Truth*.

Sacrifice is not something that can be written. The grief of loss is not something that lends itself to writing: because writing is enjoyment. Though wasn't writing itself an operation of loss insofar as the author disappeared under the weight of texts and signatures? And if this operation were only a strategic erasure, a provisional effacement of an author who is before all else religious, why give up on having the last word?

> *I cannot quite say that my work as an author is a sacrifice. It is true that I have been unspeakably unhappy ever since I was a child, but I nevertheless acknowledge that the solution God found of letting me become an author has been a rich, rich source of enjoyment for me. I may be sacrificed, then, but my authorship is not a sacrifice; it is, in fact, what I unconditionally prefer to continue as.*
>
> *Thus I cannot express the full truth here, either, for I cannot spell out in print my torment and wretchedness—so that the enjoyment ends up predominating.* (*Journal*, 6:108)

APARTÉS

What is written never has a "public." It takes the reader aside (*à part*), necessarily isolates him, draws him away, summons him to a simulated *tête-à-tête* from which the author remains absent: to write, to read, is always to enter into this aside (*aparté*). In the theater, where the term originated, the likelihood of the "aside" is not any greater, for even if the actor separates himself for a moment from those who may be with him on stage, he still remains in contact with a public or an audience that is essentially plural. He does not come down to whisper his soliloquy into the ear of one particular spectator, and even if he did, it would still function as a performance for all the others. But the reader is alone, in a solitude that is not due to the situation in which reading usually takes place—and which is relative, or contingent—but is rather due to the kind of solitude imposed by writing. There, the scene always takes place on a "private stage."

He, who by every means and every strategy wrote only in order to exhibit, or to offer to view his innermost solitude as author—a somewhat obscene gift—and as though in so doing to invite the reader to recognize his own solitude, he—whom I will call merely "him"—engages less in a self-revelation than in a description of the ordinary condition of every "author." This "essential solitude," according to Maurice Blanchot, has nothing to do with "the complacent isolation of individualism," and it does not depend on some sort of choice or decision.

*
* *

For him, Christ was the one who separated: "And Jesus took him aside . . ." (Mark, 7:33). Religion—despite its etymology [*religere*, to assemble, to bind together]—and the Christian religion in particular, would have been a work of separation. Piety demands solitude, it asks (him) to enter into a "private" relation with God, to respond to Him *aparté*, to confront Him and to obey Him at the risk, brought on by solitude, of going astray or insane. If the solitude of "the author" (it is always as such that he refers to himself) is comparable to religious solitude (the same vertigo, the same doubt, the same sacrifice, the same self-effacement, the same risk of perdition or loss), this is because it seems either to depend in some way on the religious element, or because it enters into conflict with it. So that by writing he always felt himself to be something of a traitor. He was able to excuse himself for it only by suffering, by seeking martyrdom and persecution, but without ever getting enough of them since writing, by the very isolation it drew him into, was as much an occasion of enjoyment as pain for him.

The aside, whether religious or literary, does not provide access to any kind of encounter; God or the work are not things with which a relation could be established. They only lead to solitude and to sacrifice, they only entice their prey; like greedy minotaurs, they fascinate and devour them.

For him, everything seems to end up in a scene of devouring, or even of deflowering. But let's not get ahead of ourselves.

Neither the reader nor, of course, the author does the devouring: they are what gets devoured. "To get devoured," could that be the (even unavowed) object of their desire?

There is another danger that threatens the author and the religious man: woman. She also tries to draw man away in order to get hold of him, make him lose his head, destroy him insofar as he is Spirit, and—such are the words—to devour him. Contending for man with God and the work, "woman draws man into an aside." The same scenario, then, in a mode of parody: but in this aside, man does not run the risk of death (even though as Spirit this is what he desires), since what woman is after is to keep him alive, to wrest him from his sacrifice and his death.

*
* *

Reading had to start all over again—for instance, with the *Journal*. This too could have been done in the form of a "journal" or a notebook in which, at the mercy of a deliberately haphazard reading, such and such a one of his "experiences" would have been listed.

In the *Journal*, an author encounters a genre, which, within the general aside of literature, puts him in a peculiar form of intentional isolation, but which paradoxically can also save him from a more profound solitude. This is because here he claims—again according to Blanchot—"to remind himself who he is, in other words, who he is when he is not writing." Recalling himself to himself, the author of a "journal" would be able to protect himself from a certain kind of withdrawal instead of giving himself up to it: "the journal—that book that is apparently altogether solitary—is often written out of fear and anxiety before the solitude that besets the writer on account of the work" ("The Essential Solitude," 29). K.'s journal seems to be an exception: if he often reminds himself who he is there, it is above all who he is *when he is writing*. But since this reminder is equally present throughout the "Authorship," it is not certain that the "journal" occupies a privileged position in this respect.

Solitude was always the risk for him. But it would be typical enough of his logic to consider the exposure to risk still to be the best way of parrying it. It could be that in his choice of a kind of writing given over in its entirety to the *aparté*, in this choice with every appearance of being the most risky of all, the absence of economy is not absolute. Risk, like solitude, has to do with a cut. It is also necessary to take into account the strange logic that makes an exposure to risk a means of cutting down on the risk.

The "journal," then, is tempting. It seems to sanction groping, wandering, and rehashing; it lifts the prohibition that ordinarily falls on digression; in principle it is tolerant of a certain disconnectedness. But the rules of the genre (those which apply to a real journal as well as to a fictitious one: a grounding in time, a relationship to "daily life") would still be superfluous for a journal "of reading," even if they were stretched a little. All that remained, then, was to endow this reading notebook, starting over again right now, with the bastard status of simple *notes* (and doubly bastard at that, since the main text will be missing). But notes—marginal additions, remarks, annotations, brief commentary—are normally intended to form an accompaniment. As though written in another key, by and for the left hand, they are always there in addition, in the margin or at the bottom of the page. Peripheral in the same way as prefaces, they are simultaneously subordinate and free: the dark side of the main text can find refuge in them; all sorts of wandering and casting off can take place in them. It would seem, then, as absurd to write notes without having them refer to any text as it would be to draw up a preface for no book whatsoever. It could be, though, that the author did not have time to write the main text, that he misplaced it, or that he was not able to write it. Maybe he plans on writing the book later on . . . However, should he agree to publish only the notes, this would not be without realizing that he thus condemns his commentary to a kind of philosophical abortion. There is no commentary that is not philosophical, and philosophy recognizes procedural deviations only to the extent that they contain the promise of synthetic exposition. After all, one never gives up on philosophical construction without a certain twinge of regret, even and especially if the value of the (philosophical) exposition was only a matter of form or architecture, even and especially if the constructed and systematic aspect of philosophy was at the beginning a response to an aesthetic necessity, a possibility not to be ruled out. In fact, the word *ensemble* was at first used in relation to the plastic arts, and as a noun.[34]

Not to conceive, not to construct a whole, an *ensemble*, or what with respect to writing is also called a book, can undoubtedly be the result of a choice. In some cases, it would be due rather to a failure, a paralysis, a particular incapacity to sustain a single point of view, to maintain a line of thought, to get beyond the stage of a sketch. The author who is prey to such paralysis is never able to finish with anything; even when he is a simple reader, he always gets stuck in the rough draft.

We might ask, though, whether a reading that would no longer presuppose the unity of its object in order to reconstitute it, that would no longer attempt to fill in its holes or reestablish a chain

---

34. *TN.* A preposition meaning "together," but in the sense of forming a whole, as in a musical ensemble.

of continuity, that would appear to give up on the necessity of links, whether this would still be a reading. But relinquishing control over the connections does not amount to eliminating them: they are always there. The most interesting connections are sometimes lost for want of having left anything to chance.

A reading that separates, that is more discerning than comprehending, multiplies the points of view and establishes only miniature networks—but could they ever coalesce without leaving cracks? At any rate, should it be necessary to provide a thread or gist here, then we might say that from one end to the other and in every sense of the word, it will be a question only of *breaks* or *ruptures*.

One more thing, as if by way of a notice: what draws me to him is woman, the (impossible) woman in him: his fecundity, his feminine aptitude (which is how he characterizes it) to let himself be impregnated "by the Idea" that then enters (with the male) "into a commerce that is carnal, so to speak." Woman was what he could neither have nor be, nor even less could he owe his life to her. With woman it is always a question, in one way or another, of a break-up or a rupture.

*
* *

They turn, one around the other, in a strange ballet or tournament. He writes to Regine:

> *Whenever you catch a breath of that heliotrope at home, which is still fresh, please think of me, for truly my mind and my soul are turned toward this sun, and I have a deep longing for you, thou sun of all women.* (9 December 1840, *Letters*, 66)
> (This could be a citation, since he sent her lots of them.)

Just as a whim, let's stick two sunflowers in here: one from the illustrated *London News* of 1874—a little girl pulls the flower toward her while she holds the huge stalk between her hands. The flower is so tall that the girl is stretched out on tiptoe. She closes her eyes. She is wearing a white brocade dress with pale blue satin belt, and black stockings; she has blond hair almost strawberry in color, very long, with bangs. Then there is Blake's, *Ah Sun-flower:*

> Ah Sun-flower! weary of time,
> Who countest the steps of the Sun,
> Seeking after that sweet golden clime
> Where the traveller's journey is done:
>
> Where the Youth pined away with desire,
> And the pale Virgin shrouded in snow,
> Arise from their graves, and aspire
> Where my Sun-flower wishes to go.

In the letter, *he* is the heliotrope, but she is supposed to turn (herself toward him). The last page of the "Diary of the Seducer" gives another version: "She is deflowered and the time is past when a girl suffering the pain of a faithless love can be changed into a heliotrope" (*Either/Or*, 1:371). Which is what happened to Clythia after she had been abandoned by the sun god.

Right from the start, he had to compete with her. It was a matter of finding out which one of them would give a child to the other, which one would serve as monument, guardian, tomb for the other, which one of the suns would be able to sow the other.

*
* *

This may have no connection, but one of his servants (was it the one who went mad?) told how K. had a kind of phobia about the sun: unable to live and work except by night, and in order to protect his secret, he always closed his curtains. "When the sun shuts his vigilant eye, when history is past . . ." (*Journal*, 5:178).

*
* *

23 January 1841: Regine is eighteen years old and he gives her a box of paints ("if you can find some use for them") and a pair of candlesticks ("may they shine for you even as your singing has so often charmed my gloomy spirit"). In May, he will be twenty-eight, and she will give him a lettercase which she has embroidered with pearls all by herself.

*
* *

Right away, he loved her as though for him she were dead and gone. His element seems to have been memory, or rather recollection (*Erindring*): "My recollection is ever fresh . . . For every harmonious contact with an idea and with life instantly clarifies, transfigures itself into a recollection, and while it brings close to me what happened long ago, it pushes what happened most recently far back so as to place it in the Hell-Dunkel (the light-dark) of recollection" (*Letters*, 39, p. 84).

Since he was already absent, he must have seen her right away from a distance. He liked to watch her in the city, from afar, without himself being noticed. In the future perfect: the letters of days gone by are *Old Memories*, those of the present "a potential memory": "please accept these lines, which may—who knows—soon become a representative of a time gone by" (*Letters*, 31, p. 77). He had always already finished with things.

The rose R. had brought him in blossom is returned to her by him all withered up, as though it had "forgotten its splendor" and not known about its essential immortality: what is kept is the memory.

Such is the Idea: it should have the dryness of the rose and its *former* color. But love of the past, like that of the Idea, must at a certain point have turned into fear: fascinated by dead things, he is afraid of science, of things theoretical and philosophical, of Hegel. He knows that there is no science except of what is dead: "Science and theology always come afterwards." We can't really construct the grammar of a living language. To treat being Christian in a scientific manner would be to "turn it into something from the past." He likes the penumbra too much not to take the side of the instant against the pleasures of the theoretical.

*
* *

More about the rose: "Its tomb is white and pure and your seal preserves it so. Perhaps you do not see it, but that is because it is invisible. In *A Thousand and One Nights*, a girl is described who in addition to other virtues also had a mouth like the seal of Solomon. Thus, when I press my lips to this sheet of paper, I am placing not my but your seal upon it. I know very well that border disputes may easily arise here if anywhere, but I have settled them. The seal is yours, but I watch over it. But in a seal, as you know, the letters are reversed, and from this it follows that the 'yours' by which you validate the certainty of possession appears as a 'mine' from my side. Herewith have I sealed this parcel, and I would ask you to do likewise with the enclosed rose before it is put away in temple archive.

> Your S. K.
> With this is enclosed a tracing of the seal" (*Letters*, 40, p. 85).

This double gift-giving does not go without causing some disputes of its own. There is no question of their having given themselves to each other in the sense of "letting themselves loose on each other" (*s'entre-donner*, in an absolute sense, to come to blows with one another). But neither is it a matter here of giving *something* to one another in a reciprocal manner. That one would claim to give himself to the other and the other to him would immediately become laughable; but one gives nothing by giving only what is always already something else. You have to give what is truly proper, in other words, the seal (*le seing*, the seal, the signature). Not only because *le seing* is the (most) proper noun or name, but because it "validates" and "certifies" all appropriation. To give one's *seing*, one's signature, or one's seal, is not only to give one's name, it's also to give the power which is *claimed* by the signature: the power to preserve property, propriety, proximity, and presence itself. But in order for the gift of the *seing* not to be annulled in the exchange, you need a double seal, or a double *seing* the conjugation of two signs. This is also "the conjugated spirit of the ring."

The seal is even more proper when it is the body—lips or blood—signifying *itself*, becoming sign or cachet. By means of a gift, then, one body signs the other, the mouth of one is the seal of the other. Body, letter, or stone, the seal always attests at once to an alliance and a secret: a secret distinguished by design, hidden away, destroyed, revealed. Solomon's seal is a flower whose other name is *polygonatum vulgare*.

*
* *

The ring was already a repetition (or a resumption?) of (marital) union: an anticipated marriage, a double ring ceremony. He gave his back. What did that mean?

"To send a silk cord is in the East capital punishment for the receiver; to send a ring is here capital punishment for him who sends it" (*Guilty?/Not-Guilty?*, 304). According to a dialectic in which "desire never realizes its object except through its opposite," the return of the ring does not signify a rupture of the engagement but actually its fulfillment. He gives himself dead, out for dead, because he is dead. But that is what he wants from her, too. He wants her united to him in a kind of absolute past, for eternity, for History. And for this it is enough to write her name, and in signing it to make a sepulcher and a magnificent epitaph for her.

> *My Regine!*
> <u>To our own little Regine</u>
> S. K.
>
> Such a line under a word serves to direct the typesetter to space out that particular word. To space out means to pull the words apart from one another. Therefore, when I space out the words above, I intend to pull them s o v e r y f a r a p a r t *that a typesetter presumably would lose his patience for he would very likely never get to set anything else in his life.*
>
> *Your S. K.*
(*Letters*, 15, p. 61)

Perhaps he himself would have been this typesetter who was setting, his whole life through, only one name, a name extremely large and wide—like the ones big countries have on geography maps, whose letters are spaced so far out that one does not see them. (This kind of blindness is also at work in Poe's "Purloined Letter.")

I find it everywhere now, especially in the *Journal*, this desire to praise the name, to honor it, to etch it into what we might call a "literary monument."

> *She was the beloved. My life will unconditionally accent her life, my literary work is to be regarded as a monument to her honor and praise. I take her along into history. And I who sadly had only one single desire—to enchant her—there it will not be denied to me. There I will be walking by her side: like a master of ceremonies I will lead her in triumphantly and say: Please make way for her, for "our own dear little Regine."* (*Journal*, 6:203)

(One ceremony in place of another? Elsewhere he says, "Humanly speaking, the most happy of all sights is a pair of happy lovers. But Christianly! Christianly, it is a wake—if there must be a celebration, it must be as if at a funeral" (*Journal*, 3:294). He is master of funeral ceremonies.

> *Her name will belong to my authorship and be remembered as long as I am remembered.* (*Journal*, 6:55)
> *It is all right for her to become Madam and Mrs., but no longer may she be called anything more than the one who was my beloved.* (*Journal*, 6:217–18)

Not the life, only the name; maybe not even a body: writing on an empty tomb. An epitaph on a cenotaph.

*
* *

There are several ways to read and we ought to make use of them all. For example, an "erudite" reading allows itself all the time and tools of a long process of deciphering, something which only serves to make a "partisan" reading impatient. The first type should always precede the second and make it possible. Reading *him* in translation (*en français*) makes little sense. But the first kind of reading risks causing an interminable delay for the second. Let's have a look at what he says about a love letter written in a foreign language: the fiancé makes a distinction between the dictionary reading (the deciphering) and the reading properly speaking, the "reading of the heart." After all, it is better to answer the letter right away, at the risk of making a mistake, than to take the time to translate more carefully. This is a parable; but it is another fiancée and another message.

*
* *

To cite—does that really "put in motion" (*citare*)? How can we *not* cite and how can we cite without making the text into an underlying pretext for a number of cutting inlays? Orally, one does not "cite," one lacks the space needed for the inscription of those unpronounceable marks due to some Tom, Dick, or Harry and that seem to grab words on the ends of their hooks.[35]

"Near the house where she lived, there was a church; I still remember, I can hear the heavy clapping of its bells quite distinctly" (*Journal*, 5:177).

*
* *

Regine and Isaac are in the same situation. That is what she said later when she was asked about it: "He sacrificed me to God." That is the truth, perhaps, at least the truth he wanted to lend credence to. But in more than one sense: she was a gift, an offering to God, and he chose between them by breaking with her in order to become engaged to him. "My engagement to her and my breaking of it are properly speaking my relation to God; they are, in a manner of speaking, my religious engagement to God." Ostensibly a loss, is this sacrifice pure? Does it elude a calculation in view of some profit?

For Abraham did receive Isaac a second time, by virtue of the absurd, and beyond "infinite resignation." "Nevertheless, I have faith that I will get her—that is, by virtue of the absurd, by virtue of the fact that for God all things are possible." So says the knight of faith in *Fear and Trembling* (46). Did *he* believe it?

*
* *

She, the girl, could only reign—Regina—a victim, an accursed lot. If she will not accept this role, then she loses her value, as in *Repetition* (143). Constantine gets irritated about that.

---

35. *TN.* There is a play here on the names *Guillaume, guillemets*. In French, quotation marks have taken their name from the printer, Guillaume, who invented them.

*
* *

But the poet is not "the knight of faith," and what makes him different is his speech. The knight of faith keeps quiet. Johannes de Silentio speaks, even if his words only gravitate around the silence of faith. Abraham does not speak, and Job learns from God that he must keep quiet after having spoken for so long. (Zophar the Naamathite calls him a chatterbox.) Not only is Job an interminable lamenter, he also wants to write out his complaint:

> *Oh that my words were now written!*
> *Oh that they were printed in a book*
> *that they were graven with an iron*
> *pen and lead in the rock for ever!*
>
> (Job, 19:23–24)

Job's revolt is his very speech, his speech with God—addressing God personally, entering into a private relation with him, that is also what Abraham does—*"My desire is that the Almighty would answer me,"* says Job. He wants to have him answer for all the evil that has befallen him, Job, and he thus agrees to appear alone before God—

> *I would declare unto him the number of*
> *my steps; as a prince would I go near to him . . .*
> *I will say unto God . . .*
> *Thou enquirest after mine iniquity and searchest*
> *after my sin. Thou knowest that I am not wicked . . .*
>
> (Job, 32:37, 10:2–7)

God cuts him off and delivers a long speech in his turn: a curious response that has nothing to do with Job but rather with God's omnipotence. A little naively, pridefully, God details the proofs of his omnipotence and more or less says to Job: Can you match all that?

> *Canst thou bind the sweet influences of Pleiades,*
> *or loose the bands of Orion? Canst thou bring forth*

> *Mazzaroth in his season? or canst thou guide Arcturus with his sons? . . .*
> *Does the hawk fly by thy wisdom, and stretch her wings toward the south?*
> *Does the eagle mount up at thy command, and make her rest on high?*
>
> (Job, 38:31–32, 39:26–27)

And the Lord answered Job and said:

> *Shall he that contendeth with the Almighty instruct him? He that reproveth God, let him answer it.*
>
> (Job, 40:1–2)

Then Job, vanquished by this argument, submits himself. He gives up on his complaining and his questioning, and is quiet.

> *Behold I am vile; what shall I answer thee? I will lay mine hand upon my mouth. Once have I spoken; but I will not answer: yea, twice: but I will proceed no further . . . Wherefore I abhor myself, and repent in dust and ashes.* (Job, 40:4–5, 42:6)

It's at this point that Job is given twice as much as he had before.

To *keep* silent (*garder le silence,* to preserve, protect, watch over, conserve silence)—that is also what Johannes de Silentio wants to do in his writing. This is by no means paradoxical.

To preserve the silence of Job and Abraham falls to the lot of the poet. The silence of infinite resignation has in itself nothing poetic and nothing spectacular about it. Out in the world, the knight of faith displays no distinctive trait, he appears totally in-different. If he has made the movement of infinite resignation, his very indifference retrieves finite existence for him. He lives peacefully, incognito. Should he try to imagine this knight, Johannes sees him in the guise of some tax collector or other—not the least little crack through which infinity would peek—"solid all the way through," just like "a spruced up burgher walking out to Fresberg on a Sunday afternoon" (*F&T,* 39).

According to Gilles Deleuze, we ought to take "this philosophical remark as a kind of stage direction indicating how the knight of faith should be *played.*" Yes, that is, if it did not at the same time indicate that he is *unplayable* since his faith, insofar as it is faith, can no more be staged, or represented, than it can be expressed "directly." Deleuze makes Kierkegaard and Nietzsche into men of "movement," men of the theater, philosopher-directors capable of putting metaphysics in motion, of "leading it up to the act." But isn't this passage to action, even in its refusal of any mediation, fundamentally in agreement with metaphysics? "On the contrary," says Deleuze, "it is a question of producing a motion in the work capable of removing the mind from all representation; it is a question of making movement itself into a work, *with no middle terms,* of replacing intermediate representations directly with *signs,* of creating vibrations, rotations, tourneys, gravitations, dances, and leaps that would reach *the mind directly*" (*Différence et répétition,* 16–17, emphasis added). The seductive image of these tourneys tends to make us forget that it is precisely in the "directly," in the "with no middle terms," in the "immediate action," that metaphysics always recuperates itself. It is in the very idea of a form of thought that would finally be *alive.* Deleuze goes on: "We find here a thinker who *lives* the problem of masks, who *experiences* that inner void." For Deleuze, "to live" in action, or "to put" into motion, signifies leaving behind "the element of reflection," abolishing mediations. Now, if K.'s dialectic is not or does not want to be Hegel's, it is certainly not by a (metaphysical) return to immediacy that it parts company with it; on the contrary. No one placed as little stock in immediacy as K.: "I have not known immediacy; it follows that, from a strictly human point of view, I have not lived. I started directly with reflection. I did not acquire it gradually through the years; I am reflection from start to finish."

Neither mediate nor immediate, neither end nor beginning, *His* (*Sa*) dialectic is neither lived nor spoken, at the very most it can be written . . . by preserving the silence that would have begun with Socratic irony. Or by multiplying the points of view, the repetitions and rehearsals, the returns, the anamneses.

*
* *

He who writes, remembers. He holds the past and the present at a distance in order better to present them: "it pushes what happened most recently far back in order to present it in *Hell-Dunkel* of recollection." This is the "genius of recollection." Just like the lover in *Repetition*, the poet can be recognized by this melancholy that already holds him well at a distance from his object. He is always at the point of recollection.

That's how he's lived, how he hasn't lived.

But it is not enough that God feeds off the sacrificial victims he imposes silence on; this silence falls prey to a time that would *swallow* it up. The "writer" labors against this, as though toward a particular kind of repetition that is not the same as Job's but is rather its reverent and worshipful double, stand-in, or understudy. There are grounds for distinguishing Abraham and Job from Constantine or Johannes—or Kierkegaard, who is not the mute knight. It is never a question of anything but a commentary or a memory of silence. That is how it is in *Fear and Trembling:* "If an eternal oblivion, perpetually hungry, lurked for its prey and there were no power strong enough to wrench that away from it—how empty and devoid of consolation life would be! But precisely for that reason it is not so, and just as God created man and woman, so he created the hero and the poet or orator. The poet or orator can do nothing that the hero does; he can only admire, love, and delight in him. Yet he, too, is happy—no less so than that one is, for the hero is, so to speak, his better nature, with which he is enamored—yet happy that the other is not himself, that his love can be admiration. He is recollection's genius" (*F&T,* 15). This fear of everything that is hungry shows up quite often.

*
* *

The "knight's" faith does not reside in his renunciation alone; it is the expectancy that is maintained beyond renunciation, the desire that persists beyond infinite resignation—it is a fidelity to desire.

After everything has been accounted for, this can always look like a calculation, but that is only at the end. Before, what *does not count* (itself) is the moment of madness. As time passed and Sarah became older, it was *crazy* still to desire a son. There was no longer any question of just being able still to believe in it, no more than it was possible for Abraham to believe that, in the end, at the very last moment, God would save Isaac from death. And yet, without awaiting anything, Abraham waits. What is crazy is not hoping for the impossible, it is waiting without hoping. Faith only gives up on time, in other words, each and every *present*. It affirms the nontemporality of desire.

He gives up on preserving anything. But he perhaps preserves on account of that. The poet does the same thing. He calls and recalls what he does not have, preserves what he has lost. He "can do nothing," but he has what is left of every action; he can do nothing . . . except recall. But in the case of the hero of faith, as in that of the poet, loss engenders repetition. Job receives everything "twofold." For all "eternity" the poet regains what he carefully lost–laid–deposited in his work.

Repetition is a reflux. The *present* that has been accomplished or abandoned returns through this movement.

*
* *

Repetition is the new category that must be discovered. Neither mediation nor immediate, repetition harks back to ancient recollection: "for *repetition (Erindring)* is a crucial expression for what 'recollection' was to the Greeks (anamnesis)" (*Repetition*, 131). But is this "recollection," this anamnesis, so very far from what Hegel used to write as *Er-innerung*?

For example love, "genuine" love, the passion everyone knows only bursts forth in losing its object, love starts out with recollection: "right from the start he was able to recollect his love (*erindre sin Kjaerlighed*) . . . This intensified recollection is erotic love's eternal expression at the beginning (*Denne potenserede Erindre er Elskovens evige Udtryk i Begyndelsen*), it is the sign of genuine erotic love" (*Repetition*, 136, 137).

"In the first dawning of erotic love, the present and the future contend with each other to find an eternal expression, and this recollecting (*denne Erindre*) is indeed eternity's reflux (*Tilbagestroemmen*) into the present" (*Repetition*, 137).

Erindring is a *sign* (of love), through which and in which, perhaps, the object is idealized, glorified, named, represented; and in which it is also entombed.

*
* *

All that can also be found in the treatises of Meister Eckhart. Detachment, the dialectic of detachment: another name for repetition. Especially: "Of True Obedience," "Of the Utility of Abandonment to Be Practiced Inwardly and Outwardly," "Of Detachment and the Possession of God." Abandon (yourself), detach (yourself), give in, give up . . . at the moment of absolute detachment, God will infuse you and you will possess him.

A ban don(ation): "to give up one's claim on, to desist from holding back . . ."

According to Johannes, the paradox of faith through which Abraham receives the son he sacrifices contains a dialectic. Now this dialectic of renunciation is formulated by Eckhart in *The Book of Divine Comfort* with the help of the cross: he who practices total self-renunciation is capable of taking up his cross, but in taking it up, he also takes it off himself. "A person may conclude from this that it is right for him, too, to be glad, consciously, to abandon his natural will and to practice self-renunciation, and to release himself completely in whatever God gives to him to bear. That makes good sense of what our Lord said: 'If any man will come after me, let him deny himself and take up his cross'—meaning that a man shall lay down and remove all the cross stands for in the way of suffering" (Eckhart, 63). The [French] translator adds, "Eckhart plays on the double meaning of *ûfheben*, which can mean to lift or to lift up on the one hand, and to lift off or to remove on the other." There are at least two dialectics crisscrossing each other here.

*
* *

He who is detached, the dialectician who is always already in reflection, the man of recollection, of reminiscence, of return, is the ancient one, the old man.

He had always been old, right from infancy on, *too* old—in the same way that his father was "too old" for his mother—like the young man whose confidential story is reported by Constantine in *Repetition*: "What a curious dialectic! He longs for the girl, he has to do violence to himself to keep from hanging around her all day long, and yet in the very first moment he became an old man in regard to the entire relationship" (*Repetition*, 136). Unlike this young man, though, Constantine, the author, had always been old, and that is why this love story amuses him so much. Nothing can please him as much as the narration of the sudden aging that is caused in his correspondent by romantic melancholy. He knows ahead of time the outcome—the beginning—of passion: loss and aging, in other words, the poetical. He had always known it. Consequently, he won't neglect to help things along a little and to intervene in the story in order to facilitate the advent of the *Poetiske*, for which the girl will have been only a propitious occasion. He logs, attentively and impatiently, the progress of a movement he knows quite well: the loss that appeases, interiorizes, protects, idealizes . . . Not that this loss *happens to* love: it *is* love, "characteristic of the mood of eros." It is its very delight and cause. "Recollection has the great advantage that it begins with the loss; the reason it is safe and secure is that it has nothing to lose" (*Repetition*, 136). Having begun by being missing, the object of delight—at least as an object of sense certainty—will first become *present* to memory: whence passion. "Fervor is attained only with the whip of an absolute past."

The amorous young man could not stop repeating over and over again a verse from Paul Møller:

A heartfelt longing comes over me for you,
Thou sun of women.
"If the girl dies tomorrow," muses Constantine, "it will make no essential difference." (*Repetition*, 136)

*
* *

Destined to be a memory or a memoir, a memorandum or a memorial, "her existence or non-existence was virtually meaningless to him" (*Repetition*, 138).

If *she* had understood, she would have perhaps been the first to break off. She would have had to realize that her real loss lay in the abolition of that distance which the muse must always preserve if she wants to remain the muse. "For the relations of the poet with his muse are essentially different from conjugal ties, and muses, in addition to all that is proper to them as supernatural beings, would do well to keep themselves at a distance."

But perhaps she actually did understand: that is why she married Schlegel. He sometimes suspected that perhaps she, too, had a sense for a certain dialectic.

*
* *

What a nice little couple Kierkegaard would have made with Nietzsche. They were day and night, at least when it came to the sun. Such an idea cannot be simply arbitrary, or it would not be so comical.

*
* *

Maybe she even understood a little too well; she let herself be detached a little too well. To this extent, she went along with his plans and fulfilled his own request, but so perfectly that he lost control over his dialectic. He does not know any more if she was just playing a good game, if she agreed to lose in order to keep him better . . . or if she simply forgot about him and betrayed him.

The *meaning* of the sacrifice, that is what is difficult to let go of completely. The high-style sacrifice that consisted of making himself "look like a cad" in order to spare his fiancée the pain she would not have been able to bear (since women are ignorant of dialectics), this sacrifice would he have gladly retrieved, at least in part, by at last offering a "genuine explanation" for his rupture. Since she had succeeded in overcoming the separation, in accepting the detachment—as attested to by her marriage—an explanation became "possible." For example, in '49: "Now, if she herself were to demand an explanation from me . . . I prayed God that I might be appointed to the pastoral seminary—and also to be reconciled with her, something she, the married one, would have to request herself" (*Journal*, 6:209, 410). Maybe she even got married just for that reason, so that an explanation would be possible . . . So he waits for a sign on her part, though not without a certain uneasiness. What if everything repeated itself all over again? Who knows? If she were to learn that he was not the cynical character he had been playing, "she could fall in love anew . . . suppose she breaks the bonds of marriage, runs wild, throws herself on me, asks for a separation and wants me to marry her . . ." No sooner is this possibility glimpsed (and by the same person who had just written: "I nevertheless do think about the ineffable moment when I would go back to her . . ." [*Journal*, 5:175]), than the conclusion immediately presents itself, inexorably, self-identical: "she ought to be put on an even stricter regimen so that she would never see me."

All that is enough to make us want to laugh, but after all, a rupture is a *scene*, a scenario (in order to guard against the numerous temptations to oversimplify here, we should recall that the subject is not necessarily present *as such* in a phantasy; it is possible for him to be in the syntax of the sequence in question), and there is nothing in a phantasy of "rupture" that necessarily assigns the subject the role of the abandoner, any more than it would the role of the abandoned (woman). The object of "desire" can also be the rupture itself, a detachment—who knows what sort of tear or intrusion? A desire for the repeated breaking of the marriage seal (*un hymen*)?

*
* *

The husband occupies a special place. This is so obvious that for a moment I did not suspect it. With regard to him, K. has so ingeniously rationed out indifference, sympathy, even esteem; he gives the impression of having begun a relationship with him marked by such a high degree of urbanity that it seems possible to leave the whole subject alone. "Knowing that she has been married for a long time: I couldn't care less."

The barest hint of a false note: a shade too much irony, at least in translation (*en français*), when he expresses his admiration for Schlegel's social success: "so young an age and already head of a department" (*Journal*, 6:87)—a success that is likely to satisfy Regine's desire to "shine"—and thus to keep the detached ex-fiancé happy. There are also some remarks, somewhat complacent, on *his own* qualities in comparison to those of the husband by whom he obviously does not feel replaced: "Schlegel is a likeable enough fellow, that is for certain, and I truly believe she feels happy with him. But she is an instrument which he does not know how to play: she has tones I alone know how to extract from her . . ." "She can do pretty much as she pleases: I always keep a poet at her disposal capable of explaining that to her, and precisely that is the most beautiful, the most poetic . . ." Even if he sometimes exhibits a certain irritation over the idea that in the eyes of the world she looked like the victim, whereas she in fact got married quickly enough (while he remained "faithful" and silent), he never stopped thinking of himself as master of the situation: he *could have* broken off in such a way as to make "another" marriage difficult, he *could have* then disrupted such a marriage, indeed destroyed it. Furthermore, Regine's marriage to someone else was the best out for him, one that promised him a certain tranquility and, above all, one that would allow *both* of them—who knows?—to pick up where they had left off. Maybe even this marriage would change nothing at all, "if her passion is rekindled" (*Journal*, 6:198).

He therefore never stopped reappropriating this marriage for himself: she would have gotten married for his sake, in order to keep him, in conformity with his own wishes:

> . . . *this was the only way she could possibly establish a relationship with me again, for if she were unmarried, the question of a marriage could never come up again.* (*Journal*, 6:198).
>
> *It must be remembered that the situation of* my *being the one who suggested she take Schlegel must, after all, really exasperate her and make her lose patience.* (*Journal*, 6:209)
>
> . . . *I am the pillar of this marriage, I am the one who could, at any moment, be tempted to go a little easier on myself—and the marriage would then perhaps be disrupted* . . .

On the other hand, Schlegel does not seem to have regarded K. so unfavorably—at least he showed himself to be rather adroit in taking an interest in his books. In the evening, by the fire, he reads the latest works of Søren with his wife, and when they leave for the Antilles he takes care to get hold of the sermons she wants to read. However, the day that K. finally attempts a reconciliation by writing to Schlegel and attaching a letter for Regine, he refuses categorically, "in complete agreement" with his wife, to open the letter addressed to her and returns it untouched.

By following K.'s efforts closely, though, it would seem that not only was the husband not an obstacle, but that it was in fact with him that K. wanted to be reconciled, with him that he wanted a chance to explain himself.

One day when he meets her at church, as often happens, he

tilts his head "perhaps a bit more than usual," and next thing we know he is tormented by the idea that she may have taken this gesture for an invitation. He gets to the point of devising, of rehearsing, scenes of reconciliation (but always with their corresponding ruptures) that turn about a barely perceptible gesture made by her or him in church. Then he imagines what would happen if she were to take the initiative and try to start a conversation with him: "My first question would have been to ask her if she had Schlegel's permission" (*Journal*, 6:370). The observance of certain social conventions, along with the subordinate role played by married women, explains nothing. It would be easier for me to believe that without Schlegel's consent, relations with Regine *do not interest* him. This appears to be the case if, beyond the chivalrous intentions, we take such statements as this literally: "And he [Schlegel] can truthfully say that his cause is in good hands with me; because hers does not interest me except with his consent. A relationship to her with even the slightest trace of the clandestine, of the illicit: God preserve me from it, or then no one knows me" (*Journal*, 6:370).

God preserve us from illicit relations. Schlegel, of course, has the law on his side; he has the law and he makes the law (he has at his disposal the/his woman). This is enough to give him the principal place, the "interesting" one. That is enough to assign him a privileged role within K.'s desire, his phantasmatics. He has to prohibit and permit, refuse and grant. It depends on him alone.

It is necessary for "Schlegel to be happy to consent that I speak with her." It is not only necessary for him to consent, he has to be happy about it. Regine is not desirable except on this condition.

This role does not seem to have suited Schlegel: "He was furious and would in no way 'tolerate any intervention by another in the relationship between himself and his wife' " (*Journal*, 6:368). But there was no question of that; rather what was at issue, and for some time now, was the opposite: Schlegel's intervention in the relations of Regine with Søren, who had actually specified in his letter: "my condition is that no letter from me is to reach her without its having been read by you. If the exchange is to be a *verbal* one, then my condition is that you be present during every conversation" (*Letters*, 236, p. 330). Which does not exclude the possibility that he was in fact the one who, at the moment of the rupture, suggested to Regine that she marry Schlegel.

*
* *

One of the related circumstances perhaps explains why Schlegel assumes a place, such a place, at this particular moment. Evidently, it is the father's place, occupied in turn by several people, including a father-in-law, Regine's father.

For this father had just died. At the bottom of the letter to R., sent to Schlegel, K. wrote: "This move was occasioned by the impression made upon me by the death of *Etatsraad* Olsen" (*Journal*, 6:254).

Councillor Olsen is sometimes mentioned in the *Journal*, for instance, in the narration of the engagement: "Immediately I assumed a relationship with the whole family. I turned my virtuosity toward her father in particular, whom I always liked very much anyway" (*Journal*, 6:192). After the rupture, a long time afterward, it is with him that K. first tries to be reconciled: "He is the only one I safely dare become reconciled with" (*Journal*, 6:54). On the death of the Councillor, K. supposes that R. will be unable not to think of her relationship to him: perhaps she believed her father represented an obstacle to an eventual reconciliation . . . She would have been mistaken: "This certainly is a misunderstanding. The Councillor was the very one with whom I desired reconciliation and sought it . . . in my eyes the offended father was the object of most serious concern" (*Journal*, 6:190).

K.'s attempts to resume relations with this father failed, though. One day when he tried to have a word with him, having run across him in the course of a walk, the Councillor turned away, "with tears in his eyes."

Once the Councillor is dead, Schlegel therefore becomes "the object of most serious concern." It is *by him* that K. now wants to be understood. In a draft of the letter to R.: "When I became engaged to you, I was already ancient, and I have not grown any younger. Perhaps nobody understands this as well as you do. It now depends on whether you can make Schlegel understand it" (*Letters*, 238, p. 333). The strangest thing remains K.'s comment after Schlegel's categorical refusal: "If he had understood me, if he had believed in me, then I would have become practically a servant in his hands" (*Journal*, 6:257).

*
* *

That does not mean that he did not want to see Regine again, only that this desire was subject to the order of a scene in which the law had to be present as a third party, a witness, an inverted obstacle, but by its own consent.

If all that matters is this syntax, the distribution of roles is free to vary. Here it is the husband–witness who plays the law, but elsewhere it could be the character of a phantasmatic fable, or "poetical essay" (such is the title), that is told in the *Journal*—"The King who got slapped": two lovers are separated when the man falls prey to a religious crisis. He thinks that God wants him to renounce his love. Not wanting to afflict the young woman with such a crisis, he leaves her by pretending to act like a "cad."

Several years later, the time comes for clearing things up, and all the while the young woman has remained true to her love. She is "beside herself with happiness," while the young man feels "as mighty as a God." At the climactic moment, he asks his beloved to make a wish, but she desires nothing further. Then he gets his idea: "I'll go give the king a slap!" The girl is stupefied: "How can such a thing occur to you?" But the fiancé, who is acquainted with the king and is actually "highly regarded" by him, is as good as his word. The king does not much appreciate this gesture and immediately declares his assailant "crazy." The young man is then able to tell his story and explains that he "could find no better expression for his joy than to give the king a slap in honor of his beloved." Immediately appeased by this explanation, the king proclaims: "You have provided me with one of the most sublime spiritual impressions I have ever known." What would be more natural, in fact, than to want to give one's king a slap when one feels as mighty as a God? In order to obtain complete satisfaction, the young man makes one final request—he asks the king to act as witness to the couple's happiness—which is promptly granted.

The moral of this little story is that "the might of the infinite

... breaks all boundaries and all laws."[36] It should be added: not without being reconciled simultaneously with them or with their representatives. Which laws? Whose laws? Of all kings? Of all Gods? Of all fathers? Of Michael Pedersen Kierkegaard? Of the father-in-law, Councillor Olsen? Of the husband, Schlegel? Of Bishop Mynster and a few others? ...

*
* *

He met the king of Denmark, Christian VIII, on several occasions. These were the closing moments of absolute monarchy. K. seems to have wanted, as always, to stay off on the side and keep his distance, but he enjoys relating his conversations with the king he likes so much: "a splendidly gifted man." The king assures K. of his esteem and compliments him on his intelligence. The answer: I owe it all to my father, who brought me up well. On his third visit to Sorgenfri Castle, K. brings a copy of *The Works of Love* with him. The king seems "moved." But K. is especially attracted by the feminine character of Christian VIII: "I have never seen an elderly man so animated, so stimulated, almost like a woman." "Yes, it is definitely the case ... talking with him was really like talking with a woman" (*Journal*, 6:91–94).

*
* *

Repetition—
A possible source:
"When one is a child and has no toys, one is well provided for, because then the imagination takes over. I still remember with amazement my childhood top, the only toy I had—what acquaintance was as interesting as this one?" (*Journal*, 1:120)

---

36. *TN*. This parable constitutes one of the unfortunate omissions in the present English translation of Kierkegaard's journals and papers. It can be found in the fourth volume of the German edition of the *Tagebücher* (4:33–36) and in the Danish edition of the *Papirer* (X^2 A, 168).

*
* *

How does the thunderstorm happen, in other words, repetition, the event, which is also to say, a tear, a rupture? Something, perhaps, blows or blows up, pops, pierces, opens and shows up. There it was, and now here it is. It happens.

Repetition: what does it produce, give (back), duplicate, yield, deliver, conceive, return, engender?

A child at the same time as his father and mother.

"Oneself," as Constantine's correspondent says. His last letter refers to repetition as being at the same time auto-engenderment, auto-conception, and loss of self.

> *My Silent Confidant:*
> *She is married . . . I am myself again. Here I have repetition, I understand everything, and life seems more beautiful to me than ever. Let life reward her as it will, let it give her what she loved the most; it also gave me what I love the most—myself . . .*
>
> *Isn't that a repetition, then? Did I not get everything double? Did I not get myself again and precisely in such a way that I might have a double sense of its meaning? Compared with such a repetition, what is a repetition of worldly possessions, which is indifferent toward the qualifications of the spirit? Only his children did Job not receive double again, for a human life cannot be redoubled in that way* (fordoble). *Here only repetition of the spirit* (Aandes Gjentagelse) *is possible, even though it is never so perfect in time as in eternity . . .*
>
> *I am myself again; the machinery has been set in motion. The inveiglements in which I was entrapped* (Sonderhugne ere de Besnaerelser) *have been rent asunder; the magic formula that hexed me so that I could not come back to myself has been broken. There is no longer anyone who raises his hand against me. My emancipation is assured; I am born to myself, for so long as Ilithyia folds her hands, the one who is in labor cannot give birth.* (Repetition, 220–21)

Repetition is distinguished from reproduction—to which, however, it bears a metaphorical resemblance—in that it does not add to the number of the living. It is an ideal impregnation: of the Idea, by the Idea—"I belong to the Idea (*Ideen tilhorer jeg*)."

The Idea's delivery. This is actually how *Repetition* already began, with the feminine aptitude for an impregnation by the Idea. But the fact that this aptitude is characterized as "feminine" obviously does not mean that woman is capable of it. "The inveiglements have been rent asunder," says the young man. What can it actually mean to tear apart (symbolically) these inveiglements?

"But what can it actually mean to tear this symbolical veil . . . If this birth–veil was torn, then he saw the world and was re-born . . . The necessary condition of his rebirth was that he should have an enema administered to him by a man . . . Here, therefore, the phantasy of rebirth was simply a mutilated and censored version of the homosexual wish–phantasy . . . The tearing of the veil was analogous to the opening of his eyes and to the opening of the window . . . The wish to be born of his father . . . the wish to present him with a child—and all this at the price of his own masculinity . . . in them homosexuality has found its furthest and most intimate expressions . . ."

This fragment from Freud's *Wolf-Man* (*An Infantile Neurosis*, 17:100–101) can be found in a note to Derrida's "The Double Session" (*Dissemination*, 269), a session that, beyond Freudian analysis, draws the reading here toward whatever links *Repetition* to dissemination and carries it out of the reach of the dialectical reappropriation that is, nonetheless, also at work in it. The birth to himself of the young man in the thunderstorm appears as a *resumption* since the word *Gjentagelsen* can also have that meaning (the French translator, Tisseau, even sees in it an intimation of the "resumption" of relations with Regine). A thematic reading would of course show that reappropriation, reflexivity, idealization can also be found in *Repetition*. But it is not that simple: the young man is "liberated" (and first of all from a bond: "No one coaxes out of my being an explanation that not even I myself can give to another" [*Repetition*, 221]—what is this an explanation of, if not of his [first] birth?). However, this is not in order finally to arrive at the kind of masterful self-knowledge that is required by the other. On the contrary, it is in order to abandon oneself all the more, to let oneself get carried away to the *abyss*, the *infinite*, the *stars*, through the "poetic" activity of writing. It is not his identity which he meets up with again but a kind of brilliant explosion, a dispersal with neither return nor revenue: "three cheers for the dance in the vortex of the infinite, three cheers for the cresting waves that hide me in the abyss, three cheers for the cresting waves that fling me above the stars!" (*Repetition*, 222) Through writing, he finds his deliverance and his loss.

The abyss here is not only a lyrical theme for the poet: it is above all the abyss of repetition itself, of the text that bears this title several times over. For if repetition does not allow for resumption, this is because the book is already divided and split. Through the repetition of the title, *Repetition,* on the inside of the book, it opens at least twice, thus placing *Repetition en abyme.*[37] The repetition of the same title at the heart of the text can indicate neither a simple starting over again nor another section: it shows that *Repetition* is not a *single* book. I can't help being struck by the quiet assurance of the [French] translators who note: "The resumption of the title indicates that repetition is to be henceforth understood in its religious sense." Likewise, it is not possible to ignore the *mise en abyme* of the author: the words of the young man are merely staged, mouthed by a (pseudonymous) author who effaces himself before the poet he has produced (perhaps out of himself), "just like the midwife in relation to the child she has delivered" (230). There is no taking hold of *Repetition.*[38] Let's say about it what "The Double Session" says about dissemination:

---

37. *TN. Mise en abyme* was first used in its current sense by André Gide. Based on an analogy with the procedures of heraldry and Flemish painting, it is a kind of story within a story that tells what the text itself is actually about. While it is helpful here to point to the familiar example of the Quaker Oats box that shows someone holding a Quaker Oats box that shows someone holding a Quaker Oats box, etc., we should try to remember that this is merely a pictorial analogy for a strictly linguistic structure. A more technically precise definition of the *mise en abyme* would be a text that ends up becoming an example of its own statement. Thus, in the present case, the text that is about repetition is itself a form of the repetition it tries to describe. In such an instance it becomes impossible to determine where *Repetition* as statement and *Repetition* as example begin and end, open and close.

38. *TN.* Translation, like repetition, precludes our taking hold of what is being repeated or translated in this passage. The words Agacinski uses here for "resumption" (*la reprise*), "mouthed" (*repris par*), and "taking hold" (*on n'a pas de prise*), *repeat* each other in a way that English cannot hope to reproduce in a comprehensible manner.

"*repetition* affirms the always already divided generation of meaning" (268).

Were we to destroy the scenarios one by one, there would be no more repetition, no more book.

*
* *

Just like the mime, like *Mimique*,[39] repetition, also understood as a text, turns the event into an abyss without adding anything to it. And if nothing is repeated or represented by it, this is not because it would present "it-self."

It is like the theater where, in the middle of his "story," Constantine goes looking for repetition.

Haven't we all wanted at one time or another to be actors? Mistakenly, perhaps, lured by a false image of the double, tempted by a toned-down form of repetition . . . Every "young man," admits Constantine, would like to enjoy all the possibilities he feels within himself by becoming all those he is capable of becoming. "There is probably no young person with any imagination who has not at some time been enthralled by the magic of the theater and wished to be swept along into that artificial actuality in order like a double to see and hear himself and to split himself up into every possible variation of himself, and nevertheless in such a way that every variation is still himself" (*Repetition*, 154). A "taste for the theater" is a passion for the possible: an idle dream no doubt, but perhaps momentarily necessary on account of its very futility, since "it is just as salutary for the adult to have something in his past life that he can laugh about as something past that draws his tears" (*Repetition*, 155). We will finally laugh, then, about that desired illusion, or illusioned desire, a desire for shadows, reflections, doubles, masks, fleeting scenes where "the frothing foam of words . . . sound without resonance" (*Repetition*, 156). But repetition is not a numerical multiplication; out of one it does not make several.

The actor is not all the roles, he is merely an actor, and that is his only identity.

---

39. *TN*. A short text by Mallarmé, one of the disseminating pivots in "The Double Session."

Just as a theatrical event does not take place several times; nothing gets repeated in it. Constantine learns this when he returns to the Königstädter in Berlin. His memory of this theater was as sharp as if he had just come out of it, and he was hoping once more to find a certain *"Stemning"* (mood, atmosphere, disposition). But when he attends a new performance, nothing is repeated: he can find neither the same box nor the same girl out in the audience nor the same laughter. "Beckmann could not make me laugh." Able to stand it no longer, he leaves the theater after half an hour: "There is no repetition at all. This made a deep impression on me" (*Repetition*, 169). Of all he had known in Berlin, nothing was reproduced. His apartment had changed, and even the coffee is no longer to his liking.

"I perceived that there was no repetition" (*Repetition*, 171).

The impossibility of repetition reveals itself in the very place where it had seemed to be the rule: at the theater.[40]

*
* *

"False" repetition, numerical repetition, also tempted Kierkegaard. At least once he dreamed of a Don Juan–like repetition. The *Journal* and his correspondence with Emil Boesen bear this out. There is a Viennese singer at the theater in Berlin who resembles a "certain young girl" and who, of all things, plays the part of Elvira. This striking coincidence could not fail to attract K.'s attention, causing him to imagine—come what may—a little repeat affair, of no consequence this time, a kind of game, since in the end "it does not matter much about a singer . . ." Elvira! When one has just abandoned a girl on religious grounds and is awaiting true repetition, the spiritual kind, wouldn't it be tempting to replay the Don Juan scene with an actress, and in this way to distract oneself just a little from the loftiest speculations and the gravest conflicts?

"I have no time to get married," he writes to Emil B. on the 14th of December, 1841, on a card enclosed in his letter. "But here in Berlin there is a singer from Vienna, a *Demoiselle* Schulze. She

---

40. *TN.* The word *répétition* is not only the equivalent of the English "repetition" but also names the theatrical practice of "rehearsal."

plays the part of Elvira and bears a striking resemblance to a certain young girl, so deceptive that I was extraordinarily affected to see her in the very part of Elvira. When my wild mood sweeps over me, I am almost tempted to approach her and that not exactly with the 'most honorable intentions.' Usually, it does not matter much about a singer, and she does look like her. It might be a small diversion when I am tired of speculation or sick of thinking about this or that. She lives nearby. Well, probably nothing will come of this. You know so well how I talk that you know what such stuff means, and it means no more now that I am writing about it. But meanwhile I do not want you to mention to anybody that there is such a singer in Berlin, or that she is playing Elvira, or etc." (*Letters*, 54, p. 105)

The *Journal* says only this: "Here in Berlin, a Demoiselle Hedwig Schulze, a singer from Vienna, performs the part of Elvira. She is very beautiful, decisive in bearing: in height, in the way she walks and dresses (black silk dress, bare neck, white gloves). She strikingly resembles a young lady I knew. It is a strange coincidence. I must make proper use of a little power against myself in order to dislodge this impression" (*Journal*, 5:183). But only a few lines above, in one of those little fictions that are common in the *Journal*, the following situation was described: "A seducer who already has the love of several girls on his conscience becomes enamored of a girl whom he loves to the extent that he does not have the heart to seduce her, but neither can he really decide to take up with her. He happens to see someone with a striking resemblance to her; he seduces her in order that in this pleasure he can enjoy the other" (*Journal*, 5:182).

The first girl, then, won't have been the first—since he obtains her only by way of the second. It is the second who will give him pleasure, provided she passes for the first.

Regine herself will not have been able to represent *the first* except as lost, abandoned, absent—right from the start. She will not have played, and thus repeated (in the theatrical sense [of rehearsed]), anything but a first *role*, that of Elvira, just like Demoiselle Schulze. While Søren was playing Don Juan.

If the first can be obtained only by means of the second and thereby loses its primacy, this is because repetition will have re-produced nothing, because the first will have been such only as already doubled, replaceable, a replacement. There is no Elvira except in a catalogue—but once is enough to start the catalogue. It really is a repetition, only not the one we were expecting.

*   *
   *

Repetition is not constituted from one presence to another, from one woman to another, but between the two. Nothing repeats (itself): it falls in with itself, it resonates. Starting with two—if only in anticipation. One *does not return from or get over* repetition, it will not ever have had any foundation. In Deleuze's clever formula: everything founders (*tout s'effonde*). The series has nothing to hide, it has no underside, even if we like to think so. Odette does not hide Swann's mother, Demoiselle Schulze does not double or duplicate Regine, Adrienne is not behind Aurélie—no matter what Nerval thinks.

For Nerval *believes* in the origin and the model, the only safeguard against the vertigo of "substitution"—consequently, he does not resist the desire to have the actress Aurélie come (back) to where the childhood scene took place in which he first loved Adrienne . . . *"and if they were one and the same!"* "I explained everything to her. I told her about the source of this romance, glimpsed at night, dreamed about later on, realized in her." Aurélie *thinks* she understands and yields to the evidence of an analytical and reductive interpretation of this type: so that's how it was, it was another woman, the first, the only one! Whence her disenchantment: "You don't really love me! . . . A theater scene is all you're after . . . Go on, I don't believe you any more!" The man who after all did love Aurélie does not even consider challenging her view of things. Rather, he becomes disoriented at this point, he cannot understand anything any more: "So that wasn't love? Then where is it?"

However, what the "hero" does not know, what the story does not tell us—that nothing precedes repetition, that there was no *first* love—the text of Nerval *exhibits* by organizing the scenes in a way that defies chronological sequence. Thus, it is not Adrienne who appears first: all that does *not* begin with childhood but rather with the theater and repetition: "I was on my way out of a theater where every night . . ." It starts with an image and the love of an image: the actress who is contemplated from afar, but just the actress and not the "real" woman who is Aurélie and who does not interest the author—"I was afraid of disturbing the magic mirror that sent her image back to me." Only later does the memory of Adrienne return, the girl who suddenly appeared one night from out of the middle of a roundelay. Adrienne, who sang an ancient romance "full of melancholy," and for whom Gérard had plaited a crown of laurel. But we know very well that this scene of seduction, from which the author lifts the "germ" of his love for Aurélie, was never experienced in the present; we do not even know if it was real or "half-imagined." We realize that this girl, who begins to stand for the model of the beloved woman, seduces only through her lack of reality. She seems like a "mirage," a phantom slipping across verdant meadows . . . Already she is no longer Adrienne here and now. She never was her, she was an image of the past, mythical, eternal, and lost in advance: "She was like Dante's Beatrice, who smiles at the poet as she wanders along the edge of celestial dwellings."

Adrienne was playing. It is not by accident that the actress happens into the series of loved, ideal, lost women. But that does not make Adrienne or Regine any the less virtual, ideal, absent, any the less disguised. Nor even Sylvie, the little country girl, the "first," the one who was very real, the prettiest girl in Loisy—"she really exists . . ."—but who is never loved so much as when she puts on the great dress of billowing taffetas that belonged to her aunt, as when she adorns herself with old ribbons, with lace, with pale rose silk stockings, and when disguised in this way she seems like "a legendary fairy eternally young . . ." or Greuze's "Village Fiancée."

*
* *

It is not by accident that the theater can be found at the very heart of *Repetition*. Through his apology for farce, Constantine criticizes a certain conception of theatrical *mimesis*—the lyricism of farce is no longer dependent on a classical notion of mimesis organized according to a specific model and productive of knowledge. Taste, *good taste,* that is, still requires the fictions and simulacra of a highly *finished* art that by necessity has its conventions. But this "well-executed" art, this classical art capable of satisfying the spectator who is hungry for culture, manifests "a certain limited earnestness" from which the serious man can expect nothing. Serious art is able to reach the frivolous spectator. The "serious individual" needs much stranger emotions; he is weary of comedy, of tragedy, of "well-executed" painting, of expert choreography . . . nothing less than farce will satisfy him, since in farce no model, no *bon ton* is possible any more—"Seeing a farce can produce the most unpredictable mood, and therefore a person can never be sure whether he has conducted himself in the theater as a worthy member of society who has laughed and cried at the appropriate places" (*Repetition*, 160).

If the still aesthetic young man was prey to the illusions of a certain repetition, a certain theater, then the individual whose "soul has at last integrated itself," the individual who can no longer believe in either the simple or in doubles, the "earnest" individual will no longer be able to enjoy anything but a mad art, at least as mad as that childhood in which "we had such enormous categories that they now almost make us dizzy" (*Repetition*, 158). Since here too it is a question of stages, we might say that beyond a certain *mimesis*, it is only possible to enjoy by regressing. Constantine has arrived at this point, at the stage where all mimicries "fail to please him," where nothing but "breaking into the strangest leaps" can satisfy him. He is at the stage of farce, then. And to such a degree that he doesn't look askance at joining in it himself sometimes: "and yet he had moments when he could return to his room and, indulging himself, find indescribably humorous relief in standing on one leg in a picturesque pose or, giving not a damn for the world, settling everything with an *entrechat*" (*Repetition*, 158). Whence the attraction of a return to the near side of all models and all mimicry and the desire to "return to the elemental state"—a risky diversion which we generally permit ourselves only in private and that causes fear in the cultivated public.

If, in order to divert yourself, you need to *overstep the limits,* then the aesthetic—the beautiful—will no longer be enough for you; you'll need the sublime, you'll turn to farce.

*
* *

The spectator of farce has to be willing to give up his faculty of judgment. He cannot know any more *if he has laughed at the appropriate places.* The spectacle here brings about a *lyrical explosion* that is inaccessible to "aesthetic appreciation." Deprived of models, farce brings to the stage both abstract characters, who are like the paper cut-outs made by children, as well as totally ordinary characters. As a result, farce does not require being *played* by *good* actors possessed of talent or experience. It requires "generative geniuses" (or else anybody whatsoever . . .): "They must be children of caprice, intoxicated with laughter, dancers of whimsy who, even though they are at other times like other people—yes, the very moment before—the instant they hear the stage manager's bell they are transformed and, like a thoroughbred Arabian horse, they begin to snort and puff, while their distended nostrils betoken the chaffing of spirit because they want to be off, want to cavort wildly. They are not so much reflective artists who have studied laughter as they are lyricists who themselves plunged into the abyss of laughter and now let its volcanic power hurl them out on the stage" (*Repetition*, 161).

Dropped into this abyss of drunkenness, the faculty of judgment becomes aware of its impotence. Isn't the laughter at issue here a function of the sublime as it was defined by Kant? "The *quality* of the feeling of the sublime is that it is a feeling of pain in reference to the faculty by which we judge aesthetically of an object . . . This is possible through the fact that the very incapacity in question discovers the consciousness of an unlimited faculty of the same subject, and that the mind can only judge of the latter aesthetically by means of the former." "The transcendent . . . is for the imagination like an abyss in which it fears to lose itself" (*Critique of Judgement*, 98, 97/ *Kritik*, 10:183, 181). But Kant did not think that laughter could ever become a form of expression for the sublime. That's because he was thinking only of the kind of laughter caused by jokes, amusing stories. The "amusing" stories that Kant takes the trouble to tell in his *Critique of Judgement* and that, according to him, should "send listeners into gales of laughter" leave the reader somewhat perplexed. In any case, in the third *Critique*, laughter is accorded only a *Remark* in which it is described as a "relaxation following a momentary deception of the understanding." No doubt laughter has "an advantageous effect on our bodily well-being, i.e., our health," but the art of laughter, the comical, is not one of the fine arts "because the object of the latter must always show proper worth in itself, and hence requires seriousness in one presentation" (*Critique of Judgement*, 181/ *Kritik*, 10:277).

True, laughter is not serious. Inasmuch as it lies outside the provinces of dignity and morality, it could belong to what is agreeable, but never to the beautiful. And yet, for Constantine, farce is an art and calls for the actor's genius: pure genius, such as it is conceived by Kant, which does not imitate anything but brings forth by letting nature speak through it. The genius of farce spills out in abandon, surprising itself all by itself by letting nature gush out, by not holding itself back. It is "beside itself," it is not great in commensurability, but only in disproportion: it is sublime. Why shouldn't the sublime be able to make us laugh? Things like excess, spills, audacious genius, really do make us laugh—the spasm of laughter liberates the tension created by the disproportion of the spectacle. When Kant speaks of the release that follows the interruption of vital forces and that constitutes the indirect pleasure linked to the feeling of the sublime, why does he restrict this emotion to an expression of respect and admiration for that which has "violated" the imagination? And why couldn't this "release" be *laughter?* For Kant, it is not reason, it is the understanding that laughs, and the understanding does not release itself, it only "relaxes" as a result of a deception at the outcome of a story, while in parallel fashion, a "relaxation of the body" is produced.

If the "negative pleasure" procured in admiration when the imagination is surpassed is able to constitute a kind of *economy,* a kind of reappropriation of the incommensurable, then why couldn't laughter be another form of defense, of reappropriation? The feeling of the sublime would thus have a choice between two expressions, two defenses, two releases: the pleasure linked to the feeling of respect caused in me by the admirable idea of the absolutely great—or the pleasure of laughter. Two ways of getting around the abyss into which the imagination, for just a moment, was afraid of falling.

By reserving the word *sublime* for an earnest kind of respect, Kant remains faithful to the most common usage of the word, which excludes laughter from greatness and beauty, which excludes it from art. By making genius, incommensurability, and the abyss into sources of laughter, Constantine reveals the common source of the comical and the sublime, their far-reaching complicity. It is well known that the sublime passes over quite easily into the ridiculous, that the most comical thing is one that *could have been* sublime. Over a trifle, the sublime will turn burlesque. War, says Kant, can be sublime; the courage of the warrior, of the hero, is indeed something that can arouse in us the feeling of the sublime. But who decides whether Don Quixote is admirable or laughable?

More to the point, can't he be admirable *and* laughable at one and the same time? Or to put it another way, if the ridiculous kills, or risks killing, the comic, then isn't the man who assumes the risk of the comic always sublime at the same time? Isn't the genius of farce admirable by daring to provoke laughter through disproportion?

"Ridiculous, hmmm? You find me ridiculous? And who says that I'm not sublime?" asks *the feisty character* in Jean Vauthier's play of the same name.

*
* *

The figure of the buffoon, then, the comic genius, meets up in the sublime with the figure of the religious person, the martyr, the fool, the criminal. The buffoon not only risks being ridiculous or foolish: he can risk his very life. That is how it is with Beckmann, the famous actor of farce described with admiration by Constantine: "He has sung his couplet, and now the dance begins. What B. ventures here is neck-breaking . . . He is now completely beside himself" (*Repetition*, 164).

To expose oneself deliberately to ridicule, to agree to cause laughter, such is the form of martyrdom Kierkegaard desires, which he has chosen for himself, in place of death: "A martyrdom of laughter is actually what I have endured . . . For I am the martyr of laughter and it is to this end that my life has been given. In this I find my whole reason for being. Indeed, it is almost as though I am only now beginning to understand myself, whereas I would have difficulty imagining myself being put to death, and even more difficulty seeing myself as a success in this world. No, it is as a martyr of laughter that I recognize my destiny. And for this very reason I am the wittiest one of all, I possess a *vis comica* to a rare degree."

*
* *

In the theater of farce there are no actors: the actors themselves are playing, re-presenting, making believe, rehearsing. And it isn't very funny.

The comic resides in a certain effect of inadequation between the "Idea" and its representation—this is why it requires genius, or *any old person at all*. The genius is comic by being overly great, inordinate, incommensurate. Any old person at all is comic by always being too small, too ordinary: to put an ordinary concrete individual on the stage is immediately to present him as in some way having pretensions to the ideal, to make him exemplary—a pretension that is derisory here. Some physical abnormality, some disability in a minor character would in no way detract from the comic effect; on the contrary, it would enhance it. But whatever the nature of the disproportion, excess, or deficiency, nothing would be more disappointing, nothing sorrier for the imagination, than a *good* actor who can never do more than approach the Idea.

The stage, the fictional world of the stage, opens up a space where ideality is put into question.

But what does "having pretensions to ideality" signify here? Always the same question, and always the same answers: either the thing in itself, or a copy of it, its representation in thought. The requirement of ideality would thus be a requirement of imitation, of re-presentation. But what if, as in Mallarmé's *Mimique*, the mime doesn't imitate? "The mime imitates nothing. And to begin with, he doesn't imitate. There is nothing prior to the writing of his gestures. Nothing is prescribed for him. No present has preceded or supervised the tracing of his writing. His movements form a figure that no speech anticipates or accompanies," says *The Double Session*, 194–95. The same thing ought to be said about Constantine's farce: imitation is not at issue here, as is vouched for by the absence of calculated effects and techniques on the part of the "actors" who "abandon themselves to their whimsy," rushing headlong into an abyss at one moment, only to snatch themselves back at the next, so that they even *surprise themselves*. As is also vouched for by the absence of scenario and program: Beckmann does not need to rely on a *scenario.* This means both that he "improvises," in that he neither follows closely nor illustrates a text, and that he does not even need a *setting*. Constantine might possibly have been thinking of the connotations *scenario* has in Italian [stage, scenery, set, backdrop], since further on he writes: "He does not need the support of interaction, of scenery and staging; precisely because . . . he himself carries everything along . . . he himself is painting his own scenery . . ." He paints (himself) or writes (himself) all alone; just like the Mime, "he inaugurates; he breaks into a white page . . ." (*The Double Session*, 195).

"What Baggesen says of Sara Nickels, that she comes rushing on stage with a rustic scene in tow, is true of B. in the positive sense, except that he comes walking . . . He is not only able to walk, but he is also able to *come walking*. To come walking is something very distinctive, and by means of genius he also improvises the whole scenic setting" (*Repetition*, 163). Imitation would imply a technique, a goal, a model—while Beckmann, like Münchausen, has to "take himself by the scruff of the neck and cavort in crazy capers." There is nothing of the plan about him, he paints just as Constantine writes: "without its costing [him] any more effort than it takes me to scribble this down on paper." That's what's called improvising.

Still, there remains the objection foreseen by Derrida in *The Double Session:* "Since the Mime . . . opens up in its origin the very thing he is tracing out, presenting, or producing, he must be the very movement of truth" (205)—a kind of unveiling, showing, or *aletheia*. Someone could say that "the mime produces, that is to say makes appear *in praesentia*, manifests the very meaning of what he is presently writing . . . One would thus come up with one of the most typical and tempting metaphysical reappropriations of writing . . ." (206). Someone *could say* it about Mallarmé's text *if* all mimicry had disappeared in "the spiritual production of the truth." But *"there is* mimicry," there is allusion—"but allusion to nothing." The same objection could be raised with respect to Constantine's text since the improvisation of the Königstädter theater actors evokes a kind of simple presentation or production. But here, too, *there is fiction*, everything takes place "in the fictional world of the stage," there is play, art, there is simulation. There is, therefore, neither reproduction of a past present, nor production of a present. Such perhaps is the *farce* playing at the theater, a farce made out of the metaphysics that is itself playing or being played [for a fool] there.

*
* *

We could pursue this parallel reading (*Mimique/Repetition/The Double Session*) beyond what seems like a similar subversion of *mimesis*. At any rate, the space of the stage, of the scene, is the space of writing—the clown plays (performs) "without it costing [him] any more effort than it takes me to scribble this down on paper." It is as if it were the same event, as if one and the same scene were taking place. Everything in this "event," according to *The Double Session*, "describes the very structure of the text," and this event is a "hymen, crime, suicide, spasm (of laughter or pleasure) . . ." (208). The spasm, the antre, the abyss, the tear without tear: everything is repeated in the theater scene of *Repetition*. The event, the laughter, goes (on) between the stage and the seats here in a strange atmosphere which Constantine calls "*unheimlich*": "the theater is empty. The orchestra plays an overture, the music resounds in the hall a bit *unheimlich* simply because the place is so empty" (165). This emptiness, this disquieting blankness of the theater, is mentioned several times. Then comes the antre: "Before me the vast space of the theater changed into the belly of the whale in which Jonas sat . . ." (166). The scene which is then played out in this *belly*, the laughter, is a kind of reciprocal stimulation, at a distance, of the audience and the actor who are separated and yet not separated from each other by the curtain. The music stops: "The orchestra has finished, the curtain rises slowly . . ." In the gallery there is already a presentiment that Beckmann is in the wings, another kind of music starts up: "the noise in the gallery was like the motion of the monster's viscera. From the moment the gallery has begun to perform its music, no accompaniment is necessary, for B. stimulates it and it stimulates B." (166).

If *Repetition* operates a *mise en abyme* on itself and on the concept of the book (a *mise en abyme* of the title, repeated in the center, as well as of the theme), then the farce at the heart of *Repetition* does not occur as a digression or hole in the text. It is a scene within a scene, a farce within a farce, a game within a game, an abyss within an abyss, a fiction within a fiction, etc. There has not been the slightest repetition—in the classical sense—it was all a farce. There is nothing but repetition.

*
* *

From writing to woman, from woman to repetition, to the theater and back again to writing, there are several courses to follow in every direction, and each intersects with the others.

Woman seems to have been his first reason for writing. P. E. Lund, a friend of K.'s, had published an article entitled "Defense of the Superior Origin of Woman" on 4 December 1834. On 17 December K. publishes a "New Apology for the Superior Nature of Woman." The title is obviously ironic. Unless—and this would amount to the same thing—it is one of those discourses that glorify woman's Christian qualities, like the one in *Sickness unto Death:* "the feminine nature is devotedness, abandon, and it is unfeminine if it is not that" (49–50). True woman, the only one who is any good, is the one who is herself only by *not* being herself, her own self. She has to be lost, offered up: in this way she realizes her happiness. "She loses herself in her abandon (devotion), and only then is she happy, only then is she herself; a woman who is happy without devotion, that is, without giving herself, no matter to what she gives it, is altogether unfeminine" (50). Her suffering, her particular despair, is not to realize her loss, it is to be deprived of that to which she wants to abandon herself. If a man abandons himself, it is never *properly speaking* (this term does not apply to him), if he happens to abandon himself, "his self remains behind as a sober awareness of devotion . . ."

When a woman realizes the full extent of her nature, of her abandon, she becomes a model of Christian living—this is Mary Magdalene. And yet, she remains essentially *less* religious than man since "in most cases the woman actually relates to God only through the man." Woman is ultimately less religious than man in her abandon: this is perhaps because, abandoned *by nature*, she always gives up less than him . . . It is as though man were capable of being *more* of a woman, a *better* woman than woman: in other words, religious.

*
* *

This is because it is not before God that woman submits herself, that she must submit herself, but rather before man. Man is to woman what God is to man. Silence, the mark of submission and obedience—that silence God imposes on Job—silence will be woman's lot, and it is in this way that she will be exemplary. "Let your women keep silence in the churches: for it is not permitted unto them to speak; but *they are commanded* to be under obedience, as also sayeth the law." And then this: "And if they will learn anything, let them ask their husbands at home; for it is a shame for women to speak in the church" (1 *Corinthians* 14: 34–35). The law of this silence would thus have been written, in black and white, for all time. But this is a silence before man, it is only a figure of silence, a human image for the religious position. But then, if woman, "in most cases," relates to God only through man, would she ever be directly involved with the religious?

*
* *

There is a woman in K.'s texts, just one, who incarnates at once the essence of femininity and the absolute submission of Christianity, and this is "The Sinner Woman"—perhaps the most beautiful of the *Edifying Discourses*. She provides a lesson for Simon and the others: she weeps at the feet of Christ, in silence. "A dumb personage from one end to the other of this scene." "What is it, then, that this woman from whom we are supposed to learn—did? The answer is: Nothing, she did nothing at all; she practiced the high, rare, exceedingly difficult, genuine womanly art of doing nothing at all" (268). "No doubt man has many more thoughts than woman . . . and no doubt man is stronger than weak woman" (262). This is not ironic: *of course,* man's superiority is not in question here, but woman, this woman, possesses the rarest, the most difficult, virtue—perhaps difficult for man— weakness; she is weakness itself. But from the religious point of view the affirmation of weakness signifies its opposite: "a prodigious strength."

". . . but then again woman has one—one what? Why, just 'one,' the fact that *one* is woman's element. One wish, not many wishes—no, only one wish, but that with the whole soul put into it; one thought, not many thoughts—no, only one thought, but that a prodigious strength by the power of passion, one sorrow, not many sorrows—no, one sorrow, but so deep in the heart that one sorrow is certainly infinitely more than the many . . ." (262).

Such is the case of Mary Magdalene. If such is woman, then it would seem that she is more naturally religious than man; but precisely because she is so more *naturally*, she is always *less* so than him. True Christianity requires virility—K. will always put a great deal of stress on this. "Naturally" passive, weak, mute, woman cannot know true religious castration. Which is why woman can be a *model* of religiousness without being truly religious, without ever being so as much as man, who is not religious naturally.

All things considered, it is only a matter of the image, of the idea of woman. "In most cases"—notably in the majority of cases in K.'s texts—woman is woman insofar as she signifies the opposite of this submission: she is the terrifying, voracious she-lion, egotistic, loving only herself through her progeny.

Mary Magdalene alone is complete frailty, complete submission; she is the "total impotence" required for forgiveness. She weeps, she is silent. She has understood or believed that the forgiveness of Christ, as God or man, is obtained only by not seeking to obtain it. A doctrine of grace.

Grace is what she has in fact: she is beautiful.

(I think I may have seen her, painted by Füssli. She is sitting with her legs crossed, her head resting on her bosom, her hair falling to her feet and hiding her whole face. Her arms are hanging down, too, folded elegantly over her feet, while her spreading fingers trace out, though just barely, a graceful gesture. It is called *Silence*. It could be an eternal silence, or just a pause.)

She does *nothing*, says K.: but this is not exactly true. Like the unknown man at Bethany, in Matthew's gospel, she *squanders*. Along with her tears, she pours out an expensive ointment over Christ's feet. And in the opinion of Judas, she squanders "indiscriminately." But that is because she understands that this is a festive occasion, and she knows how to spend for it. "Let us not, however, forget the festive occasion; as she for her part did not forget it" ("The Sinner Woman," 267). She pours out her tears over Christ, along with her hair and her ointment. "She weeps— "she is silent": words incessantly repeated in the *Discourse*. All of these repetitions produce an effect of fascination; she must be fascinating to be able to appear fascinated in this way—"She anoints Christ's feet with ointment and wipes them with the hairs of her head, she weeps."

Thus, she does absolutely *nothing*. And why doesn't K. talk about the kisses with which she also covers the feet of Christ?

" 'Simon,' he said, 'you see this woman? I came into your house, and you poured no water over my feet, but she has poured out her tears over my feet and wiped them away with her hair. You gave me no kiss, but she has been covering my feet with kisses ever since I came in' . . . Then he said to her, 'Your sins are forgiven' " (Luke, 7:44–49).

*
* *

The sexual difference divides every scene, organizes the distribution of all the roles, and provides the hierarchy for all the positions and oppositions. Every alternative seems to be part of the one that is most pressing of all: "Am I a man or a woman"—each of these terms dividing itself on its own, endlessly. This is not even an alternative, then, since every choice turns out to be unstable. But there is a choice only because woman is not (merely) the name for a natural being but also the name for a position, even several of them that, as such, represent a number of possibilities for man. Perhaps, even, these are his only possibilities. There are at least two of them, and they correspond to the two types of woman, to the double "nature" of woman. What if man could choose only between two ways of being a woman?

Woman is always the woman of a couple—no matter which couple—and in the couple she is able to stand for herself *as well as* her opposite: in other words, castration *or* its opposite: the power of (re)producton.

——Castrated, she is the wife as well as the son: that is the Christian position. But there is a conflict here because castration is enjoyable whereas Christianity is supposed to entail suffering.

——Powerful, she is the mother but she's also virile and paternal. So she takes the father's place, reappropriates it for herself, competes with God. She is guilty . . . unless it could be shown that she begets only in pain, that she suffers.

The conflict, then, could also be written in this way: How is it possible to be Christian *and* to write? How is it possible to be wife and mother, son and father, how can one experience enjoyment and not experience it?

The equivalence of the positions wife/son/Christian is basically a result of their common submission, their renunciation, their passivity, and their enjoyment. Christ is always, and quite explicitly, compared to the bridegroom whose bride is the Christian (*Journal*, 1:147). This feminine abandon is also explicitly presented as an enviable position: "—What horrible suffering to be superior! And what enviable happiness to be a woman!" The preliminary ruses of the husband shouldn't fool us though. That this husband should also be the "suitor" in no way signifies an inferior position; it is "the conscious superiority of man" that makes him express himself in a polite manner to "the frail sex" and to bow his head before her. In bowing down, the superior one does nothing but solicit what is due him: the abandon of the other, whose inferiority, though, he can only envy.

On the other hand, the attributes of the begetting mother are also those of man, as father or God. This can be confirmed, for instance, in the way that divine creation, the creation of the Father, is always assimilated—like poetic creation—to a begetting, a maternity. The young man in *Repetition*, once he has become a poet, says that he "effaces himself" like the midwife in relation to the child she has delivered . . . While God the Father, whose creation is similar to "poetic productions," also begets like a mother: He "allows his creation to come forth" (*Journal*, 2:147).

And what is produced by this mother's work? Like all work, it produces its own father, in a reappropriation that makes the mother, virile to such an extent, father to her father, in other words, simply father if we recall that no *son* can be father: "What does it mean to be a father? I may indeed smile to myself at the thought of being a father . . ." ". . . so here then is a contradiction, one fit both to laugh and to weep over" (*Stages on Life's Way*, 58).

"[In the world of Spirit] it does not help to have Abraham as a father or to have seventeen ancestors. The one who will not work fits what is written about the Virgins of Israel: he gives birth to wind—but the one who will work gives birth to his own father" (*Fear and Trembling*, 27).

What if there were no place for man? If I am a man, I am obliged to marry a woman, take on a virile superiority, become a father; something which, insofar as a son, I cannot do without laughing. But neither can I remain a son without being the feminine wife of the Father. But if by writing I become father, thus giving birth to myself, then I become a mother, a virile woman, who is neither Christian nor man. And even if I choose to be God's bride, my enjoyment enters into contradiction with his law, which requires me to suffer. And if I choose the paternal maternity of writing, I'm still betraying the Father's law.

In any case, femininity shows itself along with all of its enjoyment. It would be necessary to reject the feminine positions one by one, to cleave them, deny them, always to separate the good femininity from the bad . . . And finally to give back to man the good femininity. This is never simply possible. The Christian has to be wrested from the passive enjoyment of the mother. This is not possible short of denying to woman *true* submission (Christian, not natural), short of denying to woman *true* (spiritual) maternity.

*
* *

I'm not going to reconstruct all the scenes in which the question is asked, "Am I a man or a woman?" Nor is it necessary to isolate or privilege *one particular* phantasy. There are several series of contradictions and compromises, or attempts at compromise. Each series is only a link, as Freud would say, in a chain of associations, and it would be necessary, in order to resolve just one symptom, to provide the case history of a "patient" in its entirety. Where would we find this entire case history? And what is the illness? It is no use diagnosing a case of hysteria, for instance, if it does nothing but reveal, only in a more acute manner, a constitutional bisexuality. In general, it is no use even giving it a name. If such a constitutional bisexuality actually exists, then trying to define what is masculine and what is feminine is already a first symptom of it, the second being the urgency of the need to be situated with reference to these definitions. Still another would be the multiplicity and contradictory character of the responses to it.

K. will make the rounds of all the possible and impossible responses, taking time to stop at each paradoxical compromise:

virile childbirth, virile castration, feminized and feminanimalizing erection . . .

Freud: "In one case which I observed, for instance, the patient pressed her dress up against her body with one hand (as the woman), while she tried to tear it off with the other (as the man)" ("Hysterical Phantasies and Their Relation to Bisexuality," 9:166).

The eminently Christian solution to these conflicts, the one he will eventually settle on, is the rejection of sex in its entirety, of sexuality as such—let it be rejected, pushed off entirely onto one or the other of the sexes, thus eliminating the difference and the alternative. Faced with the anguish produced by bisexual phantasies, with the impossibility of a choice or compromise, the question is denied: there is no sexual difference. It is enough just to deny one of the two sexes, it is enough to take away from what is called "man" or "woman" the sexual, differential determination, for the difference to disappear (therefore sex itself), for there to remain only a sovereign indifference. To neutralize the opposition is to push the hierarchy which governed it to the limit of its violence. The old hierarchy lives on endlessly after its abolition: what remains, the indifferent, is always man—no matter what side "sex" was at first placed on.

If sex is originally and exclusively masculine, then woman represents the resurgence of a difference, due to a degeneration, a fall, or a depravation of sex itself, which divides and cuts itself off from itself. Man is original indifference. If woman is the fallen sex, then castration would be the establishment of difference here.

If sex is feminine, it signifies a setback, or animality, and man represents the indifference acquired through choosing castration. Castration, then, is the establishment of *in*difference.

In any case, it is the woman that differs, therefore it is always through *her* negation that indifference is reestablished. The desire to neutralize the opposition here is once again subject or accomplice to the desire to reinforce it.

A double desire, always, to abolish the difference while preserving it, to occupy all the positions in the opposition, and to enjoy it.

I want to be a man—I don't want to be just a man.

*
* *

What we could call "the argument of the unique masculine *and* indifferent" sex is, curiously enough, attributed to Plato: "Even Plato recognizes that, at bottom, man's state of perfection is sexual indifference. He believes that in the beginning there existed only the male (without the female, sexual difference is obviously undifferentiated), but that due to deprivation and degeneracy the female appeared. He thinks that evil and cowardly men become women when they die, though not without the hope of eventually being raised again to the status of males. In a perfect life, he believes that the male, as in the beginning, would be the only sex and that, therefore, there would be sexual indifference" (*Journal*).

A surprising reading of Plato: it obviously cannot be in reference to the Androgynous myth told by Aristophanes in *The Symposium*—besides, the Androgyne is not a man. Perhaps this comes in roundabout fashion from the speech of Pausanias? He does, in fact, distinguish two Aphrodites: the *Common* one, the daughter of Zeus and Dione, who mostly inspires a bodily love, an ephemeral love for women as well as for men; and the *Heavenly* one, the goddess of a kind of love whose attributes "are altogether male." This Aphrodite, who is called "Urania" if she is the same one Hesiod refers to, is also a goddess *with no mother* since she is born from the frothing testicles of Uranus, which were cut off by Cronus and thrown into the sea by him. In the *Concept of Irony*, the speech of Pausanias receives the following commentary: "The one love is the motherless daughter of Uranus, the heavenly; the other love is much younger, has as its basis the difference between the sexes, and is the common. He then discusses the significance of that species of heavenly pederasty which loves the spiritual in man and is not degraded or debased by the sexual" (*The Concept of Irony,* 79). By combining various elements of the Platonic myths (Androgyne, The Heavenly Aphrodite, the transmigration of souls), we could trace all the elements in K.'s dream. But to go from there to attributing to Plato the idea that sexual indifference is the state of perfection is after all quite a big step.

*
* *

The positions that at first seemed specifically feminine—submission, renunciation, or the labor of childbirth—will have to be, each one of them, divided, doubled, in such a way as to signify *virility itself* on the one hand, and the most brutish sensuality, the most feminine (beastly) stupidity (*la bêtise*) on the other. Reproduction, then, in the sense of procreation, becomes the object of the most injurious deprecations: the mother represents unenlightened selfishness, devotion to the progeny of flesh; she is "the lioness," indeed the "sot and her litter" . . . whereas man's share is the "spiritual" form of reproduction: repetition and dialectical reduplication.

By the same token, feminine submission is devalorized. When it is feminine, renunciation remains a mediocre calculation, it remains finite—whereas sacrifice, martyrdom, infinite renunciation belong properly to man, who alone is capable of choosing the absolute renunciation. This man of renunciation is the Christian: the Jew portrays his effeminate and brutish caricature.

To woman, the Jew, the animal, belongs: sex, sensuality, enjoyment, children, number, life, immediacy, the finite, temporal world.

To man, the Christian, belongs: virile castration, spirit, dialectical reduplication, the ideal, infinite sacrifice, suffering, solitude, eternity.

This basic division appears clearly in the last fragments of the *Journal*, where woman takes on a more and more threatening, more and more terrible, figure, to the point of becoming the enemy, the devourer whose sole aim is to "destroy man insofar as he is spirit." The determination of sex as *uniquely* feminine carries the day and it is *inasmuch as sex* that woman goes to war with spirit.

*
* *

". . . that is why she is also called the sex: woman is the sex" (*Journal*, 3:456).

The voice of the *Journal* is amplified here, is perhaps becoming delirious. It is no longer a question of choosing, the voice is now defending itself against an enemy on the outside: the conspiracy of sex is worldwide, historical, finding its allies in the State, the Church. The world is thus split in two: those who plot among themselves to devour the others, to take advantage of them, kill them, eat them; and those who ask nothing better than to die and to suffer but who refuse to nourish the living off their death. They do not want to be robbed of their death, to have their sacrifice recuperated, to have its exemplary meaning perverted. In the service of this historical conspiracy of the living against the dying the most powerful institutions are at work: the Protestant church, the family, the State, all of them serve feminine reproduction, all of them labor to kill spirit, to *bring back* to life what is actually the work of death, the only true "production," the work of spirit.

We can make out resonances of Blake's voice in *The Meaning of Heaven and Hell* here, too. It tells of the same kind of split—but the enemy forces there are united by their common need for one another: "Thus one portion of being, is the Prolific. The other, the Devouring: to the devourer it seems as if the producer was in his chains, but it is not so, he only takes portions of existence and fancies that the whole. But the Prolific would cease to be Prolific unless the Devourer *as a sea* received the excess of his delights . . ."

All of K.'s voices can also be heard in Blanchot: it is enough to follow *Faux Pas*, for instance, and in the following order: "The Journal of Kierkegaard"—"Meister Eckhart"—"The Meaning of Heaven and Hell," etc.

*
* *

Woman is infernal because of her "selfishness."

This means that the function of woman, her desire, is reappropriation, always. She has no relations with her children or her husband except in view of this reappropriation. In the general conspiracy, her role consists in humiliating man, destroying him, cutting him off from his spirituality, enfeebling him. The institution of the family is her instrument for this. She does not believe in marriage any more than man does, but it serves her ends and she does not seem to suffer from the lie. She feels "comfortable" with the lie and imposes it on man, for whom it is "degrading." Like him, she knows that marriage is condemned to degenerate, she is aware that it brings neither fulfillment nor happiness, but she pretends to believe in it, she acts "as though." Through the lie she imposes on him, she submits man to her law. He is also ensnared by the woman-mother, he does not see that, "as wife, as mother—well, here is an egoism of which the man has no intimation. Society has licensed it under the name of love—good heavens, no, it is the most powerful egoism in which woman most certainly does not love herself foremost but through (egotistically) loving her own she loves herself" (*Journal*, 4:576).

That is her economy. As mother of the family, and this is not anything new, woman *is* economy, in other words, finite calculation. She loves herself through her children and she also wants, *in them*, to abolish the singularity of the husband. She never gives herself except in order to preserve (herself) better, to preserve her children, and in them to preserve the (dead) father. Woman is the sole *end* of the family.

This economic law of reappropriation, this sort of *"Aufhebung,"* does not seem to be the law of *the family* as such (as the site of the sublation of sexual difference), but rather only the law of woman.

From this perspective it would be possible, though at the risk of a crude comparison, to say that *Spirit* has nothing to do with the family *here*, except insofar as it fiercely resists the family, and also insofar as the family is established in order to destroy it. Or else: if the family accomplishes only the law of woman, if reappropriation is always feminine, then it would be necessary to say that, for K., the Hegelian dialectic is feminine.

*
* *

Like femininity, Judaism divides itself in two. Sometimes it represents the *model* of religiosity, of sacrifice, or the fear of God in a *"horror religiosus"*—sometimes, and this is the version that will predominate, it is on the contrary a love of life, of the world, of reproduction, of the family. Corresponding to sexual division, degeneration, there is a religious division, or degeneration, in which, in contrast to Christianity, Protestantism awakens the "will to live"; in which it is feminine:

> The fact that the "clergyman" goes around in female attire is not, after all, devoid of deeper significance. (*Journal*, 3:455)

Men, insofar as they are living human beings, "much prefer to be Jews." But Christ is "outside the family" since he was "born of a virgin." This *conception* of Christ can only be a scandal for the Jews and their "high conception of family and lineal descent" (*Journal*, 2:511).

The Jews, like women, resist death. The first concern of the conspirators against "man's spirit" is to divert him from his wish to die, to sacrifice. The second is to pervert, retrospectively, the meaning of that death: of Christ, or the martyrs.

They live, then, only by *representing* death, and remaining at the stage of this representation. They mean to exploit it, to master it—and this is how they defend themselves against it. They become doctors of death, professors of death: "And when a witness for the truth dies a martyr's death, those liars who live by representing suffering come running as fast as they can."

"Fools! The closer they come to him the more grievous is their fault for not having followed him, but rather for having earned their living by representing him." Represented, transformed into an Idea, removed, death, or the dead body, becomes nourishment. There is an apotropaic function in representation. The meaning of blood is divided and becomes a sign of life: "It is a kind of superstitious belief [the representation of sacrifice] analogous to the crowd's practice of collecting the blood of the criminal at the scene of his execution in order to use it later as a remedy" (*Journal*).

Of course, as Hegel would say, it is not a question of remaining in the moment of representation, but this moment is indeed that of religion, where truth is merely figured. And it is Christ himself who with his death provides an image of the true. Spirit has to pass, but just pass, through its own death . . .

*
* *

If woman goes to war against spirit insofar as she is naturally sex and life, then there is no more sexual *difference* properly speaking. Virility (or spirituality) is the renunciation of sex. *Virile* would be equivalent to *castrated*. Because man alone has the possibility of castrating himself—that is where his power lies.

When it is feminine, sex constantly takes on the figure of a *tail*. That is the sign of the animal, who himself represents, as always, the "level below man." Man, man's model, is Christ: *ecce homo.* Whoever fails to recognize his kinship with him loses his kinship with God and men, and "redescends" to the level of an animal.

Now who is Christ? The crucified, the sacrificed, the castrated—more precisely, the castraterect.

Judge for yourselves with the help of this portrait: ". . . in this very instant the family of man is debased beneath what it is to be a man and is essentially animal. A humorist would say that poetic justice requires that man, in memory of the event, be decorated with a tail, and he must insist that this tail stand perpendicularly from the body in such a way that it would be impossible for any tailor's skill to hide it, and also that it could not be chopped off inasmuch as it would have the remarkable capacity of immediately growing again" (*Journal*, 1:33).

Apparently, the tailor is invoked only to clothe, hide, cover, adorn the ornament and thus to conceal it, but what follows is still of interest to him since he is just as much the one who sews as the one who cuts. The incapacity to attire or protect (*parer:* to adorn, embellish, defend, parry) is thus always the tailor's. He can attire or protect (*parer*) neither by sewing or weaving—supplemental ornaments—nor by cutting off this bizarre ornament which stems as much from the vegetable as from the animal realm. He can neither prune nor graft.

In fact, perhaps you have to be something of a "humorist" to understand how this upright tail, as though triumphant, becomes the sign or the signifier of impotence. This is because the individual who holds it, or upholds it, condemned in spite of himself to an erection, constantly hands over for castration the ornament which he exhibits and which he cannot *not* exhibit. It is perpetually exposed, threatened, offered to a cutting which he cannot control. Such an erection is therefore, paradoxically, impotent, and thus is by no means a genuine erection—one of those on the contrary which one must be able to deprive *oneself* of in order to ward off (*parer*) every other castration. Genuine castration, then, would be auto-castration itself. This is why the martyr—who alone chooses and provokes his sacrifice—is the only one to hold himself up (he must be something of a humorist), in other words, to castrate himself: therein lies his force and his virility. He alone is man, only man is Christian: "Christianity is earnestness. Obviously therefore the criterion is applied to the man; the Christian requirement is related to the man, to God's very conception of what this means; the man is the human" (*Journal*, 3:476).

Virility and Christianity are one and the same: provided virility is determined as the possibility of castration. The "perversion of Christianity" is to believe that this is a woman's affair, to lose sight of the "virile ideal," the human ideal. An unexpected "proof" for this thesis is offered by the historical origins of Christianity: where does Christianity come from?—from the Orient.

"What was the relationship there? There the man was the human; women and children were almost a kind of domesticated animal" (*Journal*, 3:477).

*   *
*

There are several ways for someone to castraterect himself; one of them consists in writing and in exposing himself to the punishment specific to the author: running the risk of ridicule, having himself persecuted as a "public figure"—etc.—that is what he is forever laying claim to.

*   *
*

To men, then, belongs auto-castration, the paradoxical mastery of humor. To the others belongs the role of priestess or beastess. The bestiality of woman-sex. The latter are condemned to devour; their only desire is to eat. The alternative is: either eat—or be eaten. But man wants none of this alternative. He wants to eat (himself) all by himself.

"Everyone understands what cannibals are, they are man-eaters. One shudders at hearing or reading about this frightful practice, that there are savages who kill their enemies in order to eat them. One shudders, one is inclined to disavow kinship with such beings, to deny that they are men. I shall now show that the priests are cannibals, and in a far more odious way" (*The Instant*, 268).

Christianity is the truth of suffering—he said. Christ wanted to be mutilated: the cannibal priests who feed off him are traitors.

Is this for sure? Didn't Christ say, "This is my body, this is my blood, take and eat of it . . ."?

What is food? It is what brings in a profit. "To eat," for K. (I say "for K." because it is still the *Journal* I'm reading here), is always *to profit*. The priest and the instructor realize a profit insofar as they exact payment but also by assimilating, by appropriating suffering for themselves through "rationalization," "doctrinalization," "dogmatization." He whose suffering included sacrificing his life will have thus been put to death twice: once by his contemporaries and persecutors, and once by the priests who converted his death into doctrine.

He does not shrink from any image for describing the great conspiracy of the man-eater.

"Here you have the cannibals, the priests who are cannibals. O ye glorious ones, departed this life; in the animal world, which is called *a parte potiori*, the world of man, it is your fate in life and after death to be eaten: while you live, you are eaten by the contemporary vermin, at last you are put to death, and when you are dead the real cannibals take hold, the priests who live by eating you. As in the farmhouses at the slaughter season provision for the winter is salted away, so the 'priest' keeps in brine tubs the glorious ones who were required to suffer for the truth" (*The Instant*, 268).

The *Journal* refers here and there to famous monsters, particularly odious in the eyes of K.: one of them—whose story K. had perhaps read in a collection of criminal cases by J. V. Neergaard (Copenhagen, 1838)—is the assassin Ole Kolleröd who owned up to the gruesome detail of having *eaten* "with the knife of his crime"! Another is Heliogabulus: "But it is like this everywhere, everywhere. This infamous, nauseating cannibalism whereby they (just like Heliogabulus ate ostrich brains) eat the thoughts, opinions, expressions, moods of the dead—but their lives, their personal qualities—no, thank you, they want nothing to do with that" (*Journal* 1:69). Wouldn't the disgust with regard to "eating" always have something to do with the fear of cannibalism? And why here, exactly, *this* fear and *this* disgust? Not only is it necessary to understand "eating" in its proper sense here, but we must also admit that this "theme" is at the heart of Christianity. It is not alien to the question of the meaning of Christ's death—nor to what becomes of his corpse.

It all turns on the question of the Kierkegaardian interpretation of Christianity: Why does K. want—always and before all else—to repeat the expiation, to imitate the sacrifice? If Christ sacrificed himself "once and for all," as Saint Paul says, if he is the Savior, then he alone had to die, he alone had to be sacrificed and could by his death liberate mankind.

Let's consider the Freudian reading for a moment: the sacrifice of the Son had to atone for the crime committed against the Father. But by dying in his turn, the Son takes the place of the Father. But, on the other hand, the act of cutting the flesh and drinking the blood of the Son would represent "a new suppression of the father, a repetition of the act that demands expiation." The disgust of eating and the desire for imitation would then be able to be explained in two ways:

K. (like Freud) would associate, consciously or not, the religion of the "once and for all" dead Son and the belief in redemption with a repetitive murder of the Father and with the reappropriation of this Father in a kind of "totemic meal." The murder would thus be accompanied by a kind of productive labor of mourning. To participate in this "meal" would thus consist in effectively realizing a profit on the Father's death and in *not* expiating the crime: which is just what the cannibal priests do. Whence, *not to eat*, which perhaps amounts to maintaining the religion of the Father in opposition to the Son's religion and implies the necessity of repeating the expiation indefinitely.

From the same perspective, it is tempting here to speak of the *real* Father. We would be hearing something like: I don't want to eat my own dead father. I don't want to perform the "labor of mourning," I don't want to take the place of my father, I want instead to die myself . . . and expiate my sin. Which sin?—Maybe I didn't kill him, but haven't I wished for his death? Like the prodigal son accused (in the *Journal*) of having insisted that the father share his wealth with him: "What injustice, for the son has not the least right to demand anything. What ingratitude, for it is almost like saying to the father: at bottom, I wish you were dead!" (*Journal*). Now, around 1837, K. had left the paternal home. His father provided him at the time with an income of 500 rigsdaler. The sixth of August, 1838, his father spent one last evening with his two sons. He was fairly merry "even though that afternoon he had scolded Søren and had refused him something" (the elder brother's journal). Michael Pedersen Kierkegaard died in the night between August 8th and 9th.

*
* *

"My father died on Wednesday (the 8th) at 2:00 A.M. I so deeply desired that he might have lived a few years more, and I regard his death as the last sacrifice of his love for me, because in dying he did not depart *from* me but he died *for* me, in order that something, if possible, might still come of me. Most precious of *all that I have inherited from him* [emphasis added] is his memory, his transfigured image, transfigured not by poetic imagination (for it does not need that), but transfigured by many little single episodes I am now learning about, and this memory I will try to keep most secret from the world" (*Journal*, 5:122). I make no comment on this page, except to emphasize "all that I inherited from him" and to compare it to the indignation manifested elsewhere with regard to the prodigal son. Finally, the same day, 11 August, he remarks, again in his *Journal:* "It's a remarkable contrast—paganism levied a tax upon bachelorhood; Christianity recommended celibacy" (*Journal*, 3:123).

——But in addition, and this would be a second possibility, the desire to sacrifice *oneself*, to expiate further, would be to want to be a witness, indeed a redeemer, in one's turn, would be to want in one's turn to take the place of the Son who had taken the Father's place. Dying for (the place of) the Father, since the Father recognizes himself by dying.

At any rate, I don't want to eat either father or son, I don't want to face having killed them, I don't want to profit from their death. I only want to die myself. Like them. This is perhaps not wholly unrelated to what could then sound like a denegation: I (don't) want to be eaten—in the way that God would have been.

He knew, of course, that the desire for martyrdom could appear presumptuous: he often tried to justify his right to sacrifice. But if he frequently and explicitly compares himself to Socrates, it is a form of denegation that predominates with respect to Christ: don't think that I dare compare myself to Christ . . . And the problem always amounts to knowing whether Christ has to be the only victim and whether, consequently, anybody else has the *right* to martyrdom. The response of the *Journal* here is very obscure and ends with a kind of hierarchy of sacrifices: a *unique* sacrifice does not exclude "subordinate" suffering: "Christ is the only sacrifice; no added sacrifice is needed. The true Christian is the one who becomes a sacrifice in order to call attention to the truth that Christ is the only sacrifice."

"Here on the one side we see that to be a Christian means to be sacrificed, and on the other side we see the relationship of subordination in relation to Christ" (*Journal*, 4:4).

A response that at the very least indicates a certain uneasiness.

*
* *

To write, to become a poet, famous perhaps: to make a name for oneself. There is another source of conflict for the son. If the young poet in *Repetition* claims to have renounced fame in his letter of 15 August, this is not only in order to punish himself for not having given his name to the woman he loved: it is also in order not to usurp the father's name (and thus take his place), *as well as* in order not to keep this name, in order better to take this place, and to rid himself of the father. To be an orphan, he says, and to have a number. "A name, my name—after all it actually belongs to her. Would that I could get rid of it. My own name is enough to remind me of everything, and all life seems to contain only allusions to this past. The day before I left, I read in the paper 'that sixteen yards of heavy black silk cloth are for sale because of a change in plan.' I wonder what the first plan could have been, perhaps a bridal dress! Would that I, too, could sell my name in the newspaper because of a change of plan. If a powerful spirit were to take away my name and offer it back to me resplendent with immortal honors, I would hurl it away, far away, and would beg for the most insignificant, the most commonplace name, to be called No. 14 like an orphan boy. Of what avail to me is a name that's not mine, of what avail to me is a glorious name, even if it were mine:

> For what is the flattering voice of fame
> To the sigh of love from a maiden's heart?"
>
> (*Repetition*, 194–95)

Renown (*Navnkundigheds*) is always the glory of the name—*Navn*—of the father.

*
* *

It is the women—the Jews, the pagans—who reproduce (themselves). Plato and Aristotle would have actually put it "in black and white": All of those functions: procreation, eating, defecation, are equally disgusting. They are a surrogate form of immortality. "They think it's simply marvelous to stuff themselves with food and drink, to relieve themselves, and then to reproduce themselves. And just imagine, Mama's managed to have three sets of twins and get herself a government citation for it" (*Journal*, XI^2 A 154).

God's jealousy is perhaps not unrelated to this disgust. If it is necessary to choose him and to abandon all else, wouldn't the sacrifice of children be the cruelest of all, *the* sacrifice, the murder *par excellence?* "Christ puts the collision in this way: He who loves father, mother, sister, brother and so on more than me is not worthy of me. Generally he does not say: One who loves his child more than me—he does not think of the Christian as married; for otherwise he might have aimed in quite another way at precisely this collision" (*Journal*, 3:136).

How can that be, "he should have?" Didn't he, as a matter of fact, envision that one, and more so than any other? Does K. forget that Matthew (19:29) actually does speak of "leaving wife and children" for the love of Christ, does he suddenly forget Abraham?

How could the possibility of such a conflict not cause, in advance, the renunciation of children, how could it not cause them to be abhorred?

*
* *

But there is perhaps another reason for this fear of children. Another conflict actually appears in two scenes from the *Journal*. The first is called *Outline:* "Once in his early youth a man allowed himself to be so far carried away in an overwrought irresponsible state as to visit a prostitute. It is all forgotten. Now he wants to get married. Then anxiety stirs. He is tortured day and night with the thought that he might possibly be a father, that somewhere in the world there could be created a being who owed his life to him. He cannot share his secret with anyone; he does not even have any reliable knowledge of the fact.—For this reason the incident must have involved a prostitute and taken place in the wantonness of youth; had it been a little infatuation or an actual seduction, it would be hard to imagine that he could know nothing about it, but now this very ignorance is the basis of his agitated torment. On the other hand, precisely because of the sickness of the whole affair, his misgivings do not really start until he actually falls in love" (*Journal* 5:219–20). We can do little more with the sketch of such a "fiction" than take notice of it. It could be functioning as either a "key" or a trap. Certainly he himself had very little idea of what was going on. But the fact remains that he returns to it elsewhere, once again in the *Journal*. This time it's a miniature portrait: "A mentally deranged person who went around scaring all children, for he believed that he had once made a girl pregnant but did not know what had become of her and now had but one concern—to find the child. No one could understand the indescribable concern with which he would look at a child" (*Journal*, 5:243). Too bad he didn't know the story about Hegel's illegitimate child. What abundant commentaries he could have provided us with . . . In any case, we are far from being finished with the accidental child.

*
* *

When Constantine goes to Berlin for the second time, in search of repetition, he returns to the home of his former host. During the first visit, this man had done his best to argue the advantages of bachelorhood. Having been married in the meantime, he goes out of his way on the contrary to praise the value of marriage during the second visit. Constantine is amused by the whole thing and concludes, "When I speak German, I am the most accommodating man in the world" (*Repetition*, 152). An anecdote. But that is not just an idle phrase, for here we are at the heart of a question which K. wants to take over from or take up again with Hegel: the question of the relationship of philosophy to *its* language. Translate *aufheben* into Danish, says Kierkegaard, and you get *ophaeve*, and that does not work any more. And from there it is easy enough for K. to pat himself on the back with a touch of irony—but just a touch—for the "felicities" of his mother tongue, preferable to those of imperialist German: ". . . one sees that repetition proper is what has mistakenly been called mediation." Or again, " 'mediation' is a foreign word; 'repetition' (*Gjentagelsen*) is a good Danish word, and I congratulate the Danish language on a philosophical term" (*Repetition*, 148, 149).

He didn't understand Hegel, he even boasted of not understanding him—something that was likely to scandalize his contemporaries. What K. and H. could agree on was the critique of a certain conception of self-identity that was both immediate and "abstract." In this sense, they are both philosophers of difference. But this is already untrue for Hegel since difference doesn't remain difference: it is annulled, recovered in the teleological movement of dialectics. It turns out to be only a kind of lure in a philosophy of immanence. It is here that K. no longer follows along. What he will not have understood, will not have accepted, is the Hegelian distinction between understanding and reason: what is posited (apart) and determined by the understanding allows its opposite to subsist alongside of it and thus remains, "for reason," un-posited. Division [*Entzweiung*] is the source of the "need for philosophy," but philosophy then refers the totality of limitations back to the Absolute and annihilates opposition. In other words, it annihilates the separate positions of the finite and the infinite. The separate position—which is opposition—subsists then, but not *apart:* it is posited in the Absolute, in other words in identity. This is Knowledge. Understanding only posits (relative) identities, speaks only in limited propositions, and necessarily maintains the oppositions. Whereas reason, though it recognizes division, does not establish it on a firm basis: "In the infinite activity of becoming and production, reason has *unified* that which was *divided,* and reduced absolute division to relative division, which is conditioned by the *original identity*" (emphasis added).

"No doubt," K. would say, "Hegel is right *from the point of view of the absolute*—from the point of view of God." He *would be* right, if he were God, and if everything were past, finite, closed, abolished. Hegel is always right when he reflects on the past. He seems to have taken himself for God . . . But should there be any more existence left, then there is more of the finite, the separate, the future; the system can't close on itself. "The systematic is a latch, the perfect joint." Existence keeps things separated. Not to take into account the Hegelian distinction between understanding and reason—since this is what his objection amounts to—is a way for K. to refuse to consider Spirit otherwise than as existing spirit, to refuse a kind of "phantom" thinking that acts as though existence were already past, as though finitude were already finished, as though *I* could be (someone else) already outside of time. If *I* exist, he'd say, I exist *apart*, I can't yet comprehend the identity of objective and subjective, without abolishing my existence ahead of time. If I remain in existence, "my effort is oriented toward the future," and "I live in the contradiction, for life is nothing if not contradictory." Hegel never claimed otherwise. But at the same time he would have acted as though he were dead, as though he, Hegel himself, didn't exist. An interesting source for the comical, this "forgetfulness," this *"absent-mindedness"* on the part of a philosopher! "If a thinker is so absent-minded as to forget that he is an existing individual . . ." (*Postscript*, 108). His system wouldn't be "false" for all that: rather, it's "laughable": "It is from this side, in the first instance, that objection must be made to modern philosophy; not that it has a mistaken presupposition, but that it has a comical presupposition, occasioned by its having forgotten, in a kind of world-historical absent-mindedness, what it means to be a human being" (*Postscript*, 109). Imagine Hegel *absent-minded*, the idea was pretty funny. Someone who puts himself in the place of a dead man (or death itself) is funny. But isn't it also a little comical, even naive, to exist and to think of oneself as existing spirit? And isn't the particular individual, K. for example, in the isolation of his body, insisting on his existence *a parte,* isn't he, in his own way, laughable? Especially if what is particular *par excellence*, the body, seems to be missing: "What I actually lack is the physical and the physical presuppositions" (*Journal*, 5:389). To have mimed death, to have done his thinking from the standpoint of death, was a means for the philosopher to *economize* on existence, on the particular, on the body, and that by losing them—ahead of time—(the other would say: by forgetting them without losing them): "With respect to particularities, the essence of philosophy is without any basis whatsoever. And if, in fact, it is the body that is actually capable of expressing the totality of particularities, well then, let's get behind it *body* and soul."

It's not because they're both dead now that Hegel dead will have had the edge over Kierkegaard existing.

Secretive K.: no one spoke as much about himself, no one was more silent.

To write: his secret.

This has nothing to do with some kind of mysterious concealment. A philosophy of "manifestation" supposes some possibility of coincidence between "interior" and "exterior," between subjective and objective. But if the subjective neither is nor ever becomes the objective, then the difference lives on and the subjective remains in reserve.

Faux pas starts with K.'s secret. Blanchot speaks there about the "problem of communication" and about the "theme of the secret" in the *Journal*. Although K. shows himself to be "sincere right up to the end," he is reserved, he does not give up everything. In a double movement, "he explains himself and veils himself. He shows himself and protects himself." Does this mean that even when he's speaking, he's keeping "something" back? Does it mean that he has an "explanation" ready, but that he dissimulates it, depriving his readers after all of "what would explain everything to them?" Blanchot's choice of words here seems to refer to the famous lines in the *Journal*: "After my death no one will find in my papers the slightest information (this is my consolation) about what really has filled my life . . ." (*Journal*, 5:226)—or again to this equivocal sentence: "*I cannot speak* about that which, in the most complete, most essential, and most intimate way, constitutes my being" (emphasis added).

No doubt he did not tell it all: no doubt he didn't write things about himself which he *knew,* at any rate, things which he *would have been able* to say and which might have constituted "explanations." (There is someone, for example, about whom he hasn't a word to say: his mother. Is there a connection between her and "the secret explanation"? Does he know what it is? Does he make conscious or unconscious assumptions about it?)

Without denying that it is also a matter of this first kind of secret—of this deliberate reserve "in the depths of his very person," a secret kept only for the public but revealed somewhere on the inside—Blanchot evokes a much more profound secret that would not simply originate in a "profound aversion to communicate" (something which he nonetheless does take into account), a secret that could never disappear by being made public because it would not even be "private."

For the thing, the thing that is known, even by just one, is never secret. Here, though, it is a kind of interior muteness, a fundamental ignorance to which Blanchot is alluding: "against Hegel, he wholeheartedly affirmed that there was something in every soul that could not become public, a mystery that constituted it in its tragic reality and that could not be pierced"—and again: "he had a very strong impression that the knight of faith was absolute isolation, that he could not speak to others, that he could not even speak *to himself* [emphasis added] and that his life was like a book under divine sequestration." The secret is unpublishable because it has no language, not even for the one it constitutes and holds in secret, from himself. This particular mystery, characteristic of "every soul," is even more so of the "exception." And this was how he always understood (did not understand) himself as *the exception:* a singularity apart, separated (from itself), sequestered, unknown *to itself* like the mission of a frigate: "When a skipper sails out in his coastal fruit boat, he usually knows the whole course in advance; but a man-of-war puts out to sea and the orders are received only after it is out on the deep. So it is with genius. He lies out in the deep and gets his orders. The rest of us know something or other about this and that which we undertake" (*Journal*, 2:82).

It seems that he is involved only with his own silence—his sea—deeper than himself; words emerge from it but cannot reduce it. We don't know where this silence comes from: from the unconscious? or, as if from even further away, from someone else's—male or female—unconscious? or from the body? There is nothing to be said about it, except that it resists.

"No, no, my silence, my secret won't allow themselves to be broken."

*
* *

The first three sections of *Faux pas* could be considered as only one, turning around a single secret, with three names: Kierkegaard, Eckhart, Blake—to which we should add that of Blanchot.

Thus, according to Blanchot, in Meister Eckhart the idea of a paradoxical dialectic and the idea of a transcendence are inseparable from the experience of an "interior abyss," from a secret that divides the soul and separates it from itself—a sequestration similar to the one K. speaks of: "It is in the soul itself that the leap is made, in the soul that the abyss opens which no thought, no act can overstep. The absolute is in us in a way that forever separates us from ourselves, and our nobility resides in this mystery: that we must give ourselves up absolutely in order to find ourselves absolutely. What there is in man, man cannot know. ('What the soul contains in its innermost depths is unknowable,' Meister Eckhart says.)"

*
* *

Once we accept the practice of a "vagabond reading" (*lecture flâneuse*), we must also accept the risks, the accidents, the swerves—which become a kind of general rule. Today I note that there actually is (as can easily be imagined) a link between the detective, the philosophic, and the religious cast of mind.

I have often thought about how, in their childhood, "analysts" such as Poe or Freud must have at some point dreamed of becoming police inspectors. I was thinking that this also might have been the case with Kierkegaard—and then I read this page in the *Journal*: "If I had followed my inclination, chosen that for which I apparently have had a definite talent: becoming a police official, I would have been far happier than I came to be later, even though everything is better now. My acuteness would have been turned outward" (*Journal*, 4:545). This is not, or is not simply, something humorous. Beyond the natural talent he supposes he has for this career, the "desire" to become a detective is also fed by his taste for "extraordinary" personalities, exceptional ones, like certain criminal types philosophers often feel inexplicably drawn to. He will give up on this vocation with no regrets, though, since he is afraid of never meeting up with the grandiose "scoundrels" he has imagined. It is with the utmost gravity that he gives an account of this renunciation: "At one time my only wish was to be a police official. It seemed to me to be an occupation for my sleepless, intriguing mind. I had the idea that there, among the criminals, were people to fight: clever, vigorous, crafty fellows. Later I realized that it was good that I did not become one, for most police cases involve misery and wretchedness—not crimes and scoundrels. They usually involve a paltry sum and some poor devil.

"My next wish was to become a pastor" (*Journal*, 5:387).

We know that for a time he often kept company with a police agent in Copenhagen; several sketches in the *Journal* attest to the intention he had of introducing a police inspector "character" into one of his fictions.

*
* *

He despised money, more precisely, he despised gainful employment as much as he despised the employment of professors or ministers. One does not write or speak in order to "earn a living." In order to think such a thing, in order to say such a thing, you have to have money; otherwise you never make it as far as this insight—it is for this very reason that today it is no longer an insight.

True, he had money. He lived and wrote to the precise extent that his wealth allowed him to, neither more nor less: he died on the brink of financial ruin. And he knew very well what he owed to his money, in other words, to his father who, fortunately, did not leave him with just "his sin" for an inheritance.

This inheritance is fairly well known thanks to a book by F. Brandt and E. Rammel, *Kierkegaard and Money—Kierkegaard og Pengene*, from which the following information is translated in the first volume of the French edition of the *Journal*:

"The father's estate was estimated at 125,000 rigsdaler and each of the two brothers received a quarter as his share, or 31,335 rigsdaler. Kierkegaard and his brother were co-owners of their father's house at No. 2 *Nytorv,* each for a share of 9,500 rigsdaler, plus a mortgage of 753 rigsdaler.

"In May, 1843, Kierkegaard bought out his brother's share and in December, 1847, he sold the property for 22,000 rigsdaler, making a profit of about 2,200 rigsdaler, according to his own reckoning.

"As his share, Kierkegaard had also received the equivalent of 17,760 rigsdaler worth of personal effects, bond certificates, or perpetual incomes, etc. which he sold off little by little from 1839 to 1847. On the 14th of December he sold his last stock. Ten days later he gave up the paternal house, where he had been living since the fall of 1844. This sale fetched him 10,000 rigsdaler in cash, which was immediately used to buy back stocks and annuities. These he sold off little by little during the following years along with the mortgages that comprised the rest of the property's value. His last holdings being sold the 25th of August, 1854, he had nothing left at the time of his death in November of 1855" (58–87).

The father did not think that his wealth would be good for his son, and had told him as much: "You won't do anything as long as you have money." "He thought I would squander it," K. will later reply, "but it was actually the opposite that happened."

"The opposite," which means that, contrary to what the father had said, had he *not* had money, he would have done nothing. Money had in fact been one of the conditions of his work: "If I became a writer, I owe it mainly to her [Regine], to my melancholy, and to my money."

"I was a spendthrift," he says with no remorse—"to be a spendthrift" was obviously already to betray the father and his ethics.

Already in 1836, at a time when relations between his father and him were none too good and he had left the paternal home, he had 1,262 rigsdaler worth of debts (a sum that would represent a decent yearly salary for most professionals). A portion of that amount was owed to coffeehouses—he was a regular patron during this period—the remainder being accounted for by purchases of perfume and colognes, of expensive handkerchiefs and linens, of wines (note the reference to Château Margaux in *In Vino Veritas*), and finally by expensive carriage rides. To that must be added the money spent later on the publication of his works. Even if they sold well (and they did) and even if, in the end, the author would receive royalties, at first he had to pay (like Nietzsche) to have himself published. K. deals directly with the printer, he orders his publications from him, he negotiates with him; for example, on 23 August 1847, the bookseller Philipsen offers K. 500 rigsdaler for a new edition of *Either/Or* (1,000 copies). K. demands 700 rigsdaler and, since Philipsen will not agree to it, turns down the second edition on 30 August. The situation here shows very little analogy to that of today's writer, and at some point, it must actually have an effect on the meaning of the "book," both for its author and its reader. For example, the way in which they are related to one another. This particular economic and social situation of the writer, which is K.'s own, cannot be without some effect on the nature of what he writes, on his very style. If it is difficult to imagine K. having to deal with today's editorial machinery, that is because he did not have to, and this is perhaps readable in his texts. For example, for a writer to claim to address himself to "his reader," for him to insist on instituting a *private* relationship with him, that too could have an economic "sense," that too is perhaps not without bearing on the place he occupied in the fabrication of his books.

*
* *

The most considerable expenditures, however, are made for what he calls his "costly distractions": his rides. These are long excursions by carriage—whose horses actually become an object of reflection for him—on the outskirts of Copenhagen and occasionally far enough outside of town to require several days: to Pedersborg, Frederiksborg, Dyrehaven, Roeyel, Rudersal. At times he is attentive to the countryside, the faces he meets; at others he travels with the curtains down. And so he flees from the city and "the stench of the tanner," his neighbor; he is also mindful of his body, which is continuously exhausted and in imminent danger: "to keep myself in form, I had to spend a lot of money on my carriage rides" (*Journal*, X^3 A 177). But all the spending has but one goal: to maintain the conditions necessary for his "productivity": "My squandering is essentially related to my productivity, which I was to consider as my sole possibility, and also as an indescribable grace from God which gave such value to my life. Thus, it was all squandered in order to maintain my productivity." ". . . It is certainly true that I would turn to God, that I would pray to him whenever I felt the need for a costly diversion, and that the good fortune of actually being able to provide myself with it simply seemed natural to me. I would pray to God to find much pleasure in these excursions and would attribute all of it to him." He calls on God as his witness, then, and leaves things up to him as though his money were coming from heaven—in the form of "good fortune" or "grace"—for the sole purpose of allowing him to accomplish a task which was itself decided on by God.

Or could it be that the "productivity" was itself the price to be paid for that good fortune, the debt owed to divine and/or paternal generosity?

*
* *

Two generations of profit:

Michael Pedersen, the father, is a kind of "self-made man." At forty years old, his fortune made, he retires from business. Søren K. never wondered about this side of his father, whose extreme religiousness is well-known—but it is not known how he became so rich, having started out as an apprentice to a hosier.

The father accumulates considerable wealth. The son spends. But the son does not consider the father from this point of view because for him, profit is a sin. In K.'s elaborate mythology or phantasmatics, it is the devourers who "profit," while the devoured lose (themselves). But the son is acquainted only with word-eaters, exploiters of doctrine, beneficiaries of martyrs. The only kinds of exploitation he is acquainted with pass by way of words. For him, accumulation and profit are always philosophical, and even if he deals with money in order to spend it, he is ignorant of work and economics. His nasty little classmates at school, though, used to call him "Søren-Socks" not just because the ones he wore were big and heavy, but also because they stood for the father's work and the source of his wealth.

But he himself had never seen his father work: he was born too late for that. The father was already elderly and was concerned only with German philosophy and religion. To his son then he was just an educated, rich, and pious man.

For the son, working, earning one's living, could mean nothing other than alienating one's soul and pen in exchange for a salary, being a professor, printer, or journalist. All of these professions, the only ones he could have imagined for himself, seemed infinitely contemptible to him. But he is able to avoid these prostitutions thanks to God. He knows that he is favored through "his money" (he often says, "thanks to my money . . ."), as if through an innate wealth cut off from any origin, appearing as if from nowhere. Where could it come from? If he imagines something like exploitation or surplus value, it is always in the domain of spirit. To devour is to appropriate (something) to oneself gratuitously ... a discourse, a suffering, a death: to be all talk. The only business he can know about or denounce is that of words or ideas, and when he concedes a material profit it is in the form of a *salary*. If it seems scandalous to him to convert Spirit into money, he still does not try to find out where the money is coming from. At most, he attacks the subversive *institutions:* Church, School, the Press, which deal only in discourse, in "pure" language, "that ideality available to everyone at no cost," that ideal medium, the element *par excellence* of trade, always ready to perform in the service of intermediaries. Like money.

Each time that words are considered essentially as a kind of money, the same hobgoblins pop out in the shape of forgers, thieves, swindlers. The "ideal" character of language makes all sorts of exploitation possible, all sorts of deception: every discourse is always capable of detaching itself from the body, from "life," from the speaking subject. Lying and "ventriloquism" are always possible. Whoever speaks can pass off a kind of counterfeit coin with his words, without it costing him a thing, and on occasion, he can even make a profit on it. In sum, it is possible to put words "to work," just as in a certain context, we say that we "are putting our money to work." (In a way that, as an owner of stock, K. himself actually did.)

Economics: Something he did, and then again did not think through. For him, everything was always a question of economics.

*
* *

When K. denounces "the lowest" of the mediators—ministers, professors, etc.—he opposes them to the hoodwinked masses of "people," to the simple man manipulated by those functionaries motivated by self-interest. In this sense, the "masses" are naive, innocent, intellectually pure and much worthier than their corruptors: "I love the common man—detest the professors. The professors are the very ones who have demoralized the race. Everything would be better if the true relationship (?) could prevail: the few who are truly in the service of the idea, or still higher, in the service of God—and then the people."

"But the infamous situation prevails in which these scoundrels press in between these few and the people, this pack of robbers who in the guise of also serving the idea betray the true servants and confuse the people, all for the sake of paltry earthly advantage."

"Were there no hell, it would have to be made in order to punish the professors, whose crime is such that it can scarcely be punished in this world" (*Journal*, 3:653).

It is as though these crooks of professors were monsters, *bastards* whose existence would not have been provided for in the "real" world; they "sneak in," these hybrid beings, in some unknown fashion, in a world where they do not belong. *In reality* they were not created by God like the masses and the handful of faithful servants of the Idea: they come in order to "cause trouble," to seduce, to contend with God and with the true geniuses over innocent people. "The human species," like a pure maiden, can only be demoralized by these vile seducers.

But the word "masses" most often has another sense that is never connected to social class: it designates number or plurality in opposition to what is isolated, or to the Individual (*den Enkelte*). "The masses" or "the crowd" therefore does not apply to any particular social category, rather they are *numerical,* numerous. The numerical as such is wholly independent of the nature or quality of the unities or individuals it comprises. A note in the *Point of View* is quite explicit on this point:

"The reader will also remember that here the word 'crowd' is understood in a purely formal sense, not in the sense one commonly attaches to the 'crowd' when it is meant as an invidious qualification, the distinction which human selfishness irreligiously erects between 'the crowd' and superior persons, etc. Good God! How could a religious man hit upon such an inhuman equality (*U-Menneske-Lighed*)! No, 'crowd' stands for number, the numerical, a number of noble men, millionaires, high dignitaries, etc.—as soon as the numerical is involved it is 'crowd,' the crowd" (*The Point of View,* 112).

It is in this sense and from this "formal" point of view that number or "the crowd" is always untruth and "the most ridiculous parody of the Idea."

For in order to find truth, you have to step *aside:* "And he took him aside . . ." (Mark, 7:33), far from the "crowd."

It is necessary to seek the truth, but this truth is not to be understood philosophically, least of all in the Greek sense (in the gospel and epistles, St. John uses the word in its Greek sense). It indicates neither disclosure nor adequation, but is closer to the Hebrew word; solidity, constancy, and fidelity. The Hebrew word *truth* is related to the word *Amen*, which first of all means affirmation, or commitment, and sometimes it simply means "yes." There have been those who have said that the word *Amen* was equivalent to a signature. God's "truth" is his faithfulness, and in the Old Testament the "God of truth" (PS. 31:6) and the "God of faithfulness" (Ex. 34:6) are interchangeable. *That* truth, of a religious order, is foreign to number and it requires singularity. No truth without signature, without commitment, without giving one's word, without witnessing.

*
* *

"Perhaps it would be best to note once and for all—and it goes without saying that I have never denied it—that with respect to all temporal, earthly, worldly goals, the crowd can have its value, and in some cases, even a decisive one. But I don't speak of that, any more than I concern myself with it."

*
* *

It is only a question of point of view: "superior persons" taken together are "the crowd"—it is enough for them to be considered from the perspective of number. On the contrary, the individual is one who simply considers his separation, who conceives his existence insofar as it is separate. "The crowd, in fact, is composed of Individuals; it must therefore be in every man's power to become what he is, an Individual. From becoming an Individual no one, no one at all, is excluded, except he who excludes himself by becoming a crowd" (*The Point of View,* 119). God knows only the second perspective, He is the name for what separates and He considers each of us *one by one.* That is the religious point of view. The one of truth.

The other, the one that has to do with number, plurality, the mass-crowd, is the political point of view.

Whence an absolute contradiction between the political and

religious orders: "The witness for the truth—who naturally has nothing to do with politics and must above everything else be most vigilantly on the watch not to be confounded with the politician—the God-fearing work of the witness to the truth is to engage himself if possible with all, but always individually, talking to everyone severally on the streets and lanes . . ." (*The Point of View,* 115).

Socrates is the only one—along with Christ—to have understood that. Socrates is always the other model, the other victim of the political order, and *The Point of View for My Work as an Author* alludes to him incessantly. "On the other hand the 'crowd,' when it is treated as an authority and its judgment regarded as the final judgment, is detested by the witness for truth . . . For (to repeat what I have said) that which in politics or in similar fields may be justifiable, wholly or in part, becomes untruth when it is transferred to the intellectual, the spiritual, the religious field" (115).

The Individual as such is a "stranger to politics"; or again, the Individual "is a category opposed to politics." It will be noted, though, that to be a "stranger" to something or to be "opposed" to it is not the same thing—and there lies the whole question.

It could be said that there is no such thing as "Kierkegaard's politics"—but also that his discourse has political implications, effects, and indeed causes. Furthermore, there are pronouncements on his part that are very directly political (monarchist, for example), and after all he did begin his "career" with lectures and articles that had as their sole objective an attack on liberalism.

*
* *

In a word: When he tries to get involved with political discourse, it's a disaster. At that point, a kind of enormous, exaggerated infantilism reveals itself. Fear is what always dominates: fear of the powers of number, fear that the law, power, or the established order will be disrupted. (Or is it the father? If there were such a thing as "K.'s politics," one could designate it with one word: paternalism.) All the many nuances of scorn are of no avail: as soon as he is forced to consider the world from a political perspective, he is overcome by fear—a fear that is too obvious to allow us to believe in some kind of "political indifference," supposing such an indifference were even possible. He is afraid of "majorities," of institutions, of the "voting machine," and especially of the State. The State, the biggest "eating" machine of them all, (worthy) rival of God insofar as it, too, produces a certain panic.

* * *

Lukács devotes a chapter of his book, *The Destruction of Reason*, to K., in the course of which he accuses K. (according to Goldmann) of having "provided the irrational-reactionary western imperialist philosophy between the two world wars with one of its most important intellectual foundations" and of having considered the private man (the Individual) independently of and in exclusion to the citizen, a conception which K.'s economic independence would have made possible. But Lukács analyzes above all the *function* of his works and what he believes to have been their political *role* in the nineteenth and early twentieth centuries. This role, in essence negative, seems to have been one of both complicity and support with respect to reactionary policy.

Goldmann does not agree with this unilateral condemnation: "His [Lukács'] opinion would have been defensible strictly speaking if there had been powerful revolutionary forces in the West, and if during the twentieth century socialism truly had been an objective possibility for Western society. In that case, one could actually have understood how Lukács could reproach existential philosophy, Kafka, and the surrealists for having provided an overly somber picture of this society and for having failed to appreciate its positive forces" (*Kierkegaard vivant*, 162).

Here, then, lumped together under the same heading, we have a somewhat curious "collection" of "overly somber" texts. No doubt we understand what a "somber" depiction might be. But what is a depiction that is *overly* somber? By what criteria— aesthetic, ethical, or political—is this excess to be judged?

Is it on the "objectively" *somber* basis of a given social reality that the "right" of a work to depict a world that is itself "somber" should be measured? *If* the "positive forces" were less important (in the nineteenth century) than Lukács believed, *then*, according to Goldmann, one cannot "criticize" certain works for having provided us with "overly somber" portrayals of this age. Goldmann is therefore less severe than Lukàcs in regard to writers of "darkness." Darkness is sometimes legitimate: furthermore, we have to recognize the "positive function" that is exercised during certain periods by a "literature and thought of radical refusal." While this nuance is underscored by Goldmann (in his contribution to the 1964 conference on Kierkegaard, *Kierkegaard vivant*), he claims, nonetheless, not to be in agreement with "the radical pessimism of these writers." There is no essential difference, then, between Lukács' reading and that of Goldmann: both of them analyze the texts—and why not—from the perspective of their political "function" or "role." This analysis has at least the advantage of simplicity since its results can be schematically summed up in two columns: the role is either "positive," or it is "negative." If the political forces are "positive," you do not have the right to be "somber"; in the opposite case, you have the right to a little pessimism, but not too much.

At any rate, what is questionable here is the effectiveness of readings that put into play notions such as "pessimism." What is a pessimistic writer? Does this question make any sense?

*
* *

It is certainly not a matter of dismissing Marxist readings as such. On the contrary: had they gone further, they would have—also and *in addition*—been able to see something else, in particular things that complicate the simplicity of the relationship Lukács establishes between Kierkegaard and "imperialist philosophy."

Goldmann says: "Lukács reproaches Kierkegaard for having developed . . . a philosophy which, on account of an insufficient knowledge of Denmark, he was incapable of analyzing, but also which, according to Lukács, provided the irrational-reactionary Western imperialist philosophy between the two world wars with one of its most important intellectual foundations" (*Kierkegaard vivant*, 158). No doubt, the wooliest forms of Spiritualism have been able to make claim to K., the most blatant and reactionary Christianism has tried to appropriate him for itself, but then maybe Denmark and imperialism have not been sufficiently discussed. With respect to "social conditioning," K.'s socioeconomic situation has often been invoked; with respect to the political "implications of the work," and this is a second point, readers have most often gone no further than the content of certain political pronouncements that are explicit, conscious, and obviously "reactionary and individualist." But perhaps we have not sufficiently analyzed the political significance of K.'s "philosophy" by taking into account the political situation of Denmark: it has not been sufficiently understood to what extent a certain "refusal" on K.'s part had something to do with what we could call a "resistance"—a resistance to imperialism, as a matter of fact.

For who is imperialistic around 1848? The king of Prussia, Frederik-Wilhelm IV, who is working toward unifying the Germanic countries and who supports the insurgents of Schleswig-Holstein against Denmark. Not only must Denmark fight against Prussia's attempts at annexation, but it has already been culturally colonized by Prussia, in particular by its philosophy and its language, its "philosophical language." Now K. had also chosen the name Vigilius Haufniensis—the Watchman of Copenhagen—and even if the city is only a "hole in the wall," even if Danish is a kind of "dialect" spoken by a small number of people, K. wanted to be a Danish writer and thinker, he wanted to affirm the particularity of his culture and the genius of his language. And could the philosophy, the culture, the cultural expansion of Prussia be conceivable independently of the political situation and movement of Prussia? Therefore, it is not only the philosophical imperialism of Hegel that K. "resists," it is also an entire troupe of Hegelio-Germanophiles (like Martensen or Heiberg) who at that moment dominate Copenhagen, it is also the German language, it is the politico-cultural imperialism of Prussia in relation to which Denmark represents a threatened particularity.

André Clair is one of the few, to my knowledge, to have seen in Kierkegaard the representative of "little, colonized Denmark"; the relatively numerous references to "the Danish Hamlet" seem to him also to move in this direction.

*
* *

There is no such thing as Kierkegaard's "politics," and yet, objectively, he speaks as a monarchist and reactionary, he condemns liberalism, and on occasion he defends absolute monarchy. But he could have defended other governments—he says so, in any case—on the condition that they be well established. As Lund put it in one of his letters, "He appeared to be very conservative, to revere the king, to love the Church, and to respect the police." Yet, no matter how naive it might seem to a political thinker, the monarchy did not represent for Kierkegaard a political choice but rather a means of keeping politics at bay, of neutralizing politics. To be a monarchist is to not want politics. The sovereign, above and beyond the conflicts of interest and the fighting for power, does not represent one form of power among others, but an exterior instance, almost transcendental, in relation to which anyone is a "private person," before which all are equals like the faithful before God or children before their father. It is a well-worn argument. Insofar as it is a government, the monarchy is of no interest to Kierkegaard: it seems to him simply to reproduce the Christian model according to which all are equals, less in rights or powers than in impotency and submission. The monarchy is a means of "liberating" men from politics, of saving them the trouble of political preoccupations, in other words, of questions of power. Not that the king represents divine power, on the contrary—there is no question of confusing absolutely different realms—he is there in order that men may renounce power, in order to exorcise political desires, in other words, the desire for power.

Christ wanted to ridicule power and he was ridiculed by being called "King of the Jews." That was the worst mockery of all: the political turns out to be the most sinister *caricature* of religiosity, its "parody."

The liberals, of course, are political animals—and they are in fact the force of politics on the move—they make claim to powers, to liberties, they risk making politics popular. That is the great danger.

Christianism, a religion of impotence, has no greater enemy than politics. More precisely, the Christian is someone who, along with Christ, understands that impotence is more powerful than power, who understands the infinite power of impotency. Such is the significance of the reed Christ carries: "therefore Christ has no scepter in his hand, only a reed, the symbol of impotence—and yet at that very moment, he is the greatest power" (*Journal*, 4:184). Such is religious logic: "in the divine order, the greatest impotence is the greatest power" (*Journal*, 4:185). Such is the irony of Christ who, like Socrates and his irony, will perish a victim of the State's ire.

It is as though the transcendence of power, like that of God, should *guarantee* the schism—denounced by others—between the *private* individual and the citizen. This frenzied individualism can obviously be interpreted politically: religious individualism dovetails with bourgeois individualism, reinforces it, serves it, indeed reflects it . . . This is why the only role that can be accorded the State from this point of view is the rational organization of self(ish)-interests. Thus, there are certain questions that belong to the collectivity: it is better to have the State attend to city lighting than to have everyone light his own door! But the State's power should be limited to this kind of task. It is necessary to maintain an absolute separation between the public domain, the exterior (represented here by the street) and the private domain, the interior (the house, the home). The State must therefore always remain an exterior instance, something other, distant. "The least State possible," as Nietzsche will put it. The model for this distant instance remains the monarchy: it is very far from you, it is not interested in you: "Would it ever occur to an emperor to concern himself with me, with my manner of life, with what time I get up in the morning, or with the books I read, etc." Unfortunately, a legitimate fear of the State, that "man-eater," competes here with an extreme political naivete: "in general [it is still a question of the emperor] he does not even know that I'm alive. But in a popular form of government, it is actually one of your 'equals' who governs. He concerns himself with my every aspect; whether my beard is like his [an unfortunate example], whether I visit the park at the same hours as he does, whether I am completely like him and the others. And if not, well then, it is a crime—a political crime, a crime against the state!"

Furthermore, Kierkegaard never imagined—whatever the political forces at play—that the supreme power of the sovereign could really be put into question. At the time of his conversations with King Christian VIII, he does his best to minimize the danger communist ideas represent for the monarchy, and about which the king is worried. It is probably all a matter of class conflict, he admits in the end, "but it would always be to the interests of the conflicting parties to get on well with the monarch" (*Journal* 6:92). In the long run, if he seems flattered by the interest Christian

VIII shows him, he remains jealous of his independence and, in keeping with his ideas, he spaces their meetings out and wants to be forgotten by the king.

*
* *

Faced with such a "political" attitude, one hesitates between laughter and disgust. It is a little too caricatured, though, a little too untimely (even for its time), too simple and excessive to be interpreted solely as a traditional political position, and not to disturb in any way what we understand by the word "political."

Had it not been the case that Kierkegaard fought the politicization *of the Church*, had he not denounced Luther and his alliance with the princes, his political attitude would be more easily analyzable. But he did not distinguish the powers of Church and State, because historically they were inseparable. He saw them doing battle on the same field, and he read in their complicity the overturning of Christianism, the advent of its parodic double, of its caricature. In any case, then, it spelled the advent of something which, insofar as it goes "counter to it," is not without a relationship to the religious, but which rather represents its demise, its risk, its temptation. There has to be something in Christianism itself that would allow for such a misunderstanding, that would justify, for example, this vigilance: "the witness for truth" must above all "be most vigilantly on the watch not to be confounded with the politician . . ." How would such a confusion be possible if, somewhere, these contraries were not dangerously close to one another?

*
* *

In the margins of Marx.

The religious and political orders exclude each other. Marx says it *as well as Kierkegaard*. An analysis of this double exclusion would in fact show that only the hierarchy is reversed, and that the pair remains the same. One is related to the other as dreaming is to reality—the question being to know *who* is dreaming. This exclusion is not possible except by supposing, at the outset, a unique desire, a common root.

Reading Marx with Kierkegaard is not a matter of noticing a

contradiction between them. There is open contradiction only on the basis of a certain shared language. And the fact that such sharing remains unexpressed prevents us from simply construing the religious (Kierkegaard) on the basis of the political (Marx). For it would still be necessary 1) to demonstrate why Marx, like Kierkegaard, has to distinguish and oppose religious neutrality to its worldly and institutional expressions, and 2) to highlight the fact that Marx recognizes in the "human grounds" of Christianism the very grounds of desire for the emancipation and sovereignty of man. What would distinguish the religious from the political, therefore, would be less a certain "ground" than the interpretation of this ground (its source, in the end) and, by the same token, the way in which the desires awakened by it are satisfied. Corresponding to which there would be at least two economies.

For Marx, it is a matter of unmasking religion, of analyzing its grounds and attacking it politically. Here he is led to oppose—and this is where he dovetails curiously with Kierkegaard—the religious *spirit* and the *desires* that propel it toward a religious reality that is politico-institutional as well. Marx interprets religion by assigning it sociopolitical origins and a human foundation, but he denounces any collusion of religiosity with the "world" and the *weltliche,* secular domain. He considers secular forms of religion corruptions of religion itself, degradations, compromises, and he does his best to disassociate these degrading compromises from true religious spirit. The Church is therefore considered as an institutional framework *exterior* to the "evangelical spirit" of original Christianism and *in contradiction* to it. All this, which appears in *The Jewish Question,* helps make apparent a certain autonomy of the *spirit* of the earliest religion in relation to whatever historico-political focus it may have assumed. According to Marx, in effect, when the State emancipates itself from religion (by emancipating itself from the *State's religion*), it merely redirects religion to what it was originally: a private affair, proper to the separate individual. Therefore, it does not touch religion itself and does not yet attain "the last form of general human emancipation." By removing religion from the public to the private realm, the State returns religion to its originary form, in other words, to the *expression* of the separation between individual and community. This understanding of religion as the "essence of difference"—and not of "human nature"—is very close to that of Kierkegaard. The Christianism of Kierkegaard is an individualism—K. always insists on this individualism in distinction to the Protestantism of his time: "it is for each individual to settle individually his relationship to God"—but his doctrine of separation and of isolation is politically interpreted as egoism: the religious mentality becomes the mentality of bourgeois society. "Man emancipates himself *politically* from religion by abolishing it from the province of public law to that of private law. It is no longer the spirit of the *state* [as when the state is itself religious] where man behaves—although in a limited way, in a particular form and a particular sphere—as a species-being [*als Gattungswesen*], in community with other men. It has become the spirit of *civil society,* the sphere of egoism and of the *bellum omnium contra omnes.* It is no longer the essence of *community* but the essence of difference [*Unterschied*]. It has become the expression of the separation [*Trennung*] of man from his *community,* from himself and from other men, which is what it was *originally*" (Karl Marx, The Jewish Question, 231). The split (*Spaltung*) between the public and private man, realized by (the spatial) political emancipation, therefore, does not abolish actual (*wirkliche*) religiosity, since religiosity is nothing other than this *Spaltung.*

On the contrary, a total emancipation of actual man (*der wirkliche Mensch*) will not simply be a political emancipation, it will not maintain the split between private person and citizen but will abolish this split. It is to be remarked that the *private person*—excepting his political condemnation—described in *The Jewish Question* is actually Kierkegaard's religious person. Analyzing the Declaration of the Rights of Man, Marx defines *person* as distinct from citizen. He is the *isolated monad,* the private and selfish person, turned in on himself, separated from mankind, apolitical; he is the member of bourgeois society. As for freedom as a human right, it is the right to *separation,* the right of the individual to be limited to himself. In relation to this isolated individual, the other is merely a limit, and society merely an "exterior framework."

Kierkegaard would have been able more or less to answer: yes, you've understood religion quite well, the religious spirit is just so, it is separation, a split, alienation, a cut, castration itself. But why are you saying that the split is bad? If I want to be castrated, it isn't in order to enjoy the world, in egoistic fashion—that is perhaps Judaism—it is in order to sacrifice myself, in order to suffer. I detest bourgeois egoism . . .

A Marxist interrupts: after all, though, you do live by spending your father's money, who was himself a model of bourgeois success . . . Kierkegaard (appreciating the weight of the argument): don't talk to me about that, it is something I can hardly stand. For me, it is an infinite debt to be paid off. Which is why I consider myself particularly called on to sacrifice. I have to justify my existence as an author . . . It is God who . . .

Marx: Yes, I see. Your religious isolation, indeed your penchant for martyrdom, sacrifice, all that is supposed to justify your bourgeois individualism. Your actual existence . . .

Kierkegaard: Why should you want to make light of my qualities? After all, there are those who don't go to so much trouble . . .

Etc.

*
* *

True freedom, total emancipation, belongs to the man, "the truly general man," who achieves unity, emancipating himself from all that divides him, in other words, that alienates him. Evil, religious or political, is the double, the division of man and the world, of the social and political, of heaven and earth. True freedom cannot belong to the *private* person—in the full sense of its particularity and partialness—but only to Man insofar as he is a truly general, actual species-being (*ein wirkliches Gattungswesen*). The religious emancipation of the State is therefore not yet the emancipation of *man*, since the State maintains the separate existence of bourgeois society, of bourgeois man distinct from the citizen. "The State can be a free state (*Freistaat*) without man's being a *free Man*." The free State, in fact, does not institute the freedom and sovereignty of men except by constituting its universality *above* the civil society of private persons and interests such as described by Hegel. The split—alienation itself—is therefore maintained: "Where the political state has attained its full degree of development man leads a double life, a life in heaven and a life on earth, not only in his mind, in his consciousness, but in *reality*. He lives in the *political community*, where he regards himself as a *communal being* (*Gemeinwesen*), and in *civil society*, where he is active as a *private individual*, regards other men as means, debases himself to a means and becomes a plaything of alien powers. The relationship of the political state to civil society is just as spiritual as the relationship of heaven to earth" (*The Jewish Question*, 220).

Thus, there is a similarity between the two oppositions; that of the State and civil society and that of heaven and earth in spiritualism. As citizen of the State, man is sovereign; he is also sovereign as religious person. But in both cases, this sovereignty and universality is chimerical, illusory, and abstract, since in his most immediate actuality (in civil society, in his concrete existence), man remains a selfish individual, different from others by his birth, condition, education, occupation, etc. The citizen is free and sovereign in his political equality with other citizens, *in the way that* the religious person, only insofar as he is religious, is free and sovereign before God. In the religious sphere, God plays the role played by the State in the political sphere; one is the mediator (*Mittler*) who recognizes the freedom and equality of the faithful, the other of its citizens. The most immediate actuality evaporates into abstraction, whence, the same abstract and partial freedom.

There is, however, a paradox, and we might be surprised by Marx's use of the celestial metaphor in regard to the political sphere.

Marx describes the original form of religion as the sphere of egoism, the essence of difference, the expression of the separation between man and his community: that is why religious Spirit is also the spirit of civil society. Now, by comparing the existence of the citizen in the State with celestial existence (while the earth takes on the figure of life in civil society), Marx uses the image of heaven as an image of *communal* life, of Man's life at the heart of the political community. So it is that, in Marx as well as elsewhere, the image of heaven is sometimes applied to the religious sphere—which is one of egoism, of individualism—and sometimes applied to the political sphere—which is one of communal life. There is, however, one constant: the *celestial* is always something illusory and abstract, opposed to a material actuality above which it is posited but by which it in fact allows itself to be dominated. The religious and political spheres are called celestial and are dependent on a "spiritualist" attitude, since they seem to be able to *double* and dominate the profane, secular world.

Despite the misunderstandings to which the text of Marx is susceptible, we know what the Marxist solution to the "Jewish question" is.[41] Religious spirit turns out to have been nothing other than a more or less spiritualized form of bourgeois spirit, and this complicity seems to be particularly visible, and in *exemplary* fashion, in Judaism. If religious alienation is nothing but the alienation that separates man from himself and makes him into a bourgeois (religious) individualist doubled by a citizen, then strictly speaking there is no longer any Jewish question. At this point, it is only a matter of denouncing whatever relates religion (in this case, Judaism) to the egoist Spirit of social society itself, and practically speaking, to bring an end to the separation between actual social man and his allegorical double, who is the abstract and artificial, political man.

However, it might seem more than just a little curious that Marx bases his argument here on a definition of Judaism as a religion essentially linked to personal interest, money, etc.—I won't retrace the discussions already alluded to—but from there he goes on to show that the actual Christian of bourgeois society is every bit as Jewish as the Jew, in other words, just as profane as he is. Christianity will never have overcome Judaism: that is where it comes from, and despite its laudable effort at spiritualization, that is where it ends up. Its mask will necessarily fall back off again.

"Christianity sprang from Judaism. It has now dissolved back into Judaism.

"The Christian was from the very beginning the theorizing Jew. The Jew is therefore the practical Christian and the practical Christian has once again become a Jew.

"Christianity overcame real Judaism only in appearance. It was too *refined* (*vornehm*), too spiritual, to do away with the crudeness of practical need except by raising it into celestial space (*in die blaue Luft*)" (*The Jewish Question*, 240).

---

41. This has been clearly demonstrated several times, among others by Elisabeth de Fontenay in her *Figures juives de Marx*.

The Jew will always have been fundamentally bourgeois, the Christian fundamentally Jewish. Mankind, Jew or Christian, will not be liberated politically, but rather by the end of bourgeois society, the reign of private interest.

However, Christianity's dream is said to be more "sublime," more "distinguished," more spiritual. Christianism *distinguishes* itself from Judaism by opposing a materialistic egoism with "an egoism of salvation," and this "distinction" seems to shelter it from the insults Marx saves for Judaism. Even if the Kierkegaardian position with respect to Judaism is double and ambivalent, it forms a partial link with that of Marx at the point where it makes Judaism appear as a materialistic egoism and affection for the world, for worldly wealth, for the body, for the family, indeed for bestiality, etc. This similarity is all the more striking in that it is supplemented by a common thesis according to which Judaism would represent a corruption (even if it were a revealing one) of secular religious spirit, a fallen state, in complicity with the world, openly betraying its most spiritual religious aspirations. Marx calls Judaism religion insofar as, in a practical manner, it enters into contradiction with itself. Judaism is the name, the figure for religion betraying itself by secularizing itself. It is perhaps there, in the choice of this figure, that Marx and Kierkegaard allow themselves to be manipulated by an age-old opposition, an ancient image whose historical origins can be traced back to the history of Christianity itself.

Nonetheless, whatever name he gives the "practical Christian," Marx in fact rejects the possibility of a "practical" form of Christianity: there is no *Christian* use or application (*Nutzanwendung*) of Christianity. As a form of sublime thought, Christianity is impractical, short of degenerating, of (re)turning to material egoism, of abandoning its dream of sovereignty—but of a sovereignty outside this world. The dissolution of Christianity is, then, the return to practical needs.

Finally, there is another fate for Christianity; where it does not dissipate into "Judaism," the religious spirit can become actualized (*verwirklicht werden*) in the democratic state. It is not religion as such that is actualized at this point, but the human grounds on which it is founded (the desire for sovereignty). Religious spirit "frees itself and constitutes itself in its profane form," ceasing at this point to be religious. In this sense, religious spirit cannot actually (*wirklich*) be secularized (*weltlich werden*), it is itself the *nonsecular* (*unweltliche*) form of a stage in the development of spirit.

So political secularization and Jewish secularization are the two threats, the two dangers for Christianity, the two forms of its decadence. Bourgeois or Jewish egoism and the exclusively political sovereignty of democracy are two forms of Christianity's secularization—but there is no good worldly form of religion as such. It is as though both Marx *and* Kierkegaard were interested in making evident the contradictions between the principles, the foundations of religion (or at least of Christian theory) and the secular and "vile" ends of every political or politicized institution claiming filiation with the Bible. The destruction of Christianity by a politicized Church or by a so-called religious State is therefore just as easily denounced from Kierkegaard's point of view as from Marx's.

*
* *

With respect to the Kierkegaardian understanding of Judaism and the historical process of "Judification," the analysis would necessarily be complicated to the extent that:

(1) Judaism is always already divided for Kierkegaard in such a way that it sometimes signifies selfish spirit bereft of any religiosity, *sometimes* (along with Abraham) religiosity *par excellence.*
(2) "Judaism" (in the first sense of the term) is in reality represented by the Protestant Church and its founder, Luther.

In fact, although Kierkegaard would not dream of considering Abraham a "Jew" (something which Hegel does), he is the one he chooses as an example of the highest form of religiosity: Abraham is a true "knight of faith" who lives in fear of God and accepts sacrifice. Abraham is a model for the *Christian.* Which goes to show the originality of the Christianity-Judaism division in Kierkegaard.

On the other hand, the corruption or Judification (in precisely the way Marx uses the term) of the Church is the work of Luther: the Reformation. Luther softened Christianity, he made it comfortable, worldly, in other words, "Jewish."

Luther reforms Christianity and so *softens* it by claiming to generalize a part of his own religious experience. Luther, as we all know, at first experienced the anguish of sin, infinite guilt, the passionate search for God, solitude and suffering, then he finally found peace in revelation and grace. With that, he gets married, has children, lives happily ever after, reforms the Church and goes into politics. By putting grace up front, so to speak, the Reformation seeks to do without suffering and sacrifice: "Luther discovers that Christianity exists to soothe and reassure" (*Journal*, 3:100). It is perhaps not entirely a Lutheran "invention"—but what is at stake here is the very meaning of Christianity. Paradoxically, a certain refusal of the peace made available through grace represents a position that is more Jewish than Christian. In any case, economizing on sacrifice (I would even say, on castration) means the end of religion: Luther becomes a politician, and more important still—inside the Church at least—a democrat. Luther toppled the pope and "set the public upon the throne." Politically, Luther gave way, he betrayed the people and he looked to the Princes; he became a politician: "he called on the Princes for help, in other words, he became a politician at heart."

Politicized religion is prostituted religion. Founded on renunciation and sacrifice, religion is not susceptible to secularization. Every collusion between Church and State is monstrous. Marx as well will denounce this collusion, demonstrating that it is contrary to religious spirit itself: "The state which allows the Gospel to speak in the language of politics or in any other language than the language of the Holy Ghost commits a sacrilegious act, if not in human eyes, then at least in its own religious eyes. The state which acknowledges Christianity as its supreme law and the *Bible* as its *charter* must be measured against the *words* of Holy Scripture" (*The Jewish Question*, 224).

Now if Kierkegaard was an inveterate enemy of the Church of his time, this is because he understood that politics does not slip into the Church from the outside, but rather that institutionalized religion is politicized from the word go insofar as it pursues secular ends and settles into worldliness. Kierkegaard radicalizes, at the same time as he pushes to its extreme consequences, the point of view according to which religion is a *private* affair.

By taking even further the adversarial relation Marx and Kierkegaard establish between the religious and political orders, we notice that this relation is the same, but reversed: a hierarchical relation that opposes dream to reality. At times, it is religion that exists in the world of dream and illusion; at others, it is politics that dreams of being able to realize in this world what belongs only to the religious sphere.

The Point of View for My Work as an Author is followed by an appendix entitled *"The Individual"* and subtitled "Two 'Notes' Concerning My Work As an Author." This appendix itself includes a small "Preface" that contains the most astonishing lines Kierkegaard ever wrote about politics and history. In the course of remarks that appear today more untimely than ever, he files his complaint against *Time*.

"In these times everything is political. Between this and the religious view the difference is as wide as heaven (*toto caelo*), as also the point of departure and the ultimate aim differ from it *toto caelo*, since politics begins on earth and remains on earth, whereas religion, deriving its beginning from above, seeks to transfigure and thereby to elevate the earthly to heaven" (*The Point of View*, 107).

"Transfigure" and "elevate" are being used here to translate the word *forklare*, which means at the same time "to explain" and "to transfigure." One and only one topic here: the high and the low, heaven and earth. The high is opposed to the low; it dominates it and explains it. Political thought, according to Kierkegaard, does not escape this opposition: it only reverses it. "The movement here is from earth to heaven," says Marx.[42] For the political man, then, the low takes the place of the high, earth the place of heaven. Or so he thinks: for the possibility of such a reversal is merely a lure. A politician reading these pages is told

---

42. In certain texts at least, it seems that Marx remains under the sway of traditional oppositions borrowed from metaphysics (such as those between heaven and earth, the real and the imaginary, etc.). This has been amply demonstrated by Sarah Kofman in her *Camera Obscura*.

that he will find "little to edify him." He should, though, recognize his own thought in them; but transfigured, idealized: "the religious is the transfigured rendering of what the politician has thought of in his happiest moments . . ." From the point of view of its content, the desire expressed in it, religious thought does not differ from the (good) politician's. But the politician will find the religious person "unpractical" because "too lofty and ideal." *"Practical"* seems to play on several meanings here: the "unpractical" is simultaneously what is too ideal and too theoretical to be applicable or "practical," and also what is difficult, uncomfortable. The politician is not wrong, because Christianity actually is an *impractical* practice: its "practice" is that of renunciation and sacrifice, it leads the practicing Christian toward persecution and death. This paradoxical practice, which consists of turning aside from the world, already belonged to a pagan philosopher, "the impractical philosopher" (whose irony already prefigures religious detachment), to a philosopher who had to suffer the consequences of his political ignorance. Here we recognize Socrates, who was "head over heels in love with *this* impracticality." "In these times, everything is political": this sentence is not simply to be understood as a criticism of an age, of a determinate moment in time. For, by following the religious point of view here, we would have to say, in *Time,* everything is political. The "practical order" of politics is the order of time, which is that of the world. The political spirit is a "spirit of the world" —to which Kierkegaard can only oppose the "eternity" in which the "religious order" resides, or toward which it strives. If the political person "dreams," this is because he cannot actualize his desire in the world and in time: "But 'impractical' as he is, the religious man is nevertheless the transfigured rendering of the politician's fairest dream."

But what does the political man dream of?—"No politics ever has, no politics ever can, no worldliness ever has, no worldliness ever can, think through or realize to its last consequences the thought of human equality." The politicized man therefore dreams of equality. We might be surprised at this narrow sense of the word, which seems to exclude from the "political" order nonegalitarian conceptions. We also ought to notice how the summary and approximate nature of this conception leaves it open to subsequent criticism. Be that as it may, the political person is dreaming, since he claims to be able to realize in this world, "in the medium of worldliness," an idea that is incompatible with the natural diversity of the world: equality. The world implies "difference" or "diversity"—here we find the outline of an unexpected philosophical argument: "as is apparent from the categories" (*The Point of View*, 107–8). The categories clearly exhibit the diverse and diversifying nature of the world, *therefore*, equality is not of this world! The argument is somewhat complicated by the fact that the word *Verdslighed* means at the same time worldliness (belonging to the world, in conformity with the world) and "the equality of things in the world." The things of the world, whatever their diversity may be, enjoy a kind of natural equality by the very fact of their belonging in common to the world. But this equality of nature is not true (ideal?) equality, on the contrary: all the things of this world, in their shared temporal and material reality, are diversified and opposed by each other. Should we want to actualize in this world what belongs exclusively to the Idea, the world would *catch fire:* "And one more word, if that be allowed me. What the age *demands*—who would ever get through with reckoning that out, seeing that now worldliness has caught fire by spontaneous combustion due to the friction of worldliness against worldliness?" (108). Along with the French translators Tisseau and Jacquet-Tisseau, we would have to admit that "Kierkegaard, who wrote these lines in 1849, is probably thinking of the events of 1848 and their countless repercussions in every area of worldly or 'practical' life, the intersection of all interests."

It would in fact be possible to see in the Kierkegaardian rejection of politics the expression of a certain coming apart at the seams. Kierkegaard interprets the upheavals of '48 as effects of the "world's" resistance to the liberal political exigencies of the moment. The old world, the old society, has tottered; Kierkegaard is perhaps experiencing the contradiction—the very same one Marx denounces—between civil society (worldliness) and the ideal of freedom and equality that tries to realize itself politically. Perhaps he is coming to terms with the distance that separates this political ideal from its realization; perhaps he too considers (solely) political freedom an abstraction, a useless dream since it is not able to reduce the conflicts and contradictions in concrete fashion. Unable to conceive a possible resolution for these contradictions, he prefers to affirm the purity and nontemporality of the Idea against the world, and to take refuge in the religious sphere. Corresponding to this choice would be Socratic and/or Christian detachment.

Kierkegaard's reaction to the events of 1848 seems to indicate that he would indeed be that bourgeois who experiences the contradiction between the ideal of "sovereignty" and the actual, material, and social world and who, having no conception of the possibility of reconciliation, takes the contradiction to its limits and chooses spiritualism. Noting a certain complicity between the Christian ideal and the democratic political ideal, he considers those involved with politics as illegitimate, incapable of realizing, totally and practically, their "dream." During the period in which it was formulated, and if we remain within Marx's point of view, this critique is not without validity: liberal democracy is still spiritualist and maintains the split between the political sphere of the State and civil society, or the material world. Marx: "The political state stands in the same opposition to civil society and overcomes it in the same way as religion overcomes the restrictions of the profane world; i.e., it has to acknowledge it again; reinstate it and allow itself to be dominated by it" (*The Jewish Question*, 220). At this stage of the political emancipation as analyzed by Marx, political and religious spiritualism resemble each other.

This resemblance cannot be fortuitous. It is only possible by considering (partial) emancipation and religion as two ways—misleading, abstract, and illusory—of overcoming an evil resulting from one source alone: alienation, division, breaking apart. But where does Marx get the idea that alienation and divestment (*Entäusserung*) would be evils, always and necessarily, whose only fate is and must be their own suppression? Where else but from a (Hegelian) philosophy of immanence for which all difference, all division is finally surmountable and never anything but a moment, if not a lure? Indeed, the Marxist analysis of economic alienation shows that a process of reappropriation is necessary and possible. But already in Hegel, alienation was more complicated. As for the difference and division at issue in Kierkegaard, they are not based on an original identity: on the contrary, they undermine it and always precede it. This is why, when all is said and done, the questions raised by a form of thinking that "begins" with division are susceptible neither to formulation nor resolution within the language of a philosophy, be it Hegelian or Marxist, that presupposes an original or final identity.

A practice of impotence, of divestment: such then, would be the definition of Kierkegaardian religion. But "impotence" is not its goal, it is *its* politics, its economy—whereas it calls "political" what is directly related to power, profit, appropriation: feminity, Judaism, animality, politics in the traditional sense. These power politics are devoid of "spirit" insofar as they depend on finite calculation: they are related to a world and a time in which power and the signs of power are vulnerable. These petty calculations are scoffed at by the grand total of the religious mentality, which makes out of impotence (even out of castration) the sign and the means of "Supreme" potency. Each of its calculations laughs at the others rather than opposing them. Or rather, the opposition here takes place on a political terrain where religious irony seeks and finds its triumphant death.

The reed turns out to be the parodic double of the scepter or staff.

"Christ has no scepter in his hand, only a reed, the symbol of impotence—and yet at that very moment he is the greatest power. As far as power is concerned, to rule the whole world with a scepter is nothing compared to ruling it with a reed—that is, by impotence—that is, divinely . . . in the divine order, the greatest impotence is the greatest power" (*Journal*, 4:184–85).

*
* *

God draws man into an *a parte*. Woman, too. Writing, too.
Notabene:

There are famous prefaces that are read independently of the books for which they were intended. And there is Lautréamont's *Preface to a Future Book*. But prefaces written for no book at all, except the one which they alone will end up by making, that is something rare, and I know of only one example, more or less.[43]

---

43. Taking into account *Prefaces*, the subtitle of Derrida's *Out-Work* in *Dissemination*. TN. Kierkegaard's *Prefaces* has not yet been translated into English. It is scheduled to appear in the new series of translations published by Princeton University Press. All references here will be to the German edition.

It is called *Prefaces* (but we ought to write *Preface[s]* since the Danish word *Forord* can be plural as well as singular), it is signed *Nicholaus Notabene,* and the author explains (in what seems like *the* preface since it comes first) why he does not write books. Notabene, like a musician who would compose only overtures, writes only prefaces. This curious practice is at once a response to a wholly subjective necessity (the author's family situation), and an objective necessity (in philosophical-literary history). The comic intersection of these two necessities allows for the separation of books and prefaces, in other words, the abandonment of the book. "The incommensurable, which in the old days was put into the preface of a book can now find its place in a preface that is no longer a preface to any book" (*Vorworte,* 174).

Prefaces: You can't make a book out of them, since you won't find anything but prefaces to read there, but they are and are not prefaces, since they don't precede any book. Prefaces we would have to call free, fictional, inhibited (as far as their goal), as well as divorced.

One of them, though, the first one, apparently prefaces the others and bears the title (*Preface*)—without our being able to decide whether it is part of the collection or "book" in the same way as the others, or whether it is detached from them, still able to represent the author's extra-textual discourse in spite of the others; without our being able to know whether it is more or less "fictional" than the others.

The book and the preface, then, are going to get confused.

This first preface confuses the book at the outset by eliminating it: he—the book—had been acting self-importantly, and now she—the preface—was going to show him how well she could get along without him. This is one way of raising the question of the preface's status. Ordinarily, notes the author, a preface is considered to be "something trivial in relation to a book" (173); it seems to bear "the imprint of contingency." Just like dialects, idioms, and "provincialisms," prefaces are subject to arbitrary fluctuations of fashion and maintained only by the respect of an imperfect reader. It is for this very reason that "modern science (*Wissenschaft*) has delivered the deathblow to the preface" (174). In opposition to the seriousness of the book, of the work properly speaking, the preface seems like an *insignificant* remark (*en hensynsløs Yttring*)—but it is precisely from that angle that it ought to catch our attention. Notabene believes in the importance of the detail, and it is with this "casual remark" that the preface begins: "It is a common experience: thanks to something trivial, a mere nothing, an insignificant remark, a spontaneous outbreak, a chance facial expression, an involuntary motion, we get the chance to delve into someone and to discover something that remains hidden from careful observation" (173). For someone who knows how to read it, then, the preface will be revealing. It would be necessary, given the peculiar literary genre represented by the preface, to consider undertaking a scientific study of the preface: "no one knows what advantages could be had if one or another man of letters could be directed to read nothing but prefaces, albeit in a thoroughly exhaustive manner . . ." To make into an object of science what seemed to be the product of chance: the suggestion is ironic, it takes the scientific requirement which claims to disqualify the preface and goes it one better. It is no less modern for all that, and literary criticism seems meanwhile to have taken up the challenge.

Apparently, Notabene does not set himself up in opposition to "modern" (Hegelian) science or philosophy; he documents the fact that it refuses the preface and belittles it as a formality, chitchat that is extraneous to the subject, a superfluous shelter for the nonconceptual. Philosophy begins by itself, it is a book without a preface (even if it still has to say so in a couple of prefaces). The author has read Hegel and has noticed that his speculative philosophy claims to dispense with the distinctions form/content or production/exposition, and that the preface, as a preliminary discourse that is exterior to the content, must disappear in the auto-development of the concept. But Notabene does not attack Hegelianism head-on: he ironizes. When you start the System out of Nothing, he says, "there's nothing much left over to say in a preface" (174). In fact, though, he does not believe in the subordination of text to meaning with nothing left over, he does not believe in the *Aufhebung* of writing in speculative discourse. But he ironizes and pretends that he does not understand, pretends that the disposal of writing could be effected by a divorce between the preface as writing and the book as content. From that point on, in a gesture that risks the appearance of situating itself all too neatly in the opposition literature/philosophy, Notabene agrees to break with the book and champions the freedom to write without discussing anything. "And so I think the quarrel is thereby settled to the mutual satisfaction of both parties; if the preface and the work are not able to pull together, then let one give the other his walking papers."

"The very latest scientific method has made me realize that things had to come to a rupture; it is my honor to take this rupture seriously." (This is probably an allusion to Hegel, who disqualifies the preface even though he continues writing them.) Once the rupture has been consummated, Notabene will not write books, he will preface. There are some wholly empirical and subjective reasons confirming him in his choice: "Every aesthetically developed writer has certainly known moments in which he had no desire whatever to write a book, though he would not have hesitated to write a preface to a book, regardless of whether his own or somebody else's. This proves that the preface is essentially different from the book, and that to write a preface is something quite different from writing a book" (175).

Emancipated, delivered, de-booked (*délivrée*), the preface does not stop acting like an introduction, but it is pure introduction, a beginning without end, a preliminary with no object. A forepleasure in the double sense of purely formal aesthetic pleasure (Freud's *Verlockungsprämie*), and of pleasure in preliminaries, in seduction, the sketch, the provocation, the offer.[44] But by offering *nothing*, the preface is the moment of pure desire, and the desire to write a preface is nothing other than self-sufficient desire. The pleasure comes uniquely from desire's *Stemning*—a word as bothersome to translate as the German *Stimmung* (disposition, mood, tuning-up, atmosphere . . .).

"A preface is a *Stemning*. Writing a preface is like sharpening a sickle, tuning a guitar, shooting the breeze with a child, spitting out the window. Without knowing why, you get the urge to throb dreamily in the *Stemning* of productivity, the urge to write a preface, the urge to feel those 'leves sub noctem sussuri.' Writing a preface is like knocking on someone's door just so you can stick

---

44. TN. *Verlockungsprämie, Vorlust,* and *Nebengewinn* are all terms that Freud uses to describe a kind of prefatory, or forepleasure. See his *Three Essays, Jokes,* and "Creative Writers and Day-Dreaming." See also Philippe Lacoue-Labarthe's essay, "Theatrum Analyticum."

your tongue out at him, it is like walking by the window of a pretty girl without lifting your eyes off the pavement, it is like beating the wind with your stick, going out of your way to lift your hat, but to no one in particular" (*Vorworte*, 175).

Everything points to the gratuitousness of the gesture, the refusal of all ends: to write a preface is to write for the sake of writing. But there is a *gesture,* even if inconsequential, there is an offer: "To write a preface is to have done something that entitles you to demand a certain amount of attention."

In any case, it is a question of getting yourself noticed. *Notabene,* by the very choice of his name, designates himself as remarkable or notable; but also, by signing with a common noun (which is not even a name in the first place), the author refers only to a pseudonymous instance to be remarked as author, without making any claim to the singularity of a proper name. This signature finally calls attention to itself only with the nonchalance, indeed the detachment, of a marginal note, or one at the bottom of the page.

This moment of writing that asks to be remarked is also figured as a moment of erection, indeed of aggression, through a series of images that are too obviously symbolic to be altogether naive ("sharpen a sickle," "spit out the window," "beat the wind with your stick," "to fill one's pipe, and then light it"). But nothing goes on here: the reader, the page, the author are still (almost) spotless: "To write a preface . . . is to notice that you've fallen in love . . . it is like pulling back the branches in the jasmine bower to see whose girlfriend is hiding there . . ." The author, though, pokes fun at everything and everybody. The "clown" or "joker" has a good time all by himself, he offers only the spectacle of his own desire and enjoyment.

It is not surprising, under these circumstances, that Mrs. Notabene looks askance at her husband's desire to write. This marital conflict will contribute, as the author explains to us in his first preface, to making an author of prefaces out of N. N.

For Notabene is married: he is even willing to admit his good fortune, until the day comes when he becomes aware of the urge (which he at first thinks he can give into with impunity) to devote himself to "some literary occupation." While he is getting ready, choosing his subject (we'll never know which one), borrowing a few books from the Royal Library, it does not take long for his wife to suspect that something is going on behind her back. Finally, when the pen is "still in the inkwell, so to speak," she extracts a full confession from him: "I was in the process of becoming a writer." War is immediately declared: she confiscates the papers, makes curlers out of them, sticks her embroidery on them, and even burns them. All of Notabene's creations are thus "nipped in the bud" (177).

"That is how things are now. I have never been able to write more than an introductory paragraph" (179).

Mrs. Notabene turns a deaf ear to her husband's explanation and simply declares that "for someone who is married, to be a writer is to be manifestly unfaithful." Furthermore: "it is the worst kind of unfaithfulness." N. tries at one point to convince her, to have her share his desire by using the customary arguments: "I pointed out to her that it would be pleasant in any case to see my name, our name, become famous; I told her that she is the muse who inspires me. She won't hear a word of it." She senses a betrayal. Indeed, she does not get lost in subtleties and shows herself to be hardly touched by the "border conflicts" which Notabene claims are likely to occur between "the conjugal and individual." But it is clear that despite a certain lack of nuance in her judgment, she is not simply wrong. She must be close to some sort of truth just to be able to put her husband into such a bother about it—since logic and rhetoric seem to hold no secrets for him. And the anecdote would not be so comical if it did not reveal, in the mode of parody, the loss, or *forfeit*, of whoever writes, always on the sly, and at the price of a guilty *a parte*.

As luck would have it, our luck that is, "writer" in Danish is *Forfatter*.[45] Isn't the forfeiture, crime, or betrayal of the husband

---

45. TN. Unfortunately, this is by no means *our* luck—but then perhaps it is not (simply) fortuitous that the reference here to "us" is bound to be disturbed by the felicities and infelicities—the luck—of translation. This passage plays on the chance encounter (paranomasia) of the Danish *Forfatter* (writer) and the French *forfait* (forfeit, loss, but also, and especially in this context, an unpardonable *crime*). We should also note how the "writing" Agacinski is talking about here necessarily assumes the shape of translation: through the translation (the writing down for "us"), what is "revealed" to us is ultimately not an understanding of the *a parte* in question, it is an example of *a parte*, the distance that leaves us not only out of luck, but out of the

to give himself over to the solitary enjoyment of writing—"a rich, rich source of enjoyment," as Kierkegaard himself puts it?

The wife's ultimate weapon will be the most terrible of all: she finally admits to her husband that she does not think him "capable" of being a writer . . . whereas he has all the requisite qualities for making a good spouse. Notabene is going to win out, though, thanks to a loophole whose deceptiveness cannot be detected by his wife this time. He pretends to give in—"I ended up by promising that I would not write any more . . ."—though not without requesting, in exchange for this promise, permission to write prefaces. "She agreed to my proposal, thinking perhaps that it was not possible to write prefaces without writing a book . . ." (183).

Reading the other prefaces, one cannot avoid altogether the suspicion that this remarkable scenario was also drawn up (and why not?) to make use of desk-drawer material and to settle scores—not only with Hegelian philosophy, but also with the entire Danish political-journalistic scene, and in particular with Heiberg, who had published several articles on the pseudonymous books.

Not all of them were written for this "book," and the seventh, for instance, was supposed to precede *The Concept of Anxiety.* Given the change of context and signature, though, we ought to forget that book and read this preface inside the "book" to which it belongs.

The prefaces following the first one bear no title and are simply numbered from I to VIII.

1. The book, like some sort of phantom, remains the necessary fictional pretext: "How delightful to have written a book!" exclaims the author (185). After which he reflects on the choice of the most propitious moment for publishing. "On this subject, the best and wisest minds are in agreement for recommending the new year." Two pages are then taken up by this delicate question, insisting on the necessity that the book be as sumptuous as it is elegant in order to constitute a tasteful present. This anecdote of the new year, on which Notabene makes a point of dwelling,

---

entire (French and Danish) scene. Translation, then, is a kind of *mise en abyme* of *aparté*.

must have been amusing in its day since it alludes to the famous teacher and critic J. L. Heiberg, who, in *Urania* (a book characterized by him in the afterword as a "New Year's book"), had written a critique of Constantine Constantius' *Repetition*. Feeling that he had not been understood, Constantius drafted several projected replies. At the time, Heiberg was a well-enough esteemed Hegelian to be considered in some quarters capable of even "going beyond Hegel." Notabene pokes fun at the pretensions of a philosopher who, in the second and last issue of his review *Perseus*, announces that the first twenty-three paragraphs of his logical System have as their sole goal the clearing of a path to an aesthetics the author has for some time wanted to elaborate . . . *A la* Heiberg, Notabene promises his own "ethical (and dogmatic) system" and finally "The System." As soon as the latter has appeared, future generations won't even have to learn how to write, for there won't be anything left to write; it will be enough simply to read "The System."

2. In the *Intelligendsblade*, No. 24, Heiberg had remarked the appearance of *Either/Or* by Victor Eremita, insisting especially on the reception which, according to him, the book would receive. This is perhaps what leads Notabene to write a small fable describing the publication of a book and ridiculing the critics. Once the book has appeared, everyone is talking about it, no one has read it, not even the critic, who only listens to what is being said: "He runs home and while the pure twaddle is still buzzing in his head, he draws up his review" (188).

But the resentment Notabene feels toward the critic will not allow him to retain his playful tone for long. In the process of drawing several comparisons likely to make apparent the persecution and the martyrdom he has to endure as an author, he turns bitter, even tragic. He is "like a cat in his barrel." According to an ancient custom, in fact, a cat was placed in a barrel on Mardi Gras day, following which the barrel was smashed to bits. A writer is treated no differently: once he recovers his wits after the assaults of the critics, he is "as stunned and dazed as the cat who is finally clubbed out of his barrel" (191).

Misunderstood and trampled upon, the author still has to undergo the humiliating experience of being placed before his examiners, just like a student. "An author is a sorry louse who does not know or understand anything, but who awaits anxiously and terror-stricken the stern judge, the wise and judicious verdict of the honorable public."

And so ends the program announced in the opening lines: "To be a writer in Denmark . . ."

3. Once again a parody, barely half a page long. An author congratulates himself on the success of his book, which has appeared, naturally, at the end of the year. "An edition of one thousand copies completely sold out after two months." He takes advantage of a second edition to announce to his public the appearance of another of his books as early as the following December: "I am taking the present opportunity to apprise my honorable neighbors of this fact so they will not go out and buy other toys or presents to put under the Christmas tree" (194).

4. Only the last lines of the fourth preface—lines I could easily believe were added to the small text they have little in common with—remind us of a Notabene preface and refer to the strange composition of the "book." This composition, in fact, rules out determining *who* the author is who is in the process of saying "I," and *which* book is at issue when reference is made to *"this"* book or to the *"present work."* For example: "My dear reader, if I were not in the habit of writing a preface for all my books [which books? Notabene does not write any], I might just as well have not written this one; for it has nothing whatsoever to do with this book [and for good reason, since there isn't any. *Prefaces* isn't one, and each of the individual prefaces is admittedly fictitious] which, either with or without preface *since it is both* [my emphasis. It is, then, a question of *Prefaces,* at once book and prefaces, but this text is not *the* preface . . . Or could each preface of the 'book' be considered preface *to* the book?], entrusts itself entirely to you" (198).

Once again, Heiberg will bear the brunt of this preface, thanks to the barb of the "New Year's Book." Either N. N. allows himself to be carried away by the bitterness he feels toward the unfortunate Heiberg—or else he is after a comic effect based on repetition. Or both.

5. The themes of individual salvation and the solitude of the writer belittled by the majority will be treated here in an unexpected context. Praise for the spoken word and number as opposed to writing and isolation.

Here we find Notabene, or a character created by him, in the role of a militant member of the "Society for Total Abstinence," drawing up an introduction to a speech on alcohol he has given in honor of the society at one of their meetings. The introduction, or preface, is supposed to precede the publication of this speech. At issue here, then, is an orator rather than a writer, who addresses a group and not some isolated individual: "To write is not to speak," he begins, "to tell the truth, only a general assembly can be truly inspiring" (198). Now the "Society for Abstinence of Copenhagen" had just been founded on the eighth of October: its members pledged to give up drinking spirits and to observe "moderation" in the consumption of wine. For a humorist such as N. N., such an affair was grist for his mill. The enthusiastic orator undertakes, then, to demonstrate that the abstinence of someone who is all alone will provide little more satisfaction than honor. If, on the contrary, he joins the illustrious society, he immediately takes on an "infinite importance for the whole." Alone, he accomplishes only his dreary duty; as a member of the society, he becomes part of a sublime mission.

6. Notabene here deplores the lack of edifying works "for educated people" in Danish literature. (Kierkegaard, however, had just published five *Edifying Discourses* . . .) Therefore, he himself will introduce the public to a book composed of twenty-four sermons that manifest a "systematic tendency" for which one would seek in vain in the sermons of Bishop Mynster. The "present sermons proceed from and refer back to the totality" (203).

7. The seventh preface upsets and complicates the schema even more. Before, it would still have been possible to make a case for a simple work of fiction published by a pseudonymous author. On closer inspection, it would even have been possible to identify an abyssal scene in which the (fictional) author of the *first* preface introduced himself as the author of prefaces for books which were themselves fictitious. Thus, there would have been a book of fiction (the prefaces) itself inscribed in the framework of a fiction (the first preface). This process of telescoping would at each point leave us in doubt as to the identity of the author—even if, by referring to the first preface and the signature of the book, it remains convenient to call him Notabene, which we already know to be a pseudonym.

Such a complicated scenario, however, is not even necessary to produce this sort of sliding. The *mise en abyme* starts with the simple exposure of writing as the scene or space of fiction. Bringing this scenario to our attention is already enough to make the discourse "indirect" and to create what Kierkegaard calls a "poetic relation" between the author and his production—something that is always related to ventriloquism. But it is extremely tempting to set these mechanisms aside, to erase the artifices of the text, to flatten it out in order to recover a direct discourse, to "bring it back" to an original source that is known and identifiable, and finally to limit its meaning.

This seventh text complicates our reading to the extent that we know that it was the original preface to *The Concept of Anxiety*, a text that was to be signed Søren Kierkegaard. Armed with this knowledge, according to which, at a given moment, Kierkegaard was to sign this preface with his own name, should we, like the [French] translators, restore to Kierkegaard the signature he wanted to erase, and consider "*with good reason* that Kierkegaard effectively assumes *responsibility* for what is said here *in the first person* [Emphasis added]?" Supposing the distinction were clear between what an author assumes "responsibility for" and a certain something left over (a distinction no one plays with more than Kierkegaard and his pseudonyms), supposing further that the signature could be considered the sign of "taking responsibility for," how can we ignore the actual substitution of one name for another here? Certainly not by reference to the author's intention, for we would then have to privilege one (anterior) intention over another. Kierkegaard *almost* signed this preface, he failed to sign it: he did not sign it. No more than he signed, in the end, *The Concept of Anxiety* (by Vigilius Haufniensis). Either we should not *ever* take into account any of the pseudonyms, nor the writing strategies part and parcel to them (something, in fact, that would go counter to all that Kierkegaard has "himself" requested), or else we must bear in mind that when a text changes its signature it no longer adds up to quite the same thing. But then maybe it doesn't "add up" at all. What must be taken into account is not so much that this or that signature has been crossed out, that one or another text has been displaced, but rather, and above all, the constant possibility of such disconnections. It would have been possible never to have known the "initial" destination of this preface. Besides, "Kierkegaard" never made a practice of concealing his strategies—on the contrary—and if he drew attention to his scratch-outs, his ruses, his scenarios, it was also as a way of indicating how not to read. Playing around with the signatures, for example, would have demonstrated how each signature has to be read along with what it is signing, as part of its text. Kierkegaard even took the trouble to explain himself somewhat in this regard by saying that each text, each implementation of an "idea," was to produce, each time, a particular author, a particular individuality. It is as though each work required, implied a particular author. Obviously, it is not a matter of anonymity: Kierkegaard, as the person holding the pen, was always willing to accept "civil responsibility" for his works. It is only a matter of recognizing a certain autonomy of the text, of its peculiar mode of functioning and communicating. Pseudonymity thus brings to light a certain arbitrary aspect of the signature (in relation to what one ordinarily considers it possible to connect the signature with: the actual identity of the person supposed to be holding the pen . . .): pseudonymity already *"represents"* the author in the text.

The signature depends on the text. Which is another way of saying that it might be less "arbitrary." The choice of a pseudonym will depend on the status of the (always fictional) author implied by the text. Thus, in the second preface to *The Concept of Anxiety,* signed Vigilius Haufniensis (the watchman of Copenhagen), the author points out that his signature is (merely) the result of a choice. He is capable of changing it; what is essential here is only that this signature in some way express the individuality the author would like to *pass himself off as.* "If to a noble envy or jealous criticism it seems too much that I bear a Latin name, I shall gladly assume the name Christen Madsen. Nothing could please me more than to *be regarded* as a layman . . ." (*The Concept of Anxiety,* 8. Emphasis added. Christen Madsen is a name like Jones or Smith; in other words, a name that is significant, or insignificant, for its very banality).

Should we recall in this context that Kierkegaard only signs with his own name those works that are properly speaking religious: edifying discourses, etc.? He signs when he is no longer writing, when he is no longer a writer or a poet, but exclusively religious. The poetic works will have never been anything but a necessary deception ("Well, obviously the poetical had to be evacuated . . ."), but at the same time foreign ("in becoming a poet,

I did not recognize myself in a deeper sense"—"I felt myself foreign to the whole poetical production . . ."). Considered retrospectively, in *The Point of View,* the poetic works are of an interim nature: "But the whole aesthetic production was put under arrest by the religious"—"One will perceive the significance of the pseudonyms and why I must be pseudonymous in relation to all aesthetic production, because I led my own life in entirely different categories and understood from the beginning that this productivity was of an interim nature, a deceit, a necessary process of elimination" (*The Point of View,* 84–86). But Kierkegaard did not publish this point of view, though he did consider publishing it . . . under a pseudonym. Nonetheless, we have to take *that* signature into account, Kierkegaard's signature, and the particular function it seems to have (were this only, perhaps, in order to designate what is owed to the father). That the author wanted to distinguish his pseudonymous production from the others cannot be dismissed, neither by making the proper name into one name among others, nor by simply subordinating the pseudonyms to a proper name that would stand up and in for them. At this point, it becomes necessary to understand the signatures in their respective roles, and to appreciate each of them, including the proper name, from the perspective of this role.

There is no reason, then, to say that "Kierkegaard" accepts "responsibility for" what is said "in the first person" in this seventh preface. And when the text refers to the "present work," it is not legitimate to note, as do the [French] translators: "In other words, *The Concept of Anxiety.*" The *here* and *now* of the text are those of Notabene's book—"the present work that will now be published . . ."—The aim which the "present work" assigns itself can be none other than that of *Prefaces,* or else that of the imaginary work that is missing from the prefaces.

Now this aim, according to the author, consists in "understanding why he wants to be an author." It is still up to the reader to determine, if he can, what author is at issue here, up to him, too, to reconcile the announcement of this aim with another, the one in the last paragraph: "I couldn't care less about being an author . . . ," and to discover a willful contradiction between them, or an unconscious denegation. For the author, who claims not to be a simple compiler-middle man, refuses to acquire "the *honor* of being a writer" cheaply; I emphasize the word "honor" and note that it is less important to write this or that (a book, or a preface) than to be a "writer"; an ambiguous honor, moreover, since elsewhere it is necessary to deny it.

8. The last text announces the editing of a philosophical review. Here we are treated to a strange scene of jealousy between the author and Hegel. Rejected as a suitor of philosophy, the author demands an explanation.

The rough draft of this preface reveals that the signature of Kierkegaard was originally supposed to figure in the text: "I am not Prof. Heiberg; in fact, I am even less than 'not Prof. Heiberg.' For I am only Mag. Kierkegaard" (219). But the final version reads: "For I am only N. N."

N. N., then, claims to found a philosophical review, an enterprise in which Heiberg had failed: *Perseus* had disappeared after only two issues. But this author's goal will be different: he does not want to communicate any knowledge to the reader—on the contrary—he wants to serve philosophy by the public admission of his own stupidity. In fact, he will admit that he *understands nothing about philosophy*, in other words, about Hegel. Such an attitude should actually be alluring for philosophy: in the face of this kind of provocation, philosophy, a distant goddess, should uncover herself more fully and make herself at last accessible . . . "A faithful lover can also have the idea of *alluring* his beloved . . . I love philosophy: I have loved her from my earliest years . . . If I try to allure her, it will only be through pleading and supplication. I don't belong to those powers that live on intimate terms with philosophy and that frequent her on an equal footing . . . For philosophy claims to be popular and makes herself accessible to everybody" (222–23, 226).

This is indeed a provocation, since stupidity will say to intelligence: you're *too* smart to understand me.

The scene takes place between a sexually indeterminate divinity ("I do not know whether I should think of philosophy in the guise of a man or woman" [234]) whose sole manifestation would be that of an invisible interior voice, and an unhappy and spurned lover.

The voice (of Hegel): "I am only for the chosen ones, those who, from the cradle on, were marked with my seal; and in order for them to belong to me, they need time, zeal, and the opportunity, a fervent love, generosity enough to risk unrequited love

... The one in whom I find all that, I repay with the Idea's kiss; for him I will make the Concept's embrace fruitful ... I cannot appear to you, I cannot be loved by you ..." (235).

The fervent admirer of the System has nothing left to do but withdraw, though not without retaining some hope: "If only we had an authentically Danish System, a one-hundred-percent-national product, and if only I were part of it" (237).

These simulacra-prefaces, by wanting to do without books, contest a certain order, a certain hierarchy, though they continue to refer to them incessantly. By means of such scenes of parody—or as their author calls them, such "entertaining" scenes—they seem to represent the critical moment of a revolt and emancipation. *Scenes:* and in more than one sense—household scenes between husband and wife, preface and book, author and critic, literature and philosophy—a *mise en scène,* too, a staging of the author by the author. The book has not disappeared, though. It becomes a pure pretext for prefacing; but it *remains* too, insofar as the prefaces themselves become a book.

Along with the preface—which has always been the place for the author's discourse about himself—it is also the author as such (as writing instance) who revolts, who refuses to let himself be excluded from the work, who displays himself, and who insists on marking his place in the text. According to a classical division, it is only in the preface that the author can discuss himself inasmuch as author (*qua Forfatter*), that he can manifest himself as "*the author,*" speaking of him in the third person, designating himself not only as the author of this particular work, but also in an absolute sense, as "author." Only here does he speak from the standpoint—indeed from the trade—of author, playing with his "authorship" and his own authority, holding this authority at a distance in order better to derive enjoyment from it, as though there were two of him. The preface is a scene in which the author can play *the role of the author, display himself as an author,* inviting the reader to come into the wings, letting himself be seen in a dressing gown, sitting at his desk, and seeming to demystify his work—even if, by exhibiting all the strings, he is actually showing them off. (The author's vanity easily finds refuge in the vanity of his prefaces. But whoever aims at emancipating himself from the constraints of "content" no longer considers vanity a vice.)

The author, like the preface, refuses to efface himself before the book. Notabene, as if in order to taunt Hegel, seems wantonly to fall into chitchat, anecdote, and minutia.

All of these more or less entertaining *mises en scènes,* however, are not what makes an exceptional "book" out of *Prefaces:* Kierkegaard and his pseudonyms do that elsewhere. Here, the strategy consists in blurring the distinction between the work and its preface, in exploding the principle of an opposition that would guarantee the preface *at one and the same time* a fundamental and privileged position (the moment of reappropriation and mastery) and an always secondary position of submission or of necessary articulation to the body of the book, without which it would lose its reason for being. But the preface is not the only "genre," the only type of text to suffer from discrimination and see itself relegated to the superfluous margins of the book of philosophy. The preface is but one possible site for all that philosophy would have liked to neutralize, expel, limit, sublate: the particular, the idiomatic, the dialectal, etc.—to retain Notabene's terms. In this sense, the emancipation of the preface is inscribed in a more general strategy that aims at contesting and subverting a certain philosophical order. Less in order simply to revalorize a regional genre (peripheral, eccentric) than to transform or blur the map of genres. For example, the emancipated preface will no longer be a preface properly speaking, "since in this case it would itself become a work, suppressing by the same token the question of the preface and the book" (*Vorworte,* 175).

Prefaces could even be considered a parody of subversive writing in comparison with the likes of *The Point of View for My Work as an Author* and the *Concluding Unscientific Postscript to the Philosophical Fragments,* in which the inside and the outside of the book and the work are confused in an even more sly and effective way.

If, for example, we were to call "preface" a redundant and superfluous form of writing, always capable of showing up all alone, of starting up all over again, of putting itself into question, of illustrating itself, spilling out over itself and over the book, all the books of K. and his pseudonyms could be considered *prefaces.*

But then a good many other "genres" that remain on the internal or external edge of the book (parasitical, parallel, para-literary, as well as para-philosophical) would constitute the body of this work; from the prolegomena or paralipomena, to the postscripts, to the notes and pieces, to the diapsalmata, to the actual or fictional journal, to the letters, to the fragments, to the remarks, and to all those para-discourses delivered by book binders, editors, and discoverers of manuscripts who thus pile up several layers of prefaces and forewords.

(End of note.)

*
* *

However, he actually seems to have wanted not to write.

He loved writing too much, he derived too much enjoyment from it, not to consider it a sin incompatible with the Christian requirement of martyrdom. His pleasure was also to be his torture—because it was pleasure. To be a writer—no, that will not have been his desire, his betrayal, his *forfait,* his crime, his vice. They were wrong about him. He will not be the one to have worn the amiable title of writer, which they like to bestow—the height of lunacy!—on Socrates himself (a Christian before the fact, as we now know): "Alas! And we who are tainted by that awful disease whose height is to be an author, we are tempted to read him [Socrates] as though he were an author, and a clever one at that . . . whereas for him the stakes are life and death." And then he adds: "My life offers an analogy on a reduced scale. For my personal existence is worth much more and costs me far more than my writings . . ."

*
* *

The writer—the *Forfatter*—is not only guilty of deriving pleasure in (and from) his solitude, he is dangerous, too. Like all technicians of language, he can turn out to be an illusionist. Illusion, that evil "worse than the plague," is to believe that you can have the Idea at your disposal "cheaply" by having at your disposal only language, the medium in which ideality can become manifest. But Truth is paid for by suffering, it is never free, as Christianity teaches us. Whereas, thanks to language, participation in the sublime "does not cost much."

The danger, the age-old danger, is not just the possibility of error or of falsity, it is not just the constant possibility of a discourse inadequate to its subject, it is also the possibility of a speaking that is empty or deceptive due to the disappearance or travesty of the speaking subject. This distance of the subject from his discourse is a function of "ventriloquism." The poet is a ventriloquist insofar as he enters into an indirect discourse, insofar as he entertains a poetic relationship with his work. But he who gives himself out for a poet does not "really" deceive, since he practices an avowed ventriloquism that gives itself out for the illusion that it is. On the contrary, poetry deceives when it conceals itself: dissimulated under the cloak of the priest, the poet will be "hypocrisy raised to the second power." So it is with speech; it is always possible not to know who is speaking nor where that speech is coming from. Language is merely an "abstraction," I can always use it without occupying it, without inhabiting it in a singular manner. Ventriloquism implies a speaking with no subject, with no *I*, with no name. To the first power, it can be simply pseudonymous and poetical; it then relates to a fictitious subject. Raised to the second power, it no longer relates to any subject, to any singularity; it becomes anonymous.

Pseudonymity—this at least is one of the explanations he will give—is the means for K. to accustom the reader, in an age when "no one dares to say 'I,'" to a subjective mode of discourse, to prepare him to hear the full and singular speech of the Christian.

Where does the voice have to come from, what does it have to come out of, in order not to seem to come already from somewhere else? Always from the body. Ventriloquism is speech without body, or without the body from which it seems to emanate, a speech that does not bring into question or into play the body that is speaking, that does not bring its body along with it, that can always disconnect itself from the body. (The texts that call language to task most violently recall those of Antonin Artaud raging against writing and articulated language.) You have to engage the body, but in order to lose it better: it is not enough to open your mouth to avoid the charge of ventriloquism and to provide the words with body. The voice, therefore, does not offer any guarantees in relation to writing. Though it does remain the model—K. asks that his reader always read out loud, probably in order to restore to the sentences their rhythm, but also their "life." Here, he is not afraid to demand of his reader a ventriloquism which he prohibits elsewhere.

If language is "an abstraction," though, how should we put this—is I even possible? How would it be possible for the I not to disconnect itself if it is itself a sign that, as such, brings whoever uses it into the universal? This is perhaps why the most proper, the most singular, the most living speaking, the speaking that would be neither prompted nor stolen, will never be as "proper" as silence. To speak is already to enter into the general. Only silence, action, and death isolate, separate; action itself being the risk of death. Speaking and writing appear at this point as substitutions for the act, for life, and for death. By representing it, they economize on the act, first and foremost on the only act through which the Individual gives himself up unreservedly, death. The critique of a certain bad use of language is always the critique of an economy. Everything that can represent, can be worth or *stand for,* can also be the basis of an advantageous exchange. Every economy is dishonest.

As always, there is not simply a condemnation of speaking and of language, but an extreme ambivalence. For language can and must coincide with thought, embody it, according to a metaphysical necessity. Being, thought, and language are but one, as Hegel had demonstrated: "Whereas the philosophy of the recent past had almost exemplified the idea that language exists to conceal thought (since thought simply cannot express *das Ding an sich* at all), Hegel in any case deserves credit for showing that language has thought immanent in itself and that thought is developed in language. The other thinking was a constant fumbling in the matter" (*Journal,* 2:214).

But on the other hand, just like "that other thinking," Kierkegaard himself never stops considering language as clothing, travesty, or mask that must be removed in order to reach truth, in other words, nakedness: "The police perform body searches on suspects—should the same sort of search be required of those hordes of rhetors, teachers and professors . . . there would result a criminal affair of considerable proportions. Search them right down to the body and order them to remain silent in these terms: 'Hold your tongue! And then let's see what your life will have to say for itself. Let your life do the talking for once, and tell us who you are!' "

The writer is ultimately guilty of naivete and vanity. The naivete resides first of all in an excessive interest in "the world" and its "people"—with whom the writer tries to communicate beyond his solitude. All communication implies an entry into generality:

concessions and mediations are necessary for whoever wants to make himself understood. But above and beyond the world and the ethical sphere in which the tragic hero still moves, there is the religious order that involves the Individual in a much more peculiar solitude, from which all communication is prohibited: "Abraham cannot be mediated; in other words, he cannot speak" (*Fear and Trembling*, 60). Without reaching the incomprehensible faith of Abraham, the humorist and the poet, such as Johannes de Silentio or Hamann, still make it as far as that strange and paradoxical situation that consists in appealing to the incommensurable, the inexpressible, and in denouncing writing *without giving it up*. This sort of "leftist" philosophical attitude that is constituted by a mysticism armed with humor and lofty irony will not be able to pass up the opportunity to discourse at length on the ridiculousness of speaking, and even more so, of writing. Each of them appeals to Christ or Socrates, thinks he can laugh at Hegel and scorn the naive vanity of a philosophy that claims to understand everything and say everything. "Christ did not go in for writing—he wrote only in the sand" (*Journal*, 1:124). Undoubtedly an allusion to the Gospel passage in which Jesus is presented an adultress by the Pharisees—"But Jesus only bent down and started writing on the ground with his finger." Pseudonymity, moreover, is perhaps itself a ruse intended to neutralize the "ridiculousness" that, for the ironist, is connected with writing, "simply because not-to-write is part of the nature of the concept, since this would betray an all-too-conciliatory position toward the world (which is why Hamann remarks somewhere that fundamentally there is nothing more ludicrous than to write for the people). Just as Socrates left no books . . ." (*Journal*, 2:258).

Finally, the ultimate sin, the ultimate denegation: it is impossible for the poet to produce or create anything *by himself*. For God alone produces and he alone is poet—consequently, Kierkegaard will never write anything but the religious works in his own name, which is also to say in the name of the father. Only then does he have the right to write: but it is no longer a question of poetic production, it is no longer a question of writing, he is no longer the one who is writing—unless it is "with guided pen"—he *witnesses* (wouldn't the word of the Christian, then, which is the word in its fulness, ever be the word proper? The poet will thus give up one form of ventriloquism for another).

The poet will always be guilty of competing with the poetic and feminine production of God, who allows his "production" to come forth in a kind of sovereign indifference: "My thought is that God is like a poet. This is why he puts up with evil and all the nonsense and wretchedness and mediocrity of triviality, etc. The poet is related in the same way to his poetic production (also called his creation), he allows it to come forth" (*Journal*, 2:147).

Having always been forbidden to conceive, he won't have been able to be either father or mother.

*
* *

He seems to have written a lot, though—but under which names and in whose name? With the question of the names, the question of the father always returns. Apparently, only the so-called "religious" work was written in his name. But we could also say that all the work is religious in the same way the erection of a slab or the construction of a monument is religious. They are always intended as a kind of witnessing. "And Jacob took a stone, and set it up for a pillar.

"And Laban said to Jacob, Behold this heap, and behold this pillar, which I have cast betwixt me and thee. This heap be witness, and this pillar be witness . . ." (Genesis, 31: 45, 51–52).

If all religion and all suffering begin with the rigor of a Law or a pact, then the most painful, most insurmountable conflict will result from a plurality of alliances.

If each pact requires its own form of blood or stone, then doesn't the plurality of works and signatures attest to the plurality of alliances and ruses set up to overcome their incompatibility?

One of the works, the one he calls his "work as an author," is supposed to attest to his posthumous marriage with the lost fiancée. Like a funeral inscription, it is written in her honor:

"My Literary work is to be regarded as a monument to her honor and praise" (*Journal*, 6:203). The literary monument he intended for her is supposed to celebrate her name: "Her name will belong to my authorship and be remembered as long as I am remembered" (*Journal*, 6:55). His name, but which one? The interminable epitaph he wanted to dedicate to her did not bear his *own* name, his father's (and perhaps his mother's). It is as though he, too, like the young man in *Repetition*, had wanted to get rid of his name: "A name, my name—after all it actually belongs to her. Would that I could get rid of it . . . My own name is enough to remind me of everything . . ." (*Repetition*, 194).

The other work, the religious one, refuses to be literary, and it is dedicated, often explicitly, to the father. It seems to attest to another pact, according to which Søren is destined for sacrifice and suffering, through which he is dispossessed in advance. How did the father impose this pact on the son? How can this sacrifice be reconciled with "the author's calling," how can the religious impregnation that engenders only tears be reconciled with paternity? The pseudonymous and "poetic" work was able to allow for a compromise: a monument in honor of the girl, it brought forth natural sons, out of wedlock but not without enjoyment, sons that the (grand)father was able not to recognize.

But what does his name recall to Søren Kierkegaard, and what can he be wanting to get rid of by ridding himself of his name, unless it is precisely the father who, among other things, leaves it to him as his inheritance?

For the impossibility of marriage is explained only by another engagement. It isn't the rupture of R. that engendered K.'s "melancholy" and that made him ask the question, "Guilty—Not Guilty?" It is because this question was already being asked, because K. had been born "melancholic," that he could not become "a husband." He had neither engendered nor chosen his melancholy and guilt through any fault of his own: he had "inherited" them. That, at least, is clear, and that alone is tragic. He was born already old—"I was not born like other children but was born already old" (*Journal*, 5:233)—already guilty. Regine had to be abandoned, since she could not enter into the darkness the father had brought down on his son, could not share with the son the secret that bound him to his father. Commenting on the impossibility of his union with her, he writes: "I would have had to initiate her into terrible things, my relationship with my father, his melancholy, the eternal night brooding within me, my going astray, my lusts and debauchery . . ." (*Journal*, 5:234).

His misfortune is truly tragic only by having its origin before birth, before consciousness, and by inscribing itself on the body and in the face of the child who will look for its traces in the mirror.

"It would be a terrible thing for a man's consciousness to have suffered a shock at the earliest age against which all of the soul's elasticity, all of freedom's efforts, remain powerless. Life's trials can certainly be oppressive, but since they occur at a later date they lack the time necessary to assume this *almost congenital* form, and eventually become simply historical factors. They cannot compare with an element which would be situated *as though beyond consciousness itself.* Someone who has had such a shock at his earliest age is like a child who has been delivered with forceps and who always retains a reminiscence of the labor pains" (*Journal*).

Such "reminiscences," whose origins are lost in childhood, or more likely in the moment of birth, seem to have their roots in the child's unconscious—indeed *even further back,* on the nether side of the child's very history, in the history of those from whom he issues. These *marks* are no less decisive for their having been cut off from their source; they are what prompt K. to a knowledge of his fate: "There are two ideas that have been part of me for so long that to tell the truth I cannot uncover their origin. The first is that there are men whose fate it is to be sacrificed, in this or that manner, for others and for the accomplishment of the Idea—and my own cross has been to be one of these. The second idea is that I would never have to undergo the ordeal of having to work to earn my living . . ." The origin of the first of these ideas, though, might not seem so very obscure. On the one hand, it could well have resulted from the image of Christianity K. received from his father (we know that it was the image of the crucifixion, and that it left a powerful impression on the child). On the other hand, it could have come from the father's certainty that he would be punished through his children for some mysterious fault, and in this way be able to reenter into God's grace. The father's despair and melancholy are sufficiently established to allow us to bring them into relation with the "congenital" character of the "most frightful" grief (K. speaks about *his father's* melancholy, and not about his own, in order to explain his rupture with R.). But it is because he was ignorant of the origin of this despair and the nature of the debt afflicting the father that the son inherited them. And it is still going too far to claim that the son received the sin as an inheritance, because he never knew its nature for certain. Anxiety is not born in knowledge, but in suspicion. And the father himself could have been tormented to such a degree only because he at least wondered about the gravity of his sins.

What seems clear is the inheritance: something was transmitted, or rather reproduced. The son seems to imitate the father—but it is as though the father himself incited, required this imitation. The son seems to be the *reflection* (of the despair) of the father:

"There was once a father and a son. A son is like a mirror in which the father beholds himself, and for the son too the father is like a mirror in which he beholds himself in the time to come . . . It sometimes happened, though, that the father came to a stop, stood before the son with a sorrowful countenance, looked at him steadily and said: 'Poor child, thou art going into a quiet despair.' Nothing was ever said to indicate how this was to be understood and to what extent it was true" (*Guilty?/Not Guilty?* 192).

The father recognizes the image of his own misfortune in his son and says: "Poor child . . ." But if the father is in his turn a mirror for the son, then the son must have looked at his father with the same compassion.

With the help of rare and scattered fragments, it is necessary to reconstruct here the "tragedy" of childhood. At the outset, there is the "patriarchal idyll"—the son loves a father who seems all-powerful to him ("nothing was impossible for the father"—"as though he were God . . .")—up to the time when the suspicion sets in. "I could perhaps reproduce in a novel called 'The Mysterious Family' the tragedy of my childhood . . . At the outset it should be thoroughly patriarchal and idyllic, so that no one would have any inkling before the words suddenly appeared and gave a terrifying explanation of everything" (*Journal*, 5:243).

With the suspicion will set in tragedy, sin, contradiction: for the father is desperate; therefore, he is guilty. The son discovers his own suffering, the worst of which, perhaps, is this one: "If there is any such thing as sympathetic pain, it is that of having to be ashamed of one's father, of him whom one loves above all and to whom one is most indebted, to have to approach him backwards, with averted face, in order not to behold his dishonor" (*Guilty?/Not Guilty?* 236).

We know what price the son had to pay for having discovered or glimpsed his father's secret (not the secret itself, but the existence of a secret, an enigma). He won't be able to preserve the father except by averting his face from the secret, by blinding himself, by remaining silent (like Periander's son), by never revealing, never "penetrating" this secret—"It is filial piety that teaches me not even to wish to penetrate the hidden, but rather to remain hidden in the father" (*Stages on Life's Way*, 58).

As the frightened guardian of the secret, the son discovers his guilt. He does not have to know the reason; it has something to do "with the family." More than just an heir to the sin that must have been committed, he is its fruit. And so from now on, he will be asking questions about himself.

"For something to become really depressing, there must be first of all, in the midst of all possible favors, a presentiment that it might just be all wrong; one does not become conscious of anything very wrong in himself, but it may have something to do with the family; then original sin displays its consuming power, which can grow [or "lead us"] into despair and have a far more frightful effect than the particular whereby the truth of the presentiment is verified. This is why Hamlet is so tragic. This is why *Robert le diable* [first duke of Burgundy], driven by a disquieting presentiment,* asks how it could ever be that he does so much evil" (*Journal*, 4:104). *Here, there is a note: "When Høgne, whom his mother had conceived by a troll, sees his reflection in the water, he asks her why his body is shaped that way."

This fragment is itself linked to a page in the *Journal* which we will soon enough have to read, and in which K. relates how he, too, had one day run to look at himself in the mirror.

It must have had something to do *with the family*, then. But with what in the family history? All the evidence points to the father. But what fault could account for the father's anguish and despair? Nothing allows us to know for sure. Is it that blasphemy, long since become legendary, which Michael Pedersen committed at twelve years of age, and which K. himself relates in his *Journal*? In a gesture worthy of Job, the father rebels against God and demands an explanation for his misfortune. Does this explain why he lived from then on in fear of punishment? To his great surprise, he was not struck down through his wealth. On the contrary, he was to know exceptional prosperity and escaped as though by miracle the crash of 1813, having put his fortune in government bonds. Søren was born that very year. Michael Pedersen then thought that he would be struck down through his children, and subsequent events seemed to confirm him in this thought: five of them were to die before their father. Only Søren and Peter Christian were to survive. A first child died at twelve years of age (the father's age at the time of the blasphemy), when Søren was six. The father's anxiety redoubled. He brought up his last son, Søren (the one with whom he had a special relationship), in the fear of God, making him the confidant of his anxiety and placing in him the little hope he could still have for salvation. Impressed early on by the image of the crucifixion—something to which several texts testify—Søren adopted it as his model. He was convinced that suffering and martyrdom were to be his destiny.

So convinced of it was he that, whatever enjoyment he was to derive from his "literary production"—an enjoyment he was often enough to recognize—in the end he wanted to interpret this whole production from a religious point of view, as a cleverly orchestrated quest for persecution.

"And he that blasphemeth the name of the Lord, he shall surely be put to death" (Leviticus, 24:16). Whatever other sins he had committed, the father knew that blasphemy was punishable by death. Just as he knew that death was also the effacement of the name along with its posterity. "And Saul said to David: Swear now therefore unto me by the Lord, that thou wilt not cut off my seed after me, and that thou wilt not destroy my name out of my father's house" (Samuel, 24:21).

Regarding the family name, let's ask one simple question here: if the punishment that strikes the children is also one through which the family name disappears, doesn't the child who abandons his father's name for another, or several others, himself strike his father, doesn't he himself inflict the punishment, doesn't he accomplish the Law? The multiplication of names would thus entail (and therein lies its ruse) not only the multiplication of descendants, as though in this way to restore to the father his lost children, but at the same time the loss for the father of sons who do not have to recall, resemble, or owe him in any way: sons which—as in the case of illegitimate children—he does not have to be able to recognize. Pure products of the Idea that impregnated their father, they will be called Johannes, Hilarius, Constantine, Vigilius, William or Nicolas, Climacus or Anti-Climacus, Frater Taciturnus, Afham, Notabene or Silentio . . .

However, it is doubtful that the blasphemy would of itself justify the certainty which the father had of his punishment. Moreover, this offense was known to the son, it was not an *enigma*. It does not account for the constant reference to the suspicion and presentiment, and even less for the allusions to the absolute secret in which the "explanation" remained shrouded.

Now if suspicion is always cast back on the father, it is rather the mother (the one to whom nothing calls our attention) who seems enveloped by the secret.

He never named his mother nor made allusion to her. Not even in the *Journal*, not even the day of her death.

Should this absolute silence not be insignificant, then it might enclose the secret which Kierkegaard was certain of having never betrayed, it might reveal an unconscious strategy. In order "not to penetrate what is hidden," in order *not to see* (the father's shame), in order neither to uncover nor to betray the (father's) secret, did the son have to turn away *from the mother?*

We know about his jealous hatred of mothers and his disgust of procreation, for sensuality as well as for sexuality: "Procreation is the fall."—"Our very existence through reproduction was a crime." But the mother cannot be ignored or rejected on the basis of this particular crime, and in any case it seems to lead us away from the suspicion and the terrible presentiment. Unless this mother were in some way linked to the father's sin, or the son were to have had at least some inkling of this. But what could be the nature of this link?

Maria Sørensdatter Lund was employed in the household of M. P. Kierkegaard at the time of his first marriage. She married M. P. (less than a year after the death of the first wife) on the 26th of April, 1797, and their first child was born on the 7th of September, less than five months later.

M. P. seems to have considered this second marriage a betrayal with respect to his first wife and to have been tormented enough by it to confide in his confessor, Mynster: "Oh dear, I have been thinking so much today of my dear wife . . . I have thought about her so long . . . Here are two hundred rigsdaler; will you please give them to the poor?" (Brandes, 266) By themselves, these facts would not warrant the father's anguish, nor the son's terror and the "earthquake" that shook him to the point of driving him to "a new infallible principle for interpreting all the phenomena." They cannot account for the suspicion that "a guilt must rest upon the entire family, a punishment of God must be upon it" (*Journal*, 5:141).

It is striking how the question of father-son relationships returns several times in *Guilty?/Not Guilty?* On the date of May 5th, K.'s birthday, Frater Taciturnus tells a curious story. It is the one about Periander, that wise and equitable tyrant who beneath his leniency concealed "the fire of passion." This easygoing and kind personage turns into "a monster," in other words, he reveals a monstrous duplicity: "two men, who could not be contained in the one man" (*Guilty?/Not Guilty?* 299). Various attempts were made to understand Periander's madness, yet it could only be a question of some terrible crime he had committed, "before he had yet heard his own fine saying 'Do not that which you have to keep secret.' " Sometimes it is related how "he lived in criminal relations with his mother," at other times, how he had "killed his beloved wife Lyside with a kick." "This," adds K., "we cannot decide. Every one of these occurrences by itself would be sufficient" (301). At any rate, Periander grows more and more desperate: "the more he was lost, the less he was repentant." Now Periander had two sons, and one day as they are returning to their father's house, their grandfather says to them: "Do you know, children, who it is that killed your mother?" It was just a question, but it completely changed one of the sons: "Upon Kypselos this saying made no impression, but Lykophron became silent."

The depiction of this family, including the reactions of the sons to the enigmatic words of the grandfather, the indifference of the one and the revolt of the other, so overcome by suspicion and even hatred that he will say to his father: "Thou thyself art deserving of death" (302), cannot help reminding us of K.'s "enigmatic family." The explanation of *the kick* might even recall the death of the first wife and the torment which seems to have been caused in the father by this death. What should attract our attention here, though, are less the facts themselves than the *Stemning*, the familial atmosphere, and what is after all the violent and sexual nature of the crimes attributed to the father. Why does

Taciturnus tell this story in the middle of a *Journal* about his "rupture"?

Recalling that at the time of his rupture with Regine, K. made reference in his own *Journal* to the impossibility of his ever being able to initiate his fiancée into "terrible things, my relationship to my father, his melancholy, the eternal night brooding within me" (*Journal*, 5:234)—we might suppose that the various fictions concerning a father and his son, a secret that silently links them together, etc., express K.'s own presentiments in a more or less displaced, more or less conscious manner.

Lycophon, Hamlet, *Robert le diable:* so many figures in which K. seems to be looking for the image of his own destiny. Each one of the stories of these somber heroes could be called: *suspicion*, or: *the birth of tragedy*. "It may have something to do with the family," said K. on that page of the *Journal* referred to earlier. According to the editors of the *Journal*, this page is supposed to be the "loose sheet of paper alluded to by K. elsewhere, when he wrote: "A certain presentiment seems to precede everything which is to happen (cf. a loose sheet)" (*Journal*, 1:38). Now in the margins of this fragment on the presentiment and its unfortunate effects, Kierkegaard makes note of a strange impression, an impression whose "frightful" character can be explained only by the memory with which it is immediately associated: a reflection by the father on sin, to which the son long ago reacted by running to look at himself in the mirror: "I was appalled the first time I heard that *letters of indulgence* stated that they absolved from *all* sins: 'etiam si matrem virginem violasset.'—I still remember how I felt when a few years ago, in my youthful, romantic enthusiasm for a *master-thief*, I said he was merely misusing his talents, that such a man could no doubt change, and my father very earnestly said: 'There are crimes that can be fought only with the constant help of God.' I hurried to my room and looked at myself in the mirror" (*Journal*, 5:92).

Etiam si matrem virginem violasset—even if he had violated the virgin mother—or, even if he had violated the mother at a time when she was still a virgin. Even that, even that particular sin could be atoned for. No doubt, it is not the atonement that could have caused the *frightful impression*. But then what? The revelation of the possibility of such a sin? But why is this impression immediately linked with another, an impression caused by the father's words? In order to explain the "frightful impression," isn't it necessary for the Latin sentence to have suddenly echoed, as is shown by what follows, the presentiment which the father had caused in the son? Isn't it necessary for there to have been a moment in which the frightful suspicion suddenly received a content: would it have been possible for the father to violate "the virgin mother" . . .? Would he have been able to violate his *own* mother (like Periander, who entered into sinful relations with his mother), or even Søren's mother—who was mother to all the children in the family—while she was still a virgin? The circumstances of the father's second marriage make the hypothesis at least plausible. (Johannes Hohlenberg [*Søren Kierkegaard*, 50–64] seems to have been the only one to have formulated such a hypothesis. His analysis, though, remains quite different from the one being attempted here.) This sin, rape, which made the mother first into a victim and then into an accomplice of the crime, *could have been* the one that weighed on "the whole family." And if the son is the reflection of the father and the heir to his offense, he would have had to see in his mirror not only the fruit of the crime, not only the image of Hamlet, of Høgne or of *Robert le diable*, but also—something that would reinforce his terror— that of Oedipus. The ambiguity of the Latin phrase—to violate the virgin mother—is more or less capable of expressing simultaneously the unspeakable desire of a son (but which one?) and the unspeakable crime of his father.

The Latin sentence, then, was enough to frighten the son. What's more, it allowed him to glimpse an overwhelming secret, it was enough to make him back up, prefer his ignorance, fall silent like Lykophron or like the confidant of *Robert le diable's* secret, who had the good fortune to be a mute: "It is an extremely poetic governance which makes the girl dumb, she who alone can comprehend what is behind *Robert le diable's* assumed madness (his penance)" (*Journal*, 4:104).

The scene of rape, of course, does not have to have been real; the proof that it was real could never be produced, and it wouldn't add anything new anyway. All that matters is the reality of the suspicion, of the doubt regarding a secret which the son both wants and does not want to penetrate—such as it is described in a little "fiction" jotted down in '44: "A father-son relationship in which the son secretly discovers everything at the bottom of it all and yet does not *dare to know it (og dog ikke tør vide det)*. The father is an important man, devout and strong; only once in a drunken condition did he let fall some words that intimated the worst. The son does not find out any more and does not dare ask the father or any other man" (*Journal*, 5:252. Emphasis added.).

He does not dare ask his father or anyone else. Is there someone else he could have asked? At any rate, the father's secret is discovered without being exposed, not only because the son lacks the means to *know*, but also because he does not dare to know. The scene of the crime had to remain something of a blank; the son had to admit it, but as a blank or a lacuna. This lacuna was not even the product of the son's own repression. One might say that it wasn't part of his "own" unconscious, of his "own" instinctual life, but that it was first of all and already dependent on the secret, indeed, on the unconscious of *another*. For it was also possible that the father was accusing himself of a desire, and not of an "actual" offense. Understood in this way, the son's legacy becomes such that he would never be successful in appropriating it. Let's say that he could neither "digest" it nor "swallow" it. Would such a legacy be liable to provoke what Nicolas Abraham and Maria Torok call "phantomatic haunting"? The image of the *phantom* suggested itself to them as a way of designating a certain "torment" felt by both analyst and analysand. Such is the case with the patient who seems to have received some secret or lacuna from a parent that is then inscribed on an unconscious incapable of doing anything with it. Such an inscription will all the more readily take on the proportions of fate in that it has nothing to do with those who receive it: "The buried speech of a parent becomes a graveless death for the child. This unknown phantom comes back from the unconscious to haunt the child and leads to phobias, madness, and obsessions. Its effects can persist through several generations and determine the fate of an entire family line" ("The Lost Object—Me," 17). Is this concept-image capable of providing us with a more illuminating psychoanalytic understanding of the Kierkegaardian legacy—of the link that so curiously unites the son's "melancholoy" with that of the father—than has previously been available? We'll have to try it out.

But first, let's put the pieces of the puzzle together once more. What will they enable us to reconstruct? Perhaps the name Søren Kierkegaard, or what is involved in the legacy of such a name, a name which he also wanted to forget. What Kierkegaard wanted at one and the same time to hide and reveal by this name, left to us along with several others. Perhaps a secret—or the secret—which this name seals and names without saying anything about it.

How many deaths are there under this name that also means "cemetery"? At least three. The monumental work written around this name could serve in some way as a family vault. A kind of crypt.

But, and the reader should be forewarned of this, the entire construction has to remain impenetrable, hermetic. No one must have the key to it. It must not reveal anything about the secret around which it has been built—"After my death no one will find in my papers the slightest information (this is my consolation) about what really has filled my life; no one will find the text in my innermost being that explains everything" (*Journal*, 5:226). "The text that explains everything": would we be unable to find it because it was not written, because it was destroyed, because K. himself would not have been able to write it, or because he would have written nothing else, and because the totality of the texts is that text—which explains everything—which is explained all by itself: would we be unable to find it because of its own holes or omissions?

Picking up the pieces of the puzzle again, then, we should also take into account the ones that are missing, the holes. Some of them are considerable, so enormous that they ought to catch our eye (*ils devraient crever les yeux*).[46] First of all, there is the gaping hole of silence that surrounds the mother. Not a thing about her, not a word. There is no place for her in the text. Then there is the silence, this time avowed, that covers up the "concrete explanation" of what has taken up his whole life. Finally, there is the uncertainty, the indetermination he is stuck with in regard to the suspicion, the enigma represented by the father. What if all these blanks referred back to each other? Suppose what the son was

---

46. *TN*. "To catch our eye," or "to grab our attention," but there are also resonances here of the eyeless blanks left by self-inflicted blindness. *"Se crever les yeux"* is what Oedipus did after "recognizing" his crime.

neither able nor willing to know were to refer to what he claimed never to have said, to what he in fact never did talk about—namely, his mother. The absolute silence in which he kept her would be less enigmatic were it also to enclose, in addition to her, that "concrete explanation" he wanted to hide, and the horrible suspicion he preferred not to look at. In appearance, nothing links the three secrets; nothing but perhaps the father's offense, the supposed or phantasmatic scene of his crime. The rape scene, perhaps. And if the theory of the phantom seems to be of some help here, that is because it makes apparent the imported or inherited character of a phantasy, rather than making it into a simple derivation of the Oedipal complex. It is likely that the Oedipal relation here and the phantasies produced by it are at the very least complicated or inhabited by the effects of a *failed* identification. Failed—since it is incapable of putting an end to either the loss or the appropriation—the identification would have to remain occult, parallel, subterranean. This is what N. Abraham and M. Torok call an endocryptic identification. The father and his silence, the father and his enigma, cannot become the object of any mourning. The son can preserve him and his dreadful secret only clandestinely—as though in a crypt. Whence the necessity of making out in Kierkegaard's text the traces of an unconscious that can also be a ventriloquist, and alongside the son's, of hearing the echo of the father's voice incessantly accusing itself and never quite done dying. (Notice the frequency of the ventriloquy theme in K. and the double valorization that surrounds it. Condemned absolutely, it can also be endorsed by the religious author who writes "with guided pen.") Everything seems to point to the mimetic nature of the son's "melancholy," of his anxiety, of his "guilt," in particular, the "congenital" character of his gloom and the frequent use of metaphors of *reflection* that recur whenever he describes his despair. "Poor child, thou art going into a quiet despair," says the father to his son; but "a son is like a mirror in which the father beholds himself"—and perhaps the son should be able to hear the father's voice inside him saying: "Poor child, don't you see that *I'm* going into a quiet despair?" Nicolas Abraham and Maria Torok, in reference to a patient they call the "Milk-Man," point out that it is as if he were experiencing "affects" that did not belong to him, and they add this: "now we understand that they were the father's affects, his ruminations, his remorse, his phantasies, his desires—all imagined and surmised [by the son]" ("The Lost Object—Me," 8). The crypt finally cracks open at the moment when the patient, passing from the *I* to the *he*, bursts into tears for the first time and says, "My father must have been so awfully miserable." Would that be the sentence Kierkegaard could not bring himself to utter, and that—because it remained unspoken—became "how miserable *I* am"?

This sort of mimetic identification of the son with the father, then, would not have had as its goal and effect the resolution of a conflict, much less the penetration of the secret that had come to trouble the "patriarchal idyll," but would rather be the avoidance of even the slightest contact with the question of the father, so as to modify in no way the paternal figure. It would thus be necessary to preserve it without seeing it, reproduce it without understanding it. Neither dead nor alive, the father still seems to gain access to the son's self, setting up his own mourning there. The originality of this cryptic formulation consists in its not having resulted from a "simple" repression but rather from a repression *en abyme*, as it were, or raised to the second power. The father's story—or his phantasies—would be transmitted to the son's unconscious "between the lines," so to speak. This, then, is the secret of a secret. But of course it would be necessary for the unconscious to have at least sensed the nature of this secret in order to produce the effects we have seen, in particular K.'s impression of being the victim of a family tragedy. But even more tragic would be the revelation of the secret, and the son might have his reasons for burying it, in other words, for preserving it as is. In reference to similar "cases," N. Abraham has further noted, "the particular difficulty connected with these analyses stems from the phobia of breaking the seal of such a rigorously maintained parental or familial secret; a secret, though, whose tenor is inscribed on the unconscious. To the phobia of the transgression properly speaking must be added the risk of infringing on the fictitious but obligatory integrity of the parental figure in question" ("Notules sur le fantôme," 430). This shows just how important the secret's tenor is, for that is what in fact unsettles the unconscious. It is the tenor that has to remain unconscious, because it represents some explosive scene.

We can now reformulate our question in these terms: could the mother's rape scene represent for K.'s unsconsciousness the father's secret? Is the son's unconscious hearing some unspeakable confession in the enigmatic words of the father, something like, "I raped your mother"? Had this been the case, such a message could not have registered completely: first of all because it would have destroyed in the son the image of a father loved and admired like a god, and further because such a "crime" would have brought to light the father's betrayal ("It wasn't you I wanted, seduced, violated . . ."), and finally because the son would have had to recognize the origin of his own birth in this scene. In addition, then, it is insofar as such a scene comes up against the phantasies connected with Oedipal conflicts that it remains unavailable to consciousness (*impensable*). This is because not only would it intersect with the inexpressible desires of the son regarding his mother, but even more importantly because it would unleash his jealousy of her, though not without the scene's being able to satisfy at the same time the son's desire to occupy his mother's place in it. Such a scene, then, would conceal just as many sources of torment liable to destroy the patriarchal idyll, as unspeakable pleasures. The crypt would thus be the preservative burial of a scene, allowing it to be kept (hidden), while at the same time removing the necessity of condemning it *and* giving it up. Such would be the Wolf-Man's "solution": the formation of a crypt that encloses the scene (that of a presumed seduction, presumed to have been perpetrated on the sister by the father)—"The disappointment at not having been the one seduced by the father would relate him to the hysteric who is never quite seduced enough; his inability to reveal such a state of affairs without having his whole world come down around him would have required him to transform his vindictive tendencies into an intrapsychic secret. Otherwise he would have to give up on his other wish as well—that of replacing his sister in the scene" ("The Lost Object—Me," 6). But such a solution works only by doubling itself with the construction of another scene substituted for the first, and which "is no less effective in being able to provide pleasure."

It would not be impossible to find the traces of such a strategy in Kierkegaard—should we only be willing to push an entirely conjectural interpretation even further. If the secret scene of the father had to be "encrypted" by the son, then the simultaneous burial of the mother would be equally necessary. It's the father, then, who from out of the crypt continues to require silence about his illicit object; he's the one who, even if it also suits the son, requires that she be forgotten. We didn't know what the father wanted to hide, but the son reveals it through his very silence.

We know that he never once named his mother, nor did he even allude to her. Perhaps it is also her he is rejecting when he refuses his own first name, Søren, for this name is also in the mother's name—her maiden (virgin) name: Maria Sørensdatter Lund. Perhaps it is also on account of what this name "recalled" to him that he would have hated it, that he would have deplored its commonness, ill-suited as it was for designating the exception: "I would have had to have had a different first name in order for Copenhagen to have believed that I was a thinker." Of course, he also wants to poke fun at "Copenhagen's" lack of discrimination—but after all.

But what other scene would be apt to represent the encrypted scene here? If we admit that the unspeakable pleasure of the son stems from his identification with his mother in this scene, it would appear that sacrifice, martyrdom, and the position of the Christian martyr are so many "scenes" capable of symbolizing what we might also call the rape *of the father*. It wouldn't do, though, to think of the sacrificial scene as providing only one kind of pleasure, and to think of the son as occupying only one position in it. He occupies all of them, and must give them all up. First there is the mother's: I wish I were myself the virgin being raped by her father! . . . (such is the place of the submissive son and the Christian "spouse of Christ"). Then there is the guilty and aggressive father, the violator (such is the position of Oedipus, who is blinded by his crime and denied the status of both father and husband). Finally, there is the position occupied by the son who is begotten in such an act, the fruit of original sin (whence the rejection of the sexual origin of birth).

The substitution of the sacrificial scene for one of rape would not so much resolve the conflicts as it would displace them, reproduce them. Whence the multiplicity of contradictory phantasies, the instability of all the positions. At once sacrificed and sacrificer, Kierkegaard can be neither one nor the other—insofar as through his father he is criminally guilty and through his mother he is victim. Through the two of them he is the impossible son, and he dreams of another (ideal or religious) birth, a *second birth*.

This phantasy of a second birth, moreover (that of the young man in *Repetition* in particular), goes hand in hand with its own reproduction or repetition of the rape scene it seems to negate. In fact, if a second, wholly spiritual birth is possible, even should it owe nothing to any mother, it will still have to include the impregnating instance of the Idea, the young man's "feminine aptitude" to let himself be impregnated by it at the very moment he renounces marriage. Liberated by repetition, the young man writes to Constantine on the 31st of May: "I am myself again; the machinery has been set in motion. The inveiglements in which I was entrapped have been rent asunder . . . My emancipation is assured, I am born to myself, for as long as Ilithyia folds her hands, the one who is in labor cannot give birth" (*Repetition*, 221). This tearing of the nets or inveiglements which reminds us of the "tearing of the veil" in the Wolf-Man's story, and which seems first of all to correspond to the expression of a homosexual desire, could just as well have the "subsidiary" status attributed it by Freud, and according to which the veil (or the snares) would represent "the hymen which is torn at the moment of intercourse with a man" (*An Infantile Neurosis*, 17:101). Repetition, that *second* conception or birth, could thus mean at one and the same time the erasure of the first (and of the role which the woman is made to play in it) *and* a symbolic repetition of the impregnation by forced entry—in other words, rape. This repetition, or (auto-) conception, is not without implying the active intervention of the father. In the same way, in the *Fragments*, the second birth is due to God alone. An impregnation that is religious and ideal but also *scandalous*—and in which the son would simultaneously occupy the place of mother and child—substitutes for the original, cryptic scene of a violent physical impregnation. The familial scandal, the son's scandalous suspicion, seems to be echoed by the religious scandal such as it appears in *Philosophical Fragments*, in other words, a resistance to the paradox and the active/passive suffering of whoever learns about his own (guilty) difference from the God (the unknown). To be scandalized, said Climacus, is to "receive a shock." The intellect, which is *wounded* by the paradox, senses that it is running headlong into its downfall. If it accepts the mortal wound and actually does lose itself, its passion is in the end glad to run the risk of faith: which is that of blindness.

Would the jealous hatred regarding women, and especially the mother (a hatred whose traces we've been able to locate in the *Journal*), then be the expression of a barrier erected against the repressed desire to be a woman? Wasn't it Kierkegaard who wrote: "What terrible suffering to be the superior, and what enviable happiness to be a woman!"? Remarks, perhaps, that take on all their significance only by being understood in the following way: What terrible suffering to be a father (like mine), and what enviable happiness to be a (raped) woman. This could be the Christian's happiness, Christ's bride, subject to abduction by the God who begets tears in her, sacrificed but impregnated: "As Jewish women regarded being without children as a disgrace, so the Christian ought to regard being without tears (which, like children, are the gift of God) as a disgrace and pray and pray, as did Rachel, that God will open the womb and viscera of the spiritual man and in the inward movements of the heart give proof of its conception" (*Journal*, 1:176). The son's sacrifice—a bloody scene in which the sacrificial victim is subjected to a beating, a violent, even deadly scene in which, like Isaac, the son is God's (or the father's) victim—this sacrifice would repeat, all the while displacing it, the original and unspeakable scene of rape. But all these scenes, of course, might also stem from phantasmatic structures—fundamental, universal, pre-subjective structures (such as those of seduction, of castration)—which would then dovetail with the father's legacy . . .

A good many of the elements belonging to what we've been calling Kierkegaard's phantasmatics might therefore attest to K.'s various efforts: sometimes to repeat, to displace the encrypted scene—and to enjoy it—sometimes to reject and erase it: the rejection of sexual difference, the position taken with respect to maternity and femininity, the Christian exaltation of virile castration, the contempt for animality as an incapacity to control erection, the disgust of a Judaism overly attached to family and lineage, and an attachment, on the contrary, to the idea that Christ was born of a virgin—"therefore outside the family"—the exclusive love of a pure young woman with whom he can only "break-up," etc.

*
* *

"At any rate, should it be necessary to provide a thread, or gist here, then we might say that from one end to the other and in every sense of the word it will be a question only of breaks or ruptures."

The question of the authorship and its names will have brought us back to this starting point.

All the same, he wrote in Regine's name. The pseudonymous authorship seems to belong to her insofar as it glorifies her loss, her death. This loss was itself prescribed by another mourning. Condemned in advance, her place was also in a crypt. But her privilege was to escape the family, for the father hadn't counted on the son's "writerly gifts." By becoming the Muse, she gave birth, through a self-effacement, to poetic conception. "She made her way into his whole being; the memory of her was forever fresh. She had meant much to him; she had made him a poet—and precisely thereby—had signed her own death sentence" (*Repetition,* 138). Writing for her, glorifying her, he would after all have celebrated their union in history and for all eternity, and through the temple so constructed (like the little chest of secrets, made for her, which he liked to call the "the temple archive") he was able to sacrifice her while preserving her. And thanks to the abandonment of his name the father remained a stranger to this alliance.

But he also wrote in his name: Kierkegaard—and we ought to consider the strictly religious authorship as the temple or tomb dedicated to the father's name, a witness to the alliance through which the son remains tied to him. Perhaps this was the price to be paid in order not to break the alliance.

(Kierkegaard is in fact the name of a temple, or church: that of Saeding, in Jutland, near where the paternal grandfather's farm [Gaard] was located: "church-yard"—Kierkegaard—became his name. The word can also mean cemetery.)

The religious authorship, witness to the son's sacrifice, would be distinguished from the pseudonymous, "poetic" authorship through which it is possible, by working at it, to "engender one's own father." The religious writing through which the author exposes himself to ridicule and persecution should not be dependent on any economy here. It is writing as sacrifice: sacrifice (of the intelligence) of the son who chooses his own undoing and blindness, an expression for the passion through which he renounces his difference in order to remain "hidden in the father," renounces his reason, convinced of being "always in the wrong with regard to the father": "and it's filial piety precisely that teaches me not to wish to penetrate the hidden, but rather to remain hidden in the father" (*Stages*, 57). It is as though, unable to conceive, he couldn't even be born.

If "penetration" never goes without some form of forced entry, the "not to penetrate" (what is hidden) can just as easily signify violent sexual penetration as a "tearing of the birthveil" and opening of the eyes. Not to penetrate, not to pierce (the father's secret, the mother's hymen) is equivalent to not leaving, not being born (staying hidden in the father)—or else, another inversion, being penetrated by him.

And under his name, under his seal or signature, no longer to write anything that would not belong to the father as his due, and that would not celebrate his memory (*sa mémoire*).

> I dedicate this little work
> In Memory
> of
> the deceased
> Michael Pedersen Kierkegaard
> My Father
> ("The Sinner Woman," 257)

Written for the father, the religious authorship would also be a reminder of what is due him, his *account* (*son mémoire*).[47]

For the father: that could indicate the destination of the authorship, its cause, or even the real author of what the son writes in his name and as though in his place.

---

47. TN. The word "mémoire" can be either masculine or feminine in French. As a feminine noun, it suggests the mental faculty that preserves the past for consciousness. As a masculine noun, it is simply a written inscription—more specifically in this case, the inscription of a debt, a bill for *accounts* due.

A usurped place, as well. Like the wife's temple, the temple or church guarding the name of the father can only celebrate the dead.

*
* *

Who to write for—Always for the dead.

He gave two versions of this answer. Two formulations of the same epigraph, inspired by Herder, and which were supposed to be used to introduce *Fear and Trembling*.

"Write."——"For Whom?"——"Write for the dead, for those in the past whom you love."——"Will they read me?"——"Yes, for they come back as posterity."

"An Old Saying"

Then, the same dialogue somewhat modified:

"Write."——"For whom?"——"Write for the dead, for those in the past whom you love."——"Will they read me?"——"No!"

"An Old Saying Slightly Altered"
(*Fear and Trembling*, 244)

The answer makes it well worth stopping there.

Selected References

Abraham, Nicolas, and Torok, Maria. "The Lost Object—Me." Translated by Nicholas Rand. *Substance*, no. 43, 1984.
———. "Notules sur le fantôme." In *L'Ecorce et le noyau*. Paris: Aubier-Flammarion, 1978.
Adorno, Theodor W. *Kierkegaard: Konstruktion des Ästhetischen*. In *Gesammelte Schriften*, vol. 2. Frankfurt: Suhrkamp, 1979.
Aristophanes. *The Clouds*. Translated by Alan H. Sommerstein. Warminster, England: Aris and Phillips, 1982.
Bataille, Georges. "Sacrificial Mutilation and the Severed Ear of Vincent Van Gogh." In *Visions of Excess*, translated by Allan Stoekl. Minneapolis: University of Minnesota Press, 1985.
Blanchot, Maurice. "The Essential Solitude." In *The Space of Literature*, translated by Ann Smock. Lincoln: University of Nebraska Press, 1982.
———. *L'Entretien infini*. Paris: NRF Gallimard, 1969.
———. *L'Espace littéraire*. Paris: NRF Gallimard, 1968.
———. *Faux pas*. Paris: NRF Gallimard, 1943.
Brandes, Georg. *Søren Kierkegaard: Ein literarisches Charakterbild*. Leipzig: J. A. Barth, 1879.
Brandt, F., and Rammel, E. *Kierkegaard og Pengene* (Kierkegaard and Money). Copenhagen: Levin & Munksgaard, 1935.
Clair, André. *Pseudonymie et paradoxe*. Paris: Librairie philosophique J. Vrin, 1976.
Deleuze, Giles. *Différence et répétition*. Paris: Presses Universitaires de France, 1968.
De Man, Paul. "Sign and Symbol in Hegel's *Aesthetics*." *Critical Inquiry* 8 (1982):4.

Derrida, Jacques. *Dissemination*. Translated by Barbara Johnson. Chicago: Chicago University Press, 1981.

———. *Margins of Philosophy*. Translated by Alan Bass. Chicago: University of Chicago Press, 1982.

Eckhart, Meister. *Meister Eckhart: A Modern Translation*. Translated by Raymond Bernard Blakney. New York: Harper Torchbooks, 1941.

Fontenay, Elisabeth de. *Les Figures juives de Marx*. Paris: Editions de Galilée, 1973.

Freud, Sigmund. *From the History of an Infantile Neurosis*. Vol. 17, *The Complete Works*. London: The Hogarth Press, 1955.

———. *Moses and Monotheism*. Vol. 22, *The Complete Works*. London: The Hogarth Press, 1964.

———. *A Seventeenth-Century Demonological Neurosis*. Vol. 19, *The Complete Works*. London: The Hogarth Press, 1961.

———. *Totem and Taboo*. Vol. 13, *The Complete Works*. London: The Hogarth Press, 1958.

Gasché, Rodolphe. "Roundtable on Translation." In *The Ear of the Other: Otobiography, Transference, Translation: Text and Discussions with Jacques Derrida*. Edited by C. V. McDonald. Translated by P. Kamuf and A. Ronell. New York: Schocken Books, 1985.

Goldmann, Lucien. Contribution in *Kierkegaard vivant*. Paris: NRF Gallimard, 1960.

Hegel, G. W. F. *Aesthetics: Lectures on Fine Art*. Translated by T. M. Knox. 2 vols. Oxford: The Clarendon Press, 1975.

———. *Der Geist des Christentums*. In *Frühe Schriften*. Vol. 1, *Theorie Werkausgabe*. Frankfurt: Suhrkamp, 1971.

———. *Entwürfe zum Geist des Judentums*. In *Hegels theologische Jugendschriften*. Edited by Hermann Nohl. Frankfurt: Minerva, 1966.

———. *Lectures on the History of Philosophy*. Translated by E. S. Haldane and Frances H. Simpson. 3 vols. New York: The Humanities Press, 1955.

———. *Phenomenology of Spirit*. Translated by A. V. Miller. Oxford: The Clarendon Press, 1977.

———. *Phänomenologie des Geistes*. Vol. 3, *Theorie Werkausgabe*. Frankfurt: Suhrkamp, 1970.

———. *The Philosophy of Right*. Translated by T. M. Knox. Oxford: The Clarendon Press, 1942.

———. *The Spirit of Christianity*. In *Early Theological Writings*, translated by T. M. Knox. Chicago: University of Chicago Press, 1948.

———. *Vorlesungen über die Asthetik.* Vols. 13–15, *Theorie Werkausgabe.* Frankfurt: Suhrkamp, 1970.

———. *Vorlesungen über die Geschichte der Philosophie.* Vol. 18, *Theorie Werkausgabe.* Frankfurt: Suhrkamp, 1970.

Hohlenberg, Johannes. *Søren Kierkegaard.* Translated by T. H. Croxall. New York: Pantheon Books, 1954.

Kant, Immanuel. *Critique of Judgement.* Translated by J. H. Bernard. New York: Hafner Press, 1951.

———. *Kritik der Urteilskraft.* Vol. 10, *Theorie Werkausgabe.* Frankfurt: Suhrkamp, 1968.

Kierkegaard, Søren. *The Concept of Anxiety.* Translated by Reidar Thomte. Princeton: Princeton University Press, 1980.

———. *The Concept of Irony with Constant Reference to Socrates.* Translated by Lee M. Capel. Bloomington: Indiana University Press, 1965.

———. *Concluding Unscientific Postscript to the Philosophical Fragments.* Translated by David Swenson. Princeton: Princeton University Press, 1941.

———. *Either/Or.* Translated by Walter Lowrie. 2 vols. Princeton: Princeton University Press, 1971.

———. *Fear and Trembling—Repetition.* Translated by Howard V. Hong and Edna H. Hong. Princeton: Princeton University Press, 1983.

———. "Has a Man the Right to Let Himself Be Put to Death for the Truth?" (*Two Minor Ethico-Religious Treatises*). In *The Present Age,* translated by Alexander Dru and Walter Lowrie. Oxford: Oxford University Press, 1940.

———. *The Instant.* In *Kierkegaard's Attack on "Christendom,"* translated by Walter Lowrie. Princeton: Princeton University Press, 1946.

———. *Philosophical Fragments.* Translated by David Swenson. Princeton: Princeton University Press, 1936, 1962.

———. *The Point of View for My Work as an Author.* Translated by Walter Lowrie. New York: Harper & Row, 1962.

———. "The Sinner Woman, An Edifying Discourse." In *Training in Christianity,* translated by Walter Lowrie. Princeton: Princeton University Press, 1941.

———. *Søren Kierkegaard's Journals and Papers.* Translated by Howard V. Hong and Edna H. Hong. 6 vols. Bloomington: Indiana University Press, 1978.

———. *Stages on Life's Way.* Translated by Walter Lowrie. Princeton: Princeton University Press, 1945.

———. *Tagebücher, Vierter Band.* In *Gesammelte Werke.* Ausgewählt, neugeordnet und übersetzt von Hayo Gerdes. Düsseldorf/Köln: Eugen Diedrichs Verlag, 1970.

———. *Vorworte.* In vols. 11–12, *Gesammelte Werke.* Ubersetzt von Emanuel Hirsch. Düsseldorf/Köln: Eugen Diedrichs Verlag, 1958.

Kofman, Sarah. *Camera Obscura.* Paris: Editions de Galilée, 1973.

Lacoue-Labarthe, Philippe. "Theatrum Analyticum." *Glyph* 2 (1977).

Leibniz, G. W. *New Essays on Human Understanding.* Translated and edited by Peter Remnant and Jonathan Bennett. Cambridge: Cambridge University Press, 1981.

Lewis, Philip. "Vers la traduction abusive." In *Les Fins de l'homme*, edited by Philippe Lacoue-Labarthe and Jean-Luc Nancy. Paris: Editions Galilée, 1981.

Lukács, Georg. *The Destruction of Reason.* Translated by Peter Palmer. Atlantic Highlands, N.J.: Humanities Press, 1981.

Mackey, Louis. *Kierkegaard: A Kind of Poet.* Philadelphia: University of Pennsylvania Press, 1971.

Marx, Karl. *The Jewish Question.* In *Early Writings.* New York: Vintage Books, 1975.

Nietzsche, Friedrich. *The Anti-Christ.* In *The Portable Nietzsche*, translated by Walter Kaufmann. New York: The Viking Press, 1968.

Nunberg, Herman. "Attempts to Reject the Circumcision." In vol. 2, *Practice and Theory of Psychoanalysis.* New York: International Universities Press, Inc., 1965.

Plato. *The Collected Dialogues.* Edited by Edith Hamilton and Huntington Cairno. Princeton: Princeton University Press, 1963.

Smyth, John Vignaux. *A Question of Eros: Irony in Sterne, Kierkegaard, and Barthes.* Tallahassee: Florida State University Press, 1986.

Vauthier, Jean. *Le Personnage combattant.* Paris: Gallimard, 1955.

Warminski, Andrzej. "Missed Crossing: Wordsworth's Apocalypses." *Modern Language Notes* 99 (1984):5.

Zenophon. *Memorabilia and Œconomicus.* Translated by E. C. Marchand. London: Heinemann, 1938.

INDEX

Abraham: as Christian model, 212; as incomprehensible, 91–92, 237; and Isaac, 81; as Jew, 93–96; and Job, 138–39; as unmediatable, 237
Abraham, Nicolaus, and Torok, Maria, 248–52
Adam, 27–28
Adorno, Theodor, 5–6
Agamemnon, 92
Alcibiades, 50–53
Allegory, 9, 29–30. *See also* History
Aparté: as inscription, 21–22; as irony, 29–30; as notes, 129–30; as parabasis, ix, 29n, 127, 232–33; as reading, 4, 127; as repetition, 3; as rupture, 131, 256; as secret, 190; as translation, ix–xi, 223–24n; as woman, 128, 131; as writing, 21–22, 127–28, 219–23
Aristophanes, 35, 41–42, 60; *Clouds*, 42–43, 47–49, 50–51, 54, 62, 63
Aristotle, 26n, 185
Artaud, Antonin, 235
Austin, J. L., 74–75

Barth, Karl, 6
Bataille, Georges, 80, 81, 117
Blake, William, 131–32, 190
Blanchot, Maurice, 7–10, 85–86n, 90–91n, 127, 129, 176, 189–91
Boesen, Emil, 156–57
Bové, Paul, 6
Brandt, F., and Rammel, E., 192
Buber, Martin, 6
Bultmann, Rudolph, 6

Charon, 43
Christian VIII, 151, 204–5
Christian: as pseudonymous writer, 8; as subjectivity, 26–28; as woman, 167–70
Christianity: as *aparté*, 128; and cannibalism, 180–82; as irony, 218; as Jewish, 213; and politics, 202–18; as rape, 253–55; as seduction, 52; as virile castration, 178–80, 218, 255
Clair, André, 202

Deleuze, Gilles, 139–40, 158
De Man, Paul, 26n, 30
Derrida, Jacques, xi, 10, 18, 37, 75n, 153, 154–55, 164–67
Diogenes, 54
Don Quixote, 163

Eckhart, Meister, 143, 190, 191

Faith: as private, 92; as sacrifice of understanding, 90, 92, 113; and temporality, 141–42; as writing, 96
Farce, 160–67
Father-Son relationship: as absolute submission, 105–6, 112–13; and children, 185–86; as contractual, 111–12, 238–39, 256–58; as crypt, 249–58; as infinite gap, 87–88, 111; and Judaism, 106–11; and the law, 150–51; and melancholy, 239–51; and memory, 240, 246, 256–58; and money, 192–93, 195–96; as

263

Father-Son relationship (*continued*)
monument, 238–39; and mother, 244–58; and politics, 199–200; and profit, 183–84; and the secret, 239–58; and the signature, 230, 237, 238–39, 243, 256–58; and writing, 184. *See also* Olsen, Terkild; Schlegel, Johan Frederik

Fichte, Johann Gottlieb, 12, 23*n*, 26*n*, 62–63

Fontenay, Elisabeth de, 210*n*

Freud, Sigmund, 104*n*, 112, 153, 173, 191, 221, 254

Gasché, Rodolphe, x
Gide, André, 154*n*
God: as absolutely different, 82–88; as arbitrary positing, 83
Goldmann, Lucien, 200–202
Grimm, 48

Hamann, 237
Hamlet, 242, 246
Hegel, G. W. F., 7, 8, 11, 23*n*; and Abraham, 93–96; as absentminded, 188; *Aesthetics*, 57–58, 63; and alienation, 217–18; and Aristophanes, 47; and Christianity, 103–4, 106–11; and Danish dialect, 186–88; and dialectical mastery, 86–87, 93, 103, 133, 140, 187–88, 231–32, 237; and feminine dialectic, 177; as fraud, 79; *History of Philosophy*, 34, 40, 43–49, 55*n*, 61, 62; and the illegitimate child, 186; and irony, 11–12; on language and thought, 236; as master of irony, 71–72; *Phenomenology*, 58–59, 86, 93, 95–96*n*, 108–9*n*; *Philosophy of Right*, 53, 61, 62; and the preface, 221; and the romantics, 62–66; and Socrates, 33–35, 39–40, 43–49, 53–54; *Spirit of Christianity*, 93–95, 106–8, 110–11; and the System, 220–21; and tragic hero, 57–58; and Xenophon, 45–47

Heiberg, Johan Ludvig, 202, 224–25, 226, 231
Heidegger, Martin, 7
Heliogabulus, 181
Herder, Johann Gottfried, 258
Hippias, 46
History, 9, 12, 28–30; as difference, 99–100; and the political, 214–15; as process, 217–18; and reading, 200–202; as tragic confrontation, 57–58. *See also* Allegory; Irony, as moment

Hohlenberg, Johannes, 247

Indirect Communication, 8–9, 76–77; and existential determinations, 8–9; as grammar, 15–16; as rhetorical prior to philosophical category, 6–7, 16; as subjectivity, 13–14, 16–17, 18–20; and ventriloquism, 234–38. *See also* Irony; Pseudonymous writing

Individual: and the crowd, 196–97; and politics, 198–99, 204–12; and the signature, 198; and the universals of grammar, 235–36

Irony: as allusion, 37–39, 51–52; as blank, 18–19, 26; and citation, 20–21, 75–78; and the erotic, 50–53; and faith, 71; as figure, 68–72; and grammar, 15–17, 20–27; history of, 11–14; as indifference, 53–54, 56, 215; as interrogation, 35–38; as linguistic displacement, 14–15; and madness, 70–71; as moment, 64–68; and negativity, 11–14, 16, 18, 24; as nonmetaphysical, 37–39; as nonmimetic, 18–20, 37–38; and nonsubjective freedom, 28–30, 74–78; as nonthematic, 72–73; as past, 13; and the performative, 74–78; as philosophical category, 11–14, 16, 25; as positing, 25–30; as rhetorical question, 15–17; as resistance, 58–60, 69; as source, 11; and subjective freedom, 11–12, 14, 22–23, 62–63, 70; as subjectivity, 11–14, 16–18, 26, 57–58, 63–65; as trope, 11, 17–18; as writing, 20–21, 76. *See also* Aparté; Napoleon

Job, 138–39, 168, 242
John the Baptist, 107
Judaism: as alienation, 93–95; as alternative, 177–78, 212–13; as bourgeois materialism, 210–12; as cult of the void, 86. *See also* Father-Son relationship; Woman

Kafka, Franz, 7, 200

INDEX

Kant, Immanuel, 7, 26; and the comical, 49; and the sublime, 161–63
Kierkegaard, Søren: *The Concept of Anxiety*, 96–105, 224, 228–31; *The Concept of Irony*, 10, 17–30, 33–78; *Concluding Unscientific Postscript*, 4, 103, 118–19, 188; *Either/Or*, 51n, 88; and existentialism, 7–9, 30; *Fear and Trembling*, 79–81, 91–96, 141, 171, 258; "Has a Man the Right?" 115–17; *Instant*, 180–81; *Journal*, 238–58; *Philosophical Fragments*, 52–53, 82–90, 254–55; *Point of View*, 120–25, 198–99, 214–16; *Prefaces*, 218–34; *Repetition*, 3, 142–44, 151–67, 186–87, 254, 256; "The Sinner Woman," 168–70, 257; *Stages on Life's Way*, 88–89, 135, 171, 241–42, 245–46, 257
Kofman, Sarah, 214n
Kollerød, Ole, 181

Lacoue-Labarthe, Philippe, 221n
La Ménardière, ix
Language. *See* Indirect Communication; Irony
Lautréamont, 218
Lewis, Philip, 29n
Lowrie, Walter, 5
Lukács, Georg, 200–202
Luke, 170
Lund, P. E., 167
Luther, 205; as Jew, 212

Mackey, Louis, 6–7
Mallarmé, Stéphane, 155; *Mimique*, 164–66
Mark, 128, 197
Martensen, Hans Lassen, 202
Marx, Karl, 26n, 205–12, 213–18
Mary Magdalene, 167–70
Matthew, 169, 185
Mimesis, 159–60
Mise en abyme, 153–54, 168
Møller, Paul, 144
Money: and language, 195–96; and writing, 193–94. *See also* Father-Son relationship
Mynster, Jakob Peter, 227, 244

Napoleon, 17–26, 37. *See also* Irony
Narcissus, 22, 23n
Nerval, Gérard de, 158–59

Niebuhr, Reinhold, 5, 6
Nietzsche, Friedrich, 58, 80, 113–15, 140, 145, 193, 204
Nunberg, Herman, 106–7n

Oedipus, 247, 249n, 250, 252, 253
Olsen, Regine; as crypt, 256; and Elvira, 156–57; as flower, 131–33; and Isaac, 137; as monument, 135–36, 144, 238–39; and repetition, 157–58; and Schlegel, 145–46; as victim, 137
Olsen, Terkild: as father, 148–49

Pascal, Blaise, 7, 91n
Paul, 106–10, 114–15, 181–82
Periander, 245–46, 247
Pilate, Pontius, 76
Plato, 35, 38, 39, 41, 50–53, 174, 185; *Apology*, 42, 51; *Cratylus*, 38; *Lysis*, 44–45, *Meno*, 44–45; as model student, 53, 60; *Protagoras*, 36–37; *Symposium*, 39, 50; *Thaetetus*, 41
Poe, Edgar Allan, 135, 191
Poet: and indirect communication, 10; and man of faith, 10–11; and memory, 140–42; and silence, 139
Proust, Marcel, 158
Pseudonymous writing: and the father, 243–44; and identity, 118; and indirect communication, 8, 228; and martyrdom, 120–24; and reappropriation, 122; and responsibility, 228–30; and the signature, 119, 221, 228–29; and ventriloquism, 235–38, 250. *See also* Indirect Communication; Secret

Recollection: as asymmetrical to repetition, 3
Repetition. *See* Aparté; Farce; Kierkegaard; Mallarmé; Nerval; Proust; Sin; Theater; Woman
Rilke, Rainer Maria, 7
Romantic Irony: as arbitrary, 13; and Hegel, 62–66, 72; and Kierkegaard, 66–68, 72

Schlegel, Friedrich, 11, 12, 62–63; *Lucinde*, 66–67
Schlegel, Johan Frederik: as husband, 146–50
Schleiermacher, Friedrich, 60

Schleifer, Ronald, 7
Searle, John, 74
Secret, 8; as blank, 248–50; and the exception, 190; and the father, 239–58; as inscription, 248; as linguistic dilemma, 8; and the mother, 189, 244–58; and the name, 248–49, 253, 256–58; and the phantom, 248–49; as signature, 134; and writing, 189. *See also* Pseudonymous writing
Silentio, Johannes, de: as religious discourse, 80–81
Sin: as difference, 84, 96–99; as extralinguistic, 10; and metaphysics, 100–101; and psychoanalysis, 101–5; as repetition, 96–98. *See also* Woman
Smyth, John, 7, 21*n*
Socrates, 11; as abstract moment, 43, 65; as barren, 41, 52; as comical, 48–49; as destructive, 41–42; and displacement, 65; in earnest, 24–25; as founder, 33–35, 41–46; as freedom without content, 47–48; as grammatical subject, 15; as ignorant, 40, 55–57; and indifference, 53–54; as individual, 199; as infinite negativity, 47–49, 64–65; as instructive, 45–47; and negativity, 24–25, 35–40, 42–49, 56–57, 58–62; as particularity, 59–60; and philosophy, 33–35; as political negativity, 55–56, 215; and the romantics, 65; as seducer, 50–54; and silence, 42; as Sophists' master, 41–42; and the state, 55–57; as vampire, 51; as without result, 44. *See also* Irony; Napoleon
Spheres of existence, 8–9
Solger, K. W. F., 11, 12, 64, 67
Soulier, F., ix
Sublime, 160–63
Sussman, Henry, 7
Swenson, David, 4

Taylor, Mark, 7
Theater, 155–59
Tieck, Ludwig, 11
Tillich, Paul, 5, 6
Tisseau, Paul, 153, 216

Unconscious: as political or psychoanalytical, 10

Vauthier, Jean, 163

Warminski, Andrzej, 20*n*
Woman: as alternative, 170–73; as *aparté*, 128, 131; as beast, 175–77, 255; as Christian, 167–70; as difference, 173–74; as repetition, 167; and writing, 167. *See also* Judaism; Sin

Xenophon, 17, 35, 45–47, 60